S0-AGK-633

On the early evening of March 18, 1980, John Favara, driving home in the face of a brilliant setting sun, did not see the twelve-year-old boy on a mini-bike suddenly dart out from behind a garbage dumpster parked on the street where Favara lived. The car slammed into the bike and the boy was instantly killed. Favara was distraught, an anguish that deepened when he learned the victim was Frank Gotti, the younger of John Gotti's two sons.

Two months later, Favara had just finished work at a Long Island convertible sofa firm when three men pulled up in a van. They jumped out and headed for Favara, who had begun packing a .22-caliber pistol. He managed to get the gun out, but one of the three men smashed him in the head with a two-by-four as he fired a shot; the shot went wild, and the limp body of Favara was thrown into the van and driven off. John Favara was never seen again.

GOOMBATA

THE IMPROBABLE RISE AND FALL OF JOHN GOTTI AND HIS GANG

JOHN CUMMINGS AND
ERNEST VOLKMAN

AVON BOOKS ● NEW YORK

AVON BOOKS
A division of
The Hearst Corporation
1350 Avenue of the Americas
New York, New York 10019

Copyright © 1990, 1992 by John Cummings and Ernest Volkman
Published by arrangement with Little, Brown and Company
Library of Congress Catalog Card Number: 89-49340
ISBN: 0-380-71487-6

The Little, Brown and Company edition contains the following Library of Congress Cataloging in Publication Data:

Cummings, John, 1931-
  Goombata : the improbable rise and fall of John Gotti and his gang
/ by John Cummings and Ernest Volkman. – 1st ed.
    p.   cm
1. Gotti, John. 2. Hoodlums – New York (N.Y.) – Biography.
3. Mafia – New York (N.Y.) I. Volkman, Ernest. II. Title.
HV6248.G615C86   1990
364.1'06'092–dc20   [B]   89–49390   CIP

First Avon Books Printing: January 1992

AVON TRADEMARK REG. U.S. PAT. OFF. AND IN OTHER COUNTRIES, MARCA REGISTRADA, HECHO EN CANADA

Printed in Canada

UNV 20 19 18 17 16 15 14 13

For
LoRetta, Bonnie, Bruce and Cheryl
J.C.

For
Eric and Michelle
E.V.

Dedicated to the Memory of
Detective John Gurnee
1936–1990

Table of Contents

Acknowledgments

THE REPORTING AND WRITING of this book required not only several years of our lives, but also the efforts of many people willing to take time out from their busy schedules (or other extenuating circumstances) to share their reminiscences and insights. The list is quite long, and includes people on both sides of the law; we are especially grateful to several persons who took extreme personal risk to talk with us.

Almost all of the people who contributed to our reporting efforts would prefer not to be named publicly, but we would like to express our thanks to the men and women of several organizations whose assistance was crucial. These include the Federal Bureau of Investigation, the United States Attorney's Office for the Eastern District of New York, the United States Attorney's Office for the Southern District of New York, the New York City Police Department, the U.S. Justice Department's Eastern District (New York) Organized Crime Strike Force, the Brooklyn District Attorney's Office, and the Manhattan District Attorney's Office (we owe a special debt of gratitude to Gerald McKelvey of the staff of Manhattan District Attorney Robert Morgenthau).

Additionally, we are grateful for the kind assistance rendered by officials of the Federal Bureau of Prisons and the New York City Department of Corrections in handling a number of matters under often-difficult circumstances.

For unfailing guidance through the intricacies of the Italian immigrant experience, we thank Bartolomo Biscardi; for insights into the separate world that is Brooklyn, we are equally indebted to a valued friend, L. J. Davis, a far greater reporter and writer than either of us could ever hope to be, and a dedicated historian of Brooklyn mores, to boot.

It should be noted that none of these people or their organizations are in any way responsible for the opinions, conclusions, and assertions in this book; these remain our own responsibility, along with any errors of fact.

Above all, we owe thanks to several people not involved in organized crime or law enforcement whose contributions were nevertheless vital in the making of this book. They include one of our researchers, Eric Volkman, now far removed from the world of organized crime in his undergraduate studies at Susquehanna University; our agent, Victoria Pryor of Arcadia Ltd., whose role in the creation and eventual fruition of this book was crucial; and our editor at Little, Brown, Jennifer Josephy, whose efforts made it a much better book.

John Cummings

Ernest Volkman

Introduction:
All in the Family

You may assume that crime, too, is incorporated.
— THOMAS E. DEWEY, 1937

LIKE MUCH ELSE about Sicily, the origins of the Sicilian slang word *goombah* (and its plural form, *goombata*) are obscure, lost in the mists of the island's ancient and bloody history. The slang is believed to be a corruption of the Italian *compare,* a word of some subtlety, for it can signify, alternately, "godfather," "accomplice," "old pal," or "old mate."

But the real meaning of *goombata* often runs to much more subtle depths, implying unquestioning loyalty, bonds of friendship forged since childhood, shared interests, and relationships so strong that they can never be betrayed. It is a word heard most often among certain people in the tradition-steeped villages of western Sicily, where time seems to stand still in the old cobbled streets. In such villages as Corleone—often besieged by tourists seeking the birthplace of the fictional clan chief of *The Godfather*—the old men still stroll arm in arm, as old men of Corleone have been doing for centuries. The goat carcasses still hang outside the butcher shop, the same display that has confronted Sicilian housewives since time immemorial. In the crooked alleys behind the buildings on the main street, the men in traditional workman's caps, with faces covered with what seems to be a permanent beard stubble, sit and exchange news and gossip in guttural Sicilian accents. Above their heads, a network of clotheslines stretches between the buildings, the wash flut-

1

tering in the soft breeze of what Sicilians call the "eternal spring."

Eternal, too, are some special *goombata* of Corleone. They are members of an organization whose existence is seldom mentioned by name in the village, or the rest of Sicily, for that matter. These *goombata* formulate narcotics deals, extort payments from businessmen, accept tributes from respectful citizens, arbitrate local disputes, bribe policemen, and, most important of all, serve as the virtual underground government for a region whose distrust of conventional government extends back centuries. Elsewhere in Sicily, in the hills and fields, the men with the *lupara* (sawed-off shotguns) patrol their domains; in the cities, villages, and towns, the elderly *dons* rule their empires amid the fawning respect of citizens who know that no matter what Rome decrees, these are the men who rule.

They are the men of the "honored society," the *goombata* of Mafia.

There are no ancient villages like Corleone in the United States, but there is a Mafia, a direct lineal descendant of the organization that so permeates life in its birthplace. The seed arrived in the United States among the great wave of Italian immigrants who came to the New World in the late nineteenth and early twentieth centuries. It was a powerful seed, representing a fusion of the ties of blood, land, family, *goombata*, and "honored society," and rooted here in fertile American soil. What finally emerged was a distinctly American Mafia, an odd hybrid of ancient traditions, American mores, and modern corporate methods. It is, fundamentally, a unique criminal organization with deep roots in the communities from which it sprang.

The American Mafia is most often portrayed as the invisible and omnipotent criminal octopus of movie melodrama. Actually, it is neither entirely invisible nor omnipotent, but the American Mafia remains the most dangerous and resilient criminal organization in the world. Until only recently, it was able to withstand every legal assault, competition from new forms of organized crime, and dramatic social change. In the past few decades, when every other social institution in

America has either been shattered or changed forever, the Mafia has continued to thrive, despite the fact that it is among the more tradition-bound of all such institutions. What made this possible was a strange contradiction: while the American Mafia continued to rely on centuries-old traditions organizationally, at the same time it demonstrated a remarkable ability to keep pace with changing conditions and social mores. Like a virulent parasite, it has adapted to the host body, fastening on whatever the law or social convention allowed: organized kidnapping was abandoned for rum-running during Prohibition, bootlegging was replaced by the black market during World War II, which was replaced by illegal gambling and narcotics trafficking, and so on. Greed is the pilot light of the Mafia, and so long as it exists, the Mafia will continue to exist.

Essentially, the Mafia is a big-city phenomenon, because the right conditions exist there for it: unholy alliances between politics, business, and crime; police corruption; and an often-blurry distinction between good guys and bad guys. Moreover, the cities are where the money is. The *Mafiosi* themselves are among the most socially mobile people in the United States. In a single generation during the 1930s, they moved from society's bottom rungs to the upper reaches of wealth and material success. (At the height of his fame, Al Capone received over a thousand letters a week from admirers.)

By now, the broad organizational outline of the American Mafia is fairly well known. It is a coalition of twenty-four separate groups of organized criminals throughout the nation, with formal membership restricted to men of Italian-American descent. Each group is known as a "family," and the overall organization is usually called *La Cosa Nostra* (this thing of ours). Administratively, the organization is overseen by a ruling "commission" that arbitrates interfamily disputes, ensures that territories and spoils are divided fairly, and sets general policy.

The organization's center of gravity is in New York, which has more than two-thirds (nearly three thousand men) of the entire *La Cosa Nostra* membership in the United States, and collects the bulk of the estimated thirty billion dollars earned by organized crime each year in this country. The five Mafia "families" in New York are preeminent in the national organization, and thus have the dominant voice in the ruling Commission.

Equally well known by this point is the American Mafia's general history, including the cataclysmic events of 1930–1931, when the frustrated "young Turks" of the New York Mafia revolted against the elderly ruling *dons* (known derisively as "Mustache Petes") who then ran the organization in an Old World style. When the revolution was finished, and most of the old-time leaders murdered or pushed aside, the modern American Mafia was born, a structure that continues unchanged to this day. Basically, the structure is a loose patriarchal organization wedded to modern American business methods. Although there is no overall *capo di tutti capi* (boss of all bosses), individual bosses of families enjoy wide latitude in making decisions, most importantly over the lives of family members. Below each boss in the organization chart is the "underboss," who functions as chief executive officer, and the *consigliere* (counsellor), who by Mafia protocol is supposed to function both as an adviser to the family boss (only rarely called "godfather") and as arbitrator of disputes between the boss and family members. The middle management of a Mafia family is represented by a *caporegime* (captain), who functions as a crew chief of a varying number of workers. Each worker, if formally inducted into the Mafia, is known as a "soldier." The rest of the crews consist of "associates," including non-Italians and Italian-Americans who have not been formally inducted.

One rule remains paramount: all money flows upward. Soldiers earn money from crime operations sanctioned from above, and the lion's share of the resulting profits is passed back up the chain of command to the family boss. Advancement in the organization is largely dependent on merit, i.e., how much money soldiers and associates earn for the organization. In turn, the organization guarantees bail money, legal help, and other services for ranking members in trouble with the law—provided, of course, that the organization's dictum of silence in the face of pressure from law enforcement is maintained.

As in all organizations, some Mafia families are more successful than others. For many years, the richest and most powerful Mafia group in the United States has been the Gambino Family of New York City. Known by that name in honor of its progenitor, the late Carlo Gambino, it is an organization of approximately two hundred fifty formally inducted members and several hundred associates.

The Gambino Family represents a rich prize to the man who is able to win control of that enterprise, for through his hands at some point will pass the millions of dollars earned every year in narcotics, extortion, illegal gambling, pornography, union racketeering, robbery, business swindles, hijacking, auto theft, loansharking, and murder. Only men of a certain rare talent can hope to rise to such a position of power, for few men have the requisite skills to achieve it: instinctive treacherousness, bloodcurdling ruthlessness, acute business sense, and ability to inspire unquestioning loyalty. And those men who do reach that pinnacle must maintain power in the face of equally ambitious and ruthless men who operate in a world where murder is an accepted means of advancement.

John Gotti, the current boss of the Gambino Family, is one of those rare men. At age forty-nine (remarkably young by Mafia standards), he is the most notorious of all organized crime leaders—and in many ways the most extraordinary.

As a man who has spent most of his life in a relentless drive to become boss of a criminal empire, his story represents a perverse American success story of sorts: teenage street gang leader becomes low-level Mafia hood, gathers a group of fiercely loyal *goombata*, and ruthlessly takes control of a criminal kingdom in the face of seemingly impossible odds.

But there is a strong element of the imponderable at work here, for nothing in the life of John Gotti and his strange crew of *goombata* would seem to have prepared any of them for criminal greatness.

1

Once Upon a Time in America

*A spirit . . . has spread deep into the hearts of the
people of the whole of southern Europe. The eyes of
the poor are turned with longing fancy to "New York."
That is the magic word everywhere. The sound of it
brings light to a hundred million faces.*
— HISTORIAN BROUGHTON BRANDENBURG, 1902

PRECISELY at one second after midnight, the bell of Our
Lady of Mount Carmel Church began pealing. From its perch
in the church campanile high above the streets of New York
City, the bell rang out slowly and sonorously; the sound
echoed far in every direction in the moist night air.

It echoed down the quiet streets, among the gray tenements
and small stores of that area of upper Manhattan along the
East River known as East—or, more commonly, Italian—
Harlem; to the west, to Lexington Avenue, the inviolable
boundary between the two worlds of black Harlem and Italian
Harlem; to the south, toward a more indefinite line that
marked the end of the Italian neighborhood and the beginning
of the Puerto Rican *mundo;* to the east, across the East River
and into the sprawling suburb of Queens; and to the north,
across the dark river separating the island of Manhattan from
the Bronx, into the small Italian enclave along the river's
shore.

There, in one of the drab, five-story tenements beside a narrow street, Mrs. Fannie Gotti and her husband John Joseph stirred. In years past, they had anticipated that first peal of the bell, the signal for them to rise, dress the children and themselves in their Sunday best, and prepare to make an annual pilgrimage south, across the river, deep into Italian Harlem and a final destination at Our Lady of Mount Carmel church at 115th Street for an important event in their lives.

But to her sorrow, Mrs. Gotti would not be making the pilgrimage that hot summer of 1940. She was having a difficult pregnancy, made even more difficult by the unusually hot summer, and could barely walk a few steps. She already had four children (she would eventually produce thirteen, two of whom died in infancy), and caring for them while pregnant with a fifth was no easy task. Certainly not in the neighborhood of the Italian immigrants in New York, where home typically meant a tenement walkup, with a single toilet for an entire floor in the hallway; where the generally large Italian families somehow managed to live in apartments of a few rooms; where children slept on the rickety fire escapes during the summer heat waves, when the tenements seemed almost to melt; where few houses had steam heat, and winters were spent around a single coal stove.

Someday, Mr. and Mrs. John Gotti were certain, they would leave their world of tenements and crowded streets; somehow, they would achieve the dream of every Italian immigrant: a home in a nice neighborhood on a quiet street, with a real yard big enough for the children to play in, and room left over to grow some tomatoes (and perhaps even a fig tree). The dream was a dim, shimmering chimera somewhere far on the horizon, for there seemed no way to achieve it—assuredly not for a day laborer such as John Joseph Gotti, who had only his brawn to sell, a man who had spent the last twenty years since his arrival in America digging ditches and hauling cement, yet had little to show for it.

Like other men in his neighborhood, John Gotti could point out buildings all over the city that bore his invisible imprint, from the brownstones whose distinctive stoops had been shaped unerringly in wet cement by hand, to the soaring

skyscrapers, great cathedrals of commerce that needed armies
of men to erect. Those silent monuments to the immigrants'
labors existed outside their own neighborhoods, in a world
that had no place for the immigrants, except as workers. In
that world, Italian immigrants like John Gotti were most often
called "wop," "dago," "greaseball," or "guinea."

But in their own neighborhood, where such slurs were
never heard, language and culture remained intact in a familiar universe of packed tenements, cages of racing pigeons on
the roofs, streets alive with noisy traffic and playing children,
and the clatter of old country accents among the people who
congregated every night on the broad stoops, the neighborhood's social halls. The neighborhood, with its culture, traditions, and deep religious faith transplanted intact from
southern Italy, was a place of refuge against what the immigrants perceived as a hostile outside world.

No matter how comforting this universe of the neighborhood, the Gottis wanted something better. But as much as
Fannie Gotti talked of moving to the suburbs, she had vowed
that no matter where she eventually settled, she would always
return each year for the one event which for several weeks
transformed the grim life of the Italian ghetto. It was the
event whose beginning was signaled by the slow pealing of
the church bell one summer night in July: the annual *festa*
of Our Lady of Carmel.

The event is difficult to describe, and had to be experienced. Part solemn religious observance, part carnival, part
block party, part family reunion, the Festival of Our Lady of
Carmel began just after midnight on July 16 every year, and
continued for weeks afterward. Proclaimed grandiloquently
in the church's monthly bulletin as an event *in alto i curori,
oggi e la grande, memorabile, solemne*, the festival virtually
consumed the more than two hundred thousand southern Italians—mostly Sicilian—who lived in the neighborhood of a
hundred square blocks known as East Harlem.

It also preoccupied several thousand other Italian-Americans who flocked into the neighborhood to participate. Those
lucky enough to have relatives or friends in East Harlem
crammed into already crowded apartments; many others simply camped out in Jefferson Park near the river. With the

sound of the church bell just after midnight, they rose and attended a solemn midnight mass, the first in a series of religious observances in honor of the Madonna of Our Lady of Mount Carmel, an especially significant religious symbol to southern Italians.

Many worshippers came from Italian neighborhoods in Brooklyn, walking barefoot all the way to East Harlem over the Brooklyn Bridge and the hot, steaming pavements as a sign of penitence. Others, Fannie Gotti among them, performed the same ritual from the Bronx, and most arrived with the swollen and bleeding feet that those of the Old World-style religion felt best demonstrated a pious remembrance of Christ's own suffering. The church's New York Archdiocese respected this and other similar acts of faith, but clearly did not approve of them. The church hierarchy was especially unhappy with another act of penance performed by many of the Italian faithful, who fell to their knees in front of Our Lady of Carmel Church, then crawled up the steps with their tongues dragging along the stone.

No amount of disapproval from the ecclesiastical establishment, however, was about to break such Old World habits, for the Italian immigrant families shared a conviction that Our Lady of Carmel was *their* church. A short while after settling in America, the first wave of Italian immigrants became unhappy with what they considered the passionless, dry atmosphere of the Catholic churches of New York, then dominated by the Irish Catholics. The Italians wanted their own church, a church in their own neighborhood, a church in which masses would be said in their own language, a church with Italian-speaking priests attuned to the nuances of southern Italian culture.

In 1884 the church was built, brick by brick, with the sweat of immigrant day laborers who worked in the evenings after they had already put in a long day of hard labor on construction sites. The foundation was dug out using only shovels; the rest was built with donated materials hauled to 115th Street by junkmen and ice haulers who lent out their carts and horses. When the masons' union objected to Italian masons working for free to build the church, their wives and other women in the neighborhood tied back their hair and did

much of the masonry work themselves, somehow managing
to push heavy wheelbarrows loaded with cement and haul
loads of cement blocks.

The result of this labor of devotion was one of the most
striking churches in New York City, a nearly exact copy of
one of the elegant edifices that grace the southern Italian
countryside. It became the real center of the Italian immigrant
community, and the annual festival in the church's honor
soon was the largest and most important such festival in the
New World. Its meaning was only partly religious, for the
festa of Our Lady of Carmel was in fact something of an
affirmation by the Gottis and the rest of the southern Italian
immigrants that they were determined to maintain their
unique identity in the New World.

The *festa* began solemnly, with the first midnight mass
opening a round of masses that continued until the following
midnight. By that point, East Harlem was in a near frenzy:
the streets, alive with people, even at 3 A.M.; the fire escapes
decorated with crepe and Italian and American flags; arches
of colored lights over 115th Street; brightly colored blankets
hanging out the apartment windows; hordes of children running excitedly among clusters of adults; the sidewalks
crowded with tables set up by local restaurants; vendors selling religious articles to the faithful—little figures of red-col-
ored hunchbacks to ward off the evil eye, holy cards, statues
of Jesus, Mary, and the saints, and the biggest seller, candles
for the church services. It was a feast of sounds and smells:
the local bands wandered the streets playing traditional tunes,
while restaurants and street vendors worked to slake the
ancient southern Italian obsession with food—from hundreds
of outdoor stands wafted the smells of beans boiled in oil
and pepper, hot waffles, boiled corn, sausages, pies of
tomato, red pepper, and garlic, great heaping bowls of pasta,
glistening pastry rings, and nougat candy.

The highlight of the *festa* was the annual procession. Thousands of marchers, accompanied by bands and fireworks,
slowly paraded through the streets. At their center was a float
carrying a statue of the Madonna from Our Lady of Carmel
Church. Decorated with flowers and white ribbons, it was

carried by a phalanx of young men from the church congregation who had been accorded this rare honor and privilege. The float moved in a slow, stately rhythm, forced to stop often as people rushed forward to pin money on a banner carried by the church congregation, or to throw themselves at the base of the Madonna statue to beg mercy or forgiveness. Others put money and jewels into a box on the float that was used to collect money for support of the church.

There was no specific time for the great *festa* to end. Generally, it ended when the community was too exhausted to go on, a point usually reached nearly two weeks after the first sound of the bell from Our Lady of Carmel Church. And when the venerated statue of the Madonna had been put back inside the church, the lighted arch stored away, and the last scrap of trash swept up from the streets, the neighborhood once again confronted the very real world of the Italian immigrants in New York, a world the gaiety of the *festa* had obscured for a brief time. It was the reality of a poor, troubled, neglected, and culturally isolated world, far different from the fantasy that had drawn them all to New York in the first place.

John Joseph and Fannie Gotti believed in that fantasy. Along with nearly a million other Italians, they had emigrated from *la miseria* of southern Italy's poverty, convinced that in the New World, astounding wealth was simply lying around in the streets, waiting to be picked up. In America, what seemed beyond attainment in Italy would be fulfilled— a good job, a house, a modest piece of land, education for the children.

It was this shimmering vision that kept hope alive for millions of Italians in the *mezzogiorno*, the region of Italy south of Rome. "Christ never reached there," many southern Italians said of the *mezzogiorno*, and perhaps they were right. The land had been ground to dust by centuries of oppression and colonization, and so had its people. They were defeated by the grinding poverty, by the indifference of the central government in Rome, and by the sheer hopelessness of it all. Despairing of a future in Italy, they heeded the siren call of the men who were recruiting throughout the *mezzogiorno*, the men who told incredible tales of a labor-hungry America, where a man could earn more *in a day* than he could during an entire year in Italy—if, as the recruiters hardly needed to add, such a remarkable thing as a steady job even existed in the poverty of southern Italy. The recruiters swore it was all true. They had seen it with their own eyes: golden opportunity for all, more money than anyone ever dreamed of, beautiful homes for even the lowliest workers.

And so in 1920, John Joseph Gotti somehow managed to accumulate the sixty dollars for steerage passage on one of the decrepit ships that regularly docked at such ports as Palermo, Salerno, and Naples to load up with starry-eyed Italian families headed for America. His sixty dollars bought one-way passage for himself and his new wife. They sailed toward a totally unknown future, for aside from the glib promises of the recruiters seeking workers in Italy, the Gottis knew nothing of their new country. They knew still less of what exactly they would be doing in that fabled land; like the other immigrants, they knew only that they were prepared to work hard in a country where a man, so it was said, could achieve anything by dint of hard work.

But Gotti did not know that as a barely literate man, with no technical skills, and speaking no English, he was in American eyes simply another in the seemingly endless legions of *giornalieri* (day workers) imported like so many beasts of burden to perform the back-breaking hard labor of America's construction boom.

From the first moment they arrived in the New World, the Gottis and their fellow immigrants learned about the reality behind the glittering visions of the recruiters. There were no streets of gold, ordinary laborers did not own beautiful homes, and trees laden with fruit did not grow everywhere, just waiting for people to pick them. Construction work, the only work available to most of the immigrants, was hard, much harder than they thought. They dug ditches and hauled cement in large gangs, armies of busy ants carving out the foundations of the skyscrapers, apartment houses, and streets for an astonishing building boom that was transforming New York City into the world's greatest metropolis.

Gotti, a short, barrel-chested man with the strength of a

bull, had done such hard work all his life. He had no sooner passed through Ellis Island than he was recruited by one of the construction outfits (a business then dominated by the Irish) to work on one of the city's biggest excavation projects, the construction of the First Avenue trolley line. It was not until some time later when he realized that he had been hired as a strikebreaker, and that he and thousands of other Italians were imported for the express purpose of breaking a strike by Irish construction workers who wanted a raise in the then-standard pay rate for such work—$1.25 for a ten-hour day. By the norms of the *mezzogiorno*, however, the pay was good, although Gotti was to discover that $1.25 a day was a bare living wage, and not nearly enough to achieve every immigrant's dream of a nice home.

For the men of the *mezzogiorno*, the dreamers of Naples, Calabria, and western Sicily, home in America for most of them was in a shantytown slapped together by the construction firms along the East River in the upper reaches of Manhattan island. Later, in what the ruling Tammany Hall politicians with straight faces described as a "temporary expedient," ramshackle tenements were constructed for the Italian construction workers to replace those shantytowns. (Those "temporary" tenements remain there to this day.)

The tenements, the kind of substandard housing the politicians built all over the city to house immigrants at immense profit, were firetraps. They were also traps for the immigrants' ambitions. Like other immigrants—the Eastern European Jews of the Lower East Side, the Chinese of Chinatown, the Irish of the West Side—the Italians were confined to specific neighborhoods, surrounded by invisible walls of ethnic prejudice and poverty. Except for day laborer, few jobs were open to them, all low-paying: barbers, pushcart vendors, rag-pickers, junk and bottle collectors, bootblacks, newsboys, beer sellers, candy makers, signmakers, and dockworkers. To the shame of many of the immigrant men, their wives were forced to supplement the husbands' meager income by either making artificial flowers at home, or working as dressmakers in sweatshops under abominable conditions.

Fannie Gotti, busy having children, had no time for any such jobs. Not too long after the annual *festa* of Our Lady of Carmel ended, she gave birth to her fifth child. It was a boy with such a startling resemblance to his father, he was immediately christened John.

Like her fellow southern Italians, Mrs. Gotti believed that the central dynamic in the life of her new child would be the family, the unassailable institution that was the single most important factor in the survival of the Italians in the New World. And yet, as she was aware, the Italian family was coming under severe strain in America.

The root cause was conflict between the first and second generations. While the second generation sought material success and achievement in the New World, it was a drive the first generation felt some ambivalence about. On one hand, Italian mothers and fathers wanted success for their children, but at the same time they were afraid of it. The drive for success, it was feared, would turn a son, especially, into a *cafone* (clodhopper, fool), since his preoccupation with success would make him forget old values and traditions.

First-generation immigrants often would tell their children that they had lived a "dog's life," and sons were firmly warned, "Live like a man and not as a beast of burden, like me." Yet, daughters who sought to work as secretaries in offices outside the neighborhood were regarded by their families and neighbors with grave suspicion; there were rumors that some Italian girls had actually gone out on *casual* dates with men who, scandalously, were not even Italian. Even worse, in the eyes of the first-generation immigrants, were reports that some second-generation sons had become engaged to Irish or Jewish girls and announced plans to live many miles from their own families. (Gossips in the Gottis' neighborhood whispered stories of how one Italian father was driven nearly to distraction by his two daughters, who spoke Yiddish to each other when they didn't want their father to understand their conversations about the non-Italian men they were dating in secret. This event was solemnly cited as an example of the terrible consequences of what happened when daughters were permitted to work outside the neighborhood, in this case as secretaries for a downtown firm owned by Jews.)

Sons of Sicilian immigrants, especially, felt the conflict of generations. The Sicilian fathers wanted something much better for their sons than life as a construction laborer, yet they retained the ancient Sicilian suspicion of education, that nefarious tool of repression which for centuries occupying powers had used in an attempt to destroy the unique Sicilian culture and language. What was the sense, for example, of studying geography? Generations of Sicilians, intensely clannish, had lived and intermarried among each other for as long as anyone could remember; since no Sicilian in the Old Country would travel more than a few miles from home, there was no demonstrable need to learn world geography. In a culture that venerated the idea of *sangu de ma sangu* (blood of my blood), higher education was regarded as a frill and a source of dangerous new ideas that threatened the sanctity of the family. Therefore, an education that prepared a child to be basically literate was sufficient. The idea of a son or daughter going off to a university—*and actually being away from the family for months on end*—seemed unthinkable.

The most intense intergenerational conflicts broke out over dating and courtship. A date between two adolescents involved all the weight and solemnity of a diplomatic treaty, in which the entire extended family might participate. Parents, aunts, uncles, and cousins interceded on both sides to consider the serious questions that such an event inspired. Was the young woman pure? Was the young man good? Was he properly educated? Did he demonstrate the proper respect toward his family and the girl's family? Girls were everlastingly subject to the complex social rituals and rigid orthodoxy that the first generation insisted upon in the matter of relations with the opposite sex. Among second-generation young women, there was a saying, "You leave the house in a wedding dress or a casket."

The Gottis were shocked by such talk, for they were strictly Old World traditionalists who followed the dictates of their culture and their church. And as such, they were convinced they could achieve the delicate balancing act their first-generation contemporaries were trying to accomplish: give their children a better life, yet at the same time keep them tightly bound to the family and the social code of the southern Italians. But the betterment part of that goal seemed far out of reach when their son John was born. The simple fact was that the Gottis were very poor, and five children on a construction worker's salary in 1940 amounted to a prescription for permanent poverty.

"I wasn't born with four fucking cents," the grown-up John Gotti was to say many years later of his entry into his parents' world, and he wasn't far wrong. At the time of his birth, no one in the neighborhood ever saw the elder Gotti without a cigarette dangling from his lips, a nervous habit that seemed to worsen as he faced the daunting task of supporting his growing family.

Like all other immigrant families, the Gottis worried most of all about the neighborhood, what their children would experience outside the apartment, in the streets. The social world of the Italian neighborhoods existed on the streets. Small children spent all their free time playing on the sidewalks, and during the warm weather ventured into the fetid waters of the East River or the Harlem River. Above them, older women, their arms resting on pillows expressly set aside for just such a purpose, leaned out of the tenement windows watching the panorama below. The most prominent symbols of the adult social world were the private "social clubs" that seemed to exist on every block. They represented another southern Italian social institution brought intact from the Old World, including the old men who smoked black, evil-smelling de Nobile cigars and drank red wine made in local basements. In the warmer months, they played cards on folding tables set up on the sidewalks, amid constant raging arguments about interpretations of the rules, or *bocce* in the alleyways, a bowling game of indefinite rules that inspired even angrier debates. Possibly, it was these furious arguments that made them seem oblivious to the neighborhood's cacophony: the constant rattle from the Third Avenue elevated subway line, the wail of police and fire sirens, the shrieks of playing children, the rumble of traffic.

Despite the concern of the Gottis and other parents about children playing in the dangerous streets and swimming in the polluted rivers—mention of the word *polio* was sufficient to make any Italian mother instantly cross herself—there was not much of an alternative. The neighborhood had only a handful of playgrounds, and very few Italian families had enough money to send their children to a summer camp. During the summer, the children virtually lived in the streets, rising early in the morning, and running down the broad stairs of their walk-up tenements and out into the asphalt and cement kingdom. They would remain there until just before nightfall, when, from a hundred thousand kitchens, the distinctive smell of large pots of tomato sauce percolating began to waft through the neighborhood, followed by the clarion calls of the mothers summoning home their children:

"AL-FON-SO! AN-GEL-O! SAL-VA-TOR-EE!"

With that call to dinner—the practiced summons of an Italian mother could carry for blocks—children would run to their buildings, bound up the steps, and, to the eternal wonderment of their parents, arrive only slightly out of breath.

As in most other immigrant households, this nightly ritual of the Gotti home was timed to the return from work of the father of the family, who expected that dinner would be on the table as he arrived. Almost invariably it was, for dinner was an important ritual in a southern Italian household, representing "family time." In that moment, with everyone seated around the behemoth dining-room table, the centerpiece of Italian households, first-generation parents felt reassured that whatever the pressures and problems of the outside world, inside their own homes the eternal verities of family, blood, and kinship prevailed.

Fannie Gotti fervently believed that the doctrine of *sangu de ma sangu* would triumph, somehow, against the "outside influences" in the largely hostile and dangerous world she perceived in the streets beyond the sanctuary of her own home. With six active sons by 1945—John, the second youngest, plus Carmine, Vincent, Gene, Richard, and Peter, the oldest—she had cause to worry, for in the streets existed a terrible temptation for the young sons of immigrant families. The temptation was known by a word that struck dread in every mother's heart: *borgata*.

East Harlem and other Italian neighborhoods were infested with *borgata,* the Italian term for gangs of boys who ran around creating mischief, or, in some cases, actually committing crimes: rolling drunks, burglarizing lofts, and stealing from the merchants with outdoor stalls. All parents prayed their sons would not join a gang, but gangs seemed endemic, and only a few boys seemed able to resist the pressure of belonging. For most of them, it was a form of protection against some of the more violent gangs of older boys, and they tended to be involved mostly in relatively innocent pranks, such as filching an apple from a grocery stand, then outrunning the beefy Irish cop on the beat.

But other *borgata* amounted to packs of baby mobsters who spent their time on the streets perfecting the criminal arts. They were busiest during the school year, terrorizing even elementary school students. The young John Gotti, when he started attending Public School 113 near his home, could see them each morning, sharks circling younger boys; brandishing knives, they demanded that the terrified younger boys give up their dimes and quarters for "protection." And there were stories about some older boys, in the local junior high school, who openly threatened teachers in the classroom. Teachers who refused to be cowed were waylaid after school by gangs who beat them with brass knuckles and lengths of garden hose filled with buckshot. These older boys strutted around the neighborhood as if they owned it, warning of the terrible things they would do to any boy who had become *sbirru* (Sicilian slang for stool pigeon)—notably, the fierce, crippling beating they would administer to any boy foolish enough to complain to school authorities about being shaken down for a few coins of lunch money.

The young John Gotti was not among the victims, for even at an early age, he was acquiring a formidable reputation. He had a volcanic temper, and in the elementary grades his school record was dotted with citations for fighting with other students. The boy seemed to be in some kind of constant rage, liable to erupt at the slightest provocation. Only those familiar with Gotti's surroundings and family life could understand that the constant battles were symptoms of the larger rage he felt toward the hand that life had dealt him. He was enraged because his family was so poor; because as a young fledgling in the nest, he had to fight constantly for attention and his rightful share; because his mother always seemed to be in a state of exhaustion; because his father had to work so hard to feed so many children; because his older brothers beat up on him; because the bathwater always seemed to be dirty by the time it was his turn in a large family; because other children snickered at the threadbare clothes he wore, patched hand-me-downs from older brothers; and because he was ashamed of who he was.

Teachers who first encountered the young John Gotti regarded his apparently uncontrollable temper as a severe handicap, for they saw an unusually bright boy (years later, his I.Q. would be measured as somewhere around 140) who nevertheless seemed to have no interest in any school subject. What they usually encountered was a boy who even in his preteen years strutted around school in a pronounced tough-guy swagger and regarded everyone with a penetrating, baleful stare. Clearly, he was carrying a large proverbial chip on his shoulder that he dared anyone to knock off.

Teachers tended to feel uncomfortable around the boy, but they also noted that he seemed to be a born leader who apparently dominated a group of boys who gathered around him. In short order, they were formed into a small *borgata* that began to explore some of the darker corners of their neighborhood. And what they encountered was the hidden world of the Italians in America, a world seldom discussed openly, yet woven deeply into the fabric of their lives.

On hot summer nights, the men could be seen sitting in wooden chairs on the sidewalk in front of such places as the misleadingly named Palma Boys Club, even in the heat wearing the then-standard 1940s mobster uniform of gray fedora with three-inch brim, and blue pinstripe suit with wide lapels. Invariably, they drove shiny black sedans, which they parked wherever they felt like it. To John Gotti and the young *borgata* boys who would come around to gawk at them, these men occasionally would turn a menacing stare through the smoke of cigarettes hanging from the corners of their lips. "G'way, kid," they might snarl, and the boys would run.

But other times, one of the men might say, "C'mere, kid." When the boy approached, a five-dollar bill—an unbelievable sum—would be pressed into his hand. "Get me a coffee—black, no sugar—and the *Telegram*. Make sure you get the final, with the racing results." The boy would run to the nearest candy store and return in Olympic-record time, but would be imperiously waved away when he tried to hand over the change. "Keep it, kid; you done good."

These were the men of mystery in the neighborhood, the men who did not go to jobs, and who apparently spent most of their time just hanging out at certain social clubs with green-painted windows. They were men who seemed to think nothing of sticking ten dollars in a shoeshine boy's pocket for a good shine, who lavished similar largesse on ten-year-old boys for the simple task of watching their cars, who casually peeled off ten- and twenty-dollar bills from huge wads of cash in their pockets, and who inspired, mysteriously, some sort of fear among other adults.

Asked about these men, parents would simply reply, "They're bad people; you stay away from them." No other explanation was forthcoming, and neighborhood boys were reduced to puzzlement: what was so bad about these people? Always dressed in the finest suits, they walked with a confident swagger. Seemingly, they spent much of their time playing cards, mostly the Sicilian games of *bris-cola* and *trisette*, chattering and laughing. The men projected the image of confidence and power. Even the local police showed great respect toward them, and for some unknown reason, never ticketed those shiny black cars that were contemptuously double-parked or pulled up beside a fire hydrant. If they were bad people, then why were the cops so friendly toward them? And why did their parents whisper about these men in awed tones of respect?

The mystery extended far deeper than John Gotti and the other young boys knew, for the people of East Harlem and the Bronx coexisted with a largely invisible and omnipotent alien force shrouded in the legends and myths of their own culture. There were many different names for that force. Immigrants from Naples knew them as the *Camorra;* those from Sicily called them *Mafia*. More often, they were known as the men of the "honored society," the "people of respect," or, more simply, "the organization." In America, they had become known by other names: The Mob. The Outfit. The Syndicate. *La Cosa Nostra.*

Whatever the name, they had been an integral part of southern Italian culture for centuries, thriving where the distinctions between the criminals and law-abiding citizens (frequently called *babbo,* Sicilian slang for "jerk") were not always clear in an essentially lawless land. The men of southern Italy many years ago began taking the law into their own hands, replacing anarchy with a system that evolved into a form of underground government.

The organization that resulted was led by men whose word was their bond, men who were expected to arbitrate local disputes, protect the people from outside marauders, and generally ensure that the distinctive southern Italian culture remained inviolate. A man entrusted with such a task was known as *un'uomo d'onore* (man of honor) and *un'uomo di rispetto* (man of respect). He was a man considered strong enough to avenge any insult to himself, and to offer "insult to his enemies."

The organization itself was most commonly known as *Mafia,* although no one knows exactly how that name came about. According to the prevailing myth among southern Italians, the name was born during a revolt of Sicilians in 1282 against their French occupiers. A French soldier allegedly raped a young Sicilian woman on her wedding day, and as her anguished mother ran through the streets crying, *"Ma fia, ma fia!"* (my daughter, my daughter), infuriated Sicilians rose up and began slaughtering French soldiers. Thousands of Frenchmen died in a bloodbath touched off by Sicilians in a frenzy over what they regarded as a direct insult to the honor of their young women.

It is a colorful story, passed down from generation to generation, but quite untrue. The historical fact is that the organization—and the concept that lay behind it—evolved gradually over a period of nearly two thousand years in southern Italy, especially Sicily. The *mezzogiorno* was conquered and reconquered many times, each conquest bringing a new set of laws. Those laws were very much a reflection of the whims of the conqueror in power at any given moment, and the people realized they were regarded merely as vassals to be exploited. In this atmosphere, they became more insular and more clannish, relying on their underground government of bandits, who stole from the rich conquerors and shared the spoils with the poor, the woeful *paesani* who tried to eke a living from the unforgiving dust.

By the time of the great migrations of southern Italians to the United States, the men usually known as *amici* (friends) or *u'omini rispettati* (men of respect) occupied a curious niche in the minds and hearts of their fellow countrymen. True, the *amici* often were violent and committed crimes, but they were also men whose word was inviolate, and who never betrayed a trust. At the same time, the vast majority of southern Italians, a remarkable and hardworking people, fervently prayed that their sons would never become one of the *amici*.

Essentially, southern Italians suffered a form of schizophrenia about the *amici*. Although life in America would seem to have obviated the need for any such organization, in fact the New World offered disturbing parallels to the Old: exploitative landlords, corrupt Tammany Hall politicians, arbitrary police who enforced the law one way for the rich, another way for immigrants; and a society whose interest in the Italian immigrants seemed restricted to how many dirty jobs they would be willing to perform for low wages. In that atmosphere, the *amici*—seen by many immigrants as a form of protection against a largely hostile American society—thrived anew. Granted, they were criminals, but they were the men who could run the Italian lottery (immigrants did not understand why such an innocent thing was illegal in America), guarantee that a man could make his own red wine in a home distillery (another mysterious illegality in American culture), and intervene with authority so that men could play card games in the open air for money—which southern Italians had been doing for centuries, until told that such a thing was against the law in America. The *amici* could be approached to intervene with the authorities to solve various problems, and in a culture suspicious of banks—which in any event did little to underwrite immigrant dreams of business success—they could provide the loans that started a small business or helped another to expand.

There was a price to be paid. All children who grew up

in Italian immigrant neighborhoods could tell stories about encountering occasional victims of gangland rubouts lying in the streets. Similarly, they would see the bleeding and broken men staggering around after having received a severe beating for failure to repay a debt, or some other transgression. And there were the recurring whispers about some family funerals, where the brawn of several beefy, sweating pallbearers would be required to carry the casket of someone's deceased grandmother. Several mourners would wink knowingly at each other, aware that the body of that frail woman who weighed less than a hundred pounds at her death hardly needed all that strength to carry to her final resting place; in fact, the funeral home had participated in the common practice of disposing of a gangland murder victim by squeezing that body into the coffin of a more legitimately deceased person.

Worst of all, the depredations of the *amici* cast a shadow over the reputation of the immigrants as a people, the vast majority of whom were decent, law-abiding citizens intent only on forging a life of success in a world that retained a deep suspicion about anyone whose name ended in a vowel. Yet, too many of them persisted in an odd duality, insisting on one hand that their children have nothing to do with the "evil" Mafia, yet on the other venerating its members. To outsiders, the *amici* of the Mafia were described as some sort of strange aberration that existed in the Italian community, having no connection with its lawful citizens. Yet, as everyone was aware, the *amici* could not survive a moment were it not for the favorable climate of the neighborhood in which they lived.

The duality that existed in the minds of the immigrants was best summarized in East Harlem by the lives of its two most famous native sons. One of them was named Fiorello La Guardia. Known affectionately as "The Little Flower," the diminutive La Guardia worked his way through school, and burst onto the political scene as a congressman representing New York's Eighteenth Congressional District, which then included East Harlem and the Bronx. He was a remarkable man, a tireless fighter for the poor of his district, who startled the staid chamber of the House of Representatives in one of his first speeches on the floor when he pulled lamb chops and steaks from his pockets, slammed them on his desk, and decried high meat prices that made such food impossible for poor families to buy.

Totally incorruptible, La Guardia was worshipped by his constituents. Like an icon, his picture hung on the walls of many apartments in his district; parents would point out the picture to their children as the man they were to emulate. The "little flower," the children were instructed, was an inspiration to all: the son of poor immigrants, he had overcome prejudice, the hostility of corrupt Tammany Hall politicians (who sneeringly called him "Blackguardia"), and his humble roots to become not only a congressman, but later mayor of the entire City of New York. This product of the *mezzogiorno* was proud to be an Italian; he had never sought to change his name, as some second-generation Italians had done, and was never ashamed to demonstrate the exuberance and sheer joy of life that was most characteristic of his people.

And yet, while La Guardia was building a dazzling political career that was to make him the most famous mayor in the country—his name is still venerated in New York City many years later—another son of southern Italian immigrants in East Harlem was beginning his own career. He, too, in his time would become just as famous as La Guardia, although the two men hated each other. More to the point, this son of immigrants came to be held as a curious mirror image of the respect of his people that La Guardia enjoyed. That fact tells much about the dichotomy the southern Italians of the Eighteenth Congressional District felt about two very different kinds of men their neighborhood produced.

The man whose fame would rival La Guardia's was born with the name Salvatore Lucania, although he would become better known by his assumed name of Charles (Lucky) Luciano.

The story of Luciano was, in most respects, typical of East Harlem: large family, life in a drab tenement, construction worker father, mother supplementing husband's meager income by taking in laundry, the young Salvatore Lucania, a child of the streets, forming his own *borgata*. What made

Salvatore Lucania different, however, was his demonstrable talent in the kingdom of the streets: with extraordinary organizational and business acumen, by the age of eighteen, a school dropout, he was a full-fledged crime czar, already formulating plans for a huge, nationwide confederacy of crime.

He ultimately succeeded, and although he was later convicted and deported to Italy, Lucky Luciano had become a legend in the streets that spawned him. By the time John Gotti was a boy playing in those very same streets, he heard the stories that everyone seemed to know about Luciano: how at age fifteen he was thrown out of his home by a father despairing that even severe beatings could forestall the son's drift into crime; how the boy rented his own apartment, recruiting local boys like Francisco Castiglia (later, Frank Costello), Gaetano (Three Fingers Brown) Lucchese, Albert Anastasia, and Vito Genovese for a *borgata;* how he changed his last name to Luciano so he would not shame the family name; how he changed his first name to Charles because he hated the nickname "Sal"; how his mother would sneak out of her home to his apartment and deliver jars of his favorite homemade tomato sauce; how he miraculously survived an assassination attempt by knife and acquired the nickname "Lucky"; how he formed an alliance with Jewish gangsters Maier Sucholjowsky (later, Meyer Lansky) and Benjamin (Bugsy) Siegel from the Lower East Side; how he went to work for the *don* of the *amici,* Giussepe (Joe the Boss) Masseria, who infuriatingly patronized him by calling him *"bambino"* and demanded that he "get rid of those fucking hebes"; how he arranged for Masseria's murder; how he became second in command to Masseria's replacement, Salvatore Maranzano, a Sicilian traditionalist who read volumes of Roman history for inspiration; how he decided that Maranzano would never agree to his ideas for a modern Mafia using American business techniques; how he arranged for the death of Maranzano and his supporters in a bloodbath known as the "Night of the Sicilian Vespers"; how, at the remarkably young age of thirty-four, he formed the greatest and most powerful criminal organization that the world had ever seen;

and how he was finally defeated by a determined prosecutor named Thomas E. Dewey—although it was whispered in the neighborhood that the case that brought him to earth, running a prostitution ring, was a total frameup.

These stories had the effect of transforming Luciano into some kind of folk hero, and they left a disturbing legacy among the boys of the neighborhood: Luciano, as well as La Guardia, was a role model. Other, similar role models existed, notably the men who ran East Harlem and the Bronx for Luciano, also "men of respect," men who, the neighborhood boys learned, enjoyed an ambiguous reputation among their parents. Some parents called Michael (Trigger Mike) Coppola "bad," but there were other parents who related how Trigger Mike each Christmas handed out turkeys and hams to needy families, and who gave five hundred dollars to other families down on their luck, refusing all talk of repayment. True, Coppola among other acts had murdered an election district worker who had the temerity to complain about a rigged local election, but that was "business," and did not in the least detract from his reputation as a "man of respect" eager to help out anybody in the neighborhood with a problem. Coppola's chief lieutenant, Joseph (Joey) Rao was also called "bad" by some people, but there were plenty of others who boasted about how this son of poor immigrants had enjoyed spectacular success in the New World: it was rumored he had made *millions*, and there was a great deal of gossip about the beautiful suits he always wore, and the large estate he had bought in New Jersey, where he kindly had set aside land so his aged father could grow tomatoes and tend fig trees.

No wonder that the *borgatas* of John Gotti and other boys took as their role models the "men of respect" like Luciano, Coppola, and Rao. Their parents might talk about the virtues of hard work and dedication, as exemplified by the life of Fiorello La Guardia, but that paled beside the inspiration provided by a man like Joey Rao, ostentatiously strolling the sidewalk outside an East Harlem social club, his two-hundred-dollar suit perfectly tailored, his fedora precisely correct, like a movie star's, his shoes shined to a mirrorlike gleam, his car at the curb looking as though it had just come out of the showroom.

There were no boys of the *borgata* hanging around City Hall, watching La Guardia wrestle with the problems of where to locate that sewer line, or how to find the money for a needed new wharf. But there were knots of the boys around Rao, imitating his every move, eagerly trailing after him, hoping that Rao might favor them at some point—a ten-dollar bill snapped from a huge bankroll just to hold open a car door for him, a five-dollar bill to get him a bar of candy, a twenty-dollar bill ready for any of the competing shoeshine boys who could keep his handmade Italian shoes in a high gloss. And why not? The boys had seen how adults acted when a man like Luciano, Coppola, or Rao walked into a store and ignited displays of obsequious respect and fawning service.

Nothing so distressed the parents of John Gotti as the realization that most of his time on the streets seemed devoted to his little junior *borgata* and hanging around outside those social clubs with the green-painted windows, fawning over men like Joey Rao. Just as they despaired of a solution, one arrived in the form of a highly sought prize, the security of a civil service job. John Gotti, Sr., who had taught himself English, passed the civil service test and was hired by the Sanitation Department.

The security and increased pay allowed Gotti Sr. to take a significant step: rental of a two-story home on the Brooklyn waterfront to house his large family. It was short of his eventual dream of a home of his own in the suburbs, but to a family jammed into four rooms of a fifth-floor walkup tenement, the move seemed like an advance to the Taj Mahal.

If Gotti Sr. hoped that the new neighborhood would be free of what the sociologists liked to call "environmental factors" that had lured some of his sons—including his favorite, John Jr.—into the world of the *borgata*, he was to be sadly disappointed. Unfortunately, although he assumed that the move across the East River meant his children would now be able to play on real grass and away from the menacing concrete shadows of Manhattan, he was quite wrong. He did not know that in the Brooklyn waterfront of 1950, there existed a world that in many ways was much more dangerous than the one he was leaving.

He could not have guessed that his favorite son would flourish in this world of violence and death.

2

Borgata Nostra

I killed him, that's true. But it wasn't nothing personal.
—ABRAHAM (KID TWIST) RELES

LIKE A RAILROAD WATCH, the daily schedule of Thomas
(Toddo) Marino was so precise, a man could stake his life
on the certainty that Marino would perform his daily rituals
at exactly the same time for each and every day of each and
every year. Indeed, for anyone doing business with him, it
was considered wise to observe the same sort of rigid
schedule.

Marino rose at 1 P.M. exactly. He allowed himself exactly
twenty-five minutes to get ready for his workday, a process
that included dressing himself in one of his many expensive
suits, complete with large tie clip decorated with forty-eight
diamonds and belt buckle with an even larger number of
diamonds. He would then eat a light breakfast—he scheduled
six minutes for it—and walk out of his Brooklyn home into
a waiting chauffeur-driven car whose driver had learned to
begin idling the motor a precise two minutes before his boss
exited the house.

Marino was driven to a nearby tavern he owned, where a
cook already had waiting for him his second breakfast. Its
preparation had been precisely timed to be on the table just
as Marino walked in the door. Other men, who had gathered
in the tavern to discuss business with Marino while he ate
his second breakfast, girded their digestive systems for this
ordeal, for the meal consisted of a dish known as "eggs in
purgatory"—several sunny-side eggs in a thick tomato sauce.

To their unfailing disgust, Marino would seize a fork, then mash the concoction into a bloody-looking mess. He would insist on talking while eating, and the other men in the tavern would try not to look as some of his breakfast dribbled down his chin.

The second breakfast concluded—in Marino's allotted time of sixteen minutes—he would adjourn to a coffee shop a few doors away. There, Marino would spend the next twelve hours discussing business with a constant stream of visitors. Without fail, he would leave the coffee shop at 4 A.M. Exactly one hour later, he would retire for the night, rise again at 1 P.M. the following day, and begin the process all over again.

Marino's persona was a source of some amusement to his business associates, who privately mocked this strange man of precise schedule, garish adornment, and table manners of a warthog. But no one dared openly to mock Marino, a humorless man, for Toddo was not somebody to tolerate mockery of himself. A flat-out Mafia hood, Marino had risen through the ranks of the Brooklyn branch of the Mafia to become boss of the waterfront. It was a tough world, and only a man like Marino, who bore the scars of knife fights and bullet wounds, along with a reputation as a killer with a dozen murders to his credit, could rise to such a position of prominence.

The pre–World War II Brooklyn waterfront that Marino oversaw—and for which he set a certain criminal style that endured—was a savage world, a world where everything seemed to perch on the edge of violence. By its very definition, the waterfront and its jungle of piers and loading docks was a place for only the hardiest of men, capable of the back-breaking labor of moving crates in and out of ships by hand. The strong survived and the weak were pushed aside in this world, immortalized by Marlon Brando in *On the Waterfront*.

The Brooklyn waterfront was notorious, the kind of place, it was rumored, where bodies of murder victims and gangland rubouts were never found. They were dumped into the ocean and set upon by voracious sea crabs that had developed a taste for human flesh. The crabs, so it was said, could strip a body of its flesh in less than a half hour. Perhaps so; fed a steady diet of bodies by the violent world above them, the sea crabs that lived in the waters around Brooklyn had grown to immense sizes.

The world of the Brooklyn waterfront included Red Hook, so named by the Dutch, who originally settled the place, in honor of the wild cranberries that flourished there. The Dutch unintentionally got the name just right, for three hundred years later, Red Hook's dominant color was that of blood. The home of southern Italian immigrants recruited for the docks, Red Hook attracted the lowliest dregs of the *mezzogiorno,* people whom other Italian immigrants looked down upon. The life of brutal work on the docks produced hardened men who walked around with cargo hooks stuck in their belts. Often, arguments were settled by duels with these hooks, and losers were known by the horrible scars across their faces. Red Hook probably had more one-eyed men than any other place in the world.

Nearby was another tough community, Sheepshead Bay. It was a fishing community, peopled largely by immigrant Sicilian fishermen already toughened by the unforgiving life of trying to catch fish in the unpredictable Atlantic Ocean. They were further toughened by the intense competition among the various groups of fishermen for the finite supply of fish. Almost all of them wore large knives, ostensibly for the purpose of cutting nets and fish carcasses, but more commonly used to settle disputes.

All in all, the Brooklyn waterfront was a perfect environment for the Mafia to operate in: large numbers of immigrants who spoke little English, communities dominated by a single industry, and that industry at the mercy of one labor force. The first inroad was made as early as 1907, when a local thug named Paul Kelly—his real name was Paolo Vaccarelli— formed the Garbage Scow Union to represent the men who worked the huge barges that transported garbage. As Kelly realized, shipping firms were eager to keep labor peace, for nobody wanted strikebound scows loaded with garbage anchored at dockside, stinking up the entire waterfront. The shippers discovered that paying bribes to Kelly would insure peace. Meanwhile, Kelly plundered the union treasury and with his union members cowed by a platoon of thugs, he allowed the Mafia to plunder them further by extortionate loans and gambling operations.

For the next eighty-two years, the Mafia would come to regard the Brooklyn waterfront as its private preserve for plunder. The key was the waterfront unions that represented the dock workers, whose locals remained firmly in the grip of the Mafia. The grip was enhanced by the antiquated "shape-up" system used on the waterfront: gangs of long-shoremen would show up early each morning, from which a foreman would arbitrarily select a certain number of men to work that day, depending on how many ships were waiting at dockside. The rest of the men would be sent home.

An ordinary longshoreman, totally at the mercy of this system, was in no position to argue. Those who did exhibit too independent a turn of mind would encounter the Mafia hoods who lurked all over the waterfront, enforcing discipline. Back in the early days, they included a local hood named Alphonse (Big Al) Capone, who later ducked a murder charge by fleeing to Chicago, where he began a different career path. He was succeeded by plenty of other later-famous hoods—among them Albert Anastasia, Carlo Gambino, and Vito Genovese—who all cut their teeth in the waterfront rackets.

The waterfront attracted a small army of *Mafiosi*, for there were seemingly unlimited riches to be plundered there. In addition to the union local racket, the Mafia also used its control of the docks to steal just about any shipment worth stealing. The losses were enormous, but insurance companies—controlled by crooked politicians—quietly paid the claims, then collected even greater commissions on still more expensive policies. In turn, the shipping companies absorbed the losses and simply passed on the costs in the form of increased shipping charges to their customers. Meanwhile, the ultimate victims in this giant clockwork of racketeering—the longshoremen—were victimized further by the Mafia loan sharks eager to advance money to workers hard put to support families on their pay. Those who tried to avoid repayment would find themselves victims of the many "accidents" that occurred every day on the docks: a cargo pallet that suddenly slipped from a crane and fell atop a man's head, or the box of heavy machinery that somehow tumbled from atop a pile and smashed a man's foot. Or, there was the less complicated way, the method that occurred daily in the streets of Red Hook: a recalcitrant debtor, waylaid by several hoods, would have his teeth smashed in with a lead pipe, or get his knees broken with baseball bats. The "message," as it was called, was accompanied by the standard admonition: "You better fuckin' pay next time!"

It was into this violent world that John Gotti, Sr., brought his family in the late winter of 1950. Among other things, the two-story wooden house he was renting in Sheepshead Bay had the advantage of being within walking distance of local schools, including Public School 209, in which his son John was enrolled.

The change in environment did not alter the young John Gotti. He still had that explosive temper, and his sixth-grade teacher, a lady with the unlikely name of Miss Doody, tried to figure out some way of channeling that rage. As other teachers had been, she was struck by how bright the boy was, yet she seemed to spend most of her time separating him from fights with other boys. John Gotti, she quickly understood, was a boy very angry at the world.

She never did succeed in her project of redirecting the boy's energies, for after less than two years in P.S. 209, John Gotti was gone: the house his father was renting was about to be torn down to make way for an apartment building project. Forced to move quickly, Gotti Sr. decided on East New York, a working-class community in Brooklyn's interior flatlands, where there were some similar two-story houses for rent.

In terms of environment, it was another terrible mistake, for East New York was an area whose savagery made places like East Harlem and even the Brooklyn waterfront seem tame. The savage reputation of East New York could be summed up in one name: Murder Incorporated. And the heritage of that infamous organization would do much to shape the mind of the young John Gotti.

*   *   *

Years before the urbanization of Brooklyn began, the small and sparsely settled villages of Williamsburg, Brownsville, and East New York existed in a rural stupor. But just prior to World War I, the overflow from the increasingly crowded Jewish quarter of the Lower East Side in Manhattan and the Italian neighborhoods of Little Italy and East Harlem began to move eastward, across the East River, into the vast interior plains of Brooklyn. Organized crime followed these immigrants across the river, and by 1930, flourishing Mafia and Jewish organized crime groups existed side by side, with elaborate arrangements to overcome ethnic differences in the name of common profit.

While the Italian Mafia concentrated on its conventional interests—primarily loansharking and illegal gambling—the Jewish mobsters went after the small garment manufacturers who had sought to escape the Garment Center in Manhattan, badly infested by the criminals that preyed on manufacturers and unions alike. Chiefly, the manufacturers were trying to outrun their greatest nemesis, Louis (Lepke) Buchalter, the mobster who dominated the Garment Center. Buchalter some years before had been invited by the manufacturers to break union organizing drives; when Buchalter discovered that he could make even more money by extorting labor peace from the manufacturers, their ordeal began. By the mid-1930s, Buchalter was extorting nearly fifty million dollars a year from them. He had a crew of two hundred fifty hoods, including his chief assistant, the infamous Jacob (Gurrah) Shapiro, who walked around with lead window sash weights in his coat pockets, used to smash in the skulls of manufacturers and union leaders who did not want to "cooperate."

Buchalter followed the runaway manufacturers into East New York, and in short order had matters under control. To do so required the murder of seven local punks who made the mistake of attempting to muscle into a territory Buchalter considered his private preserve. And in carrying out these murders, Buchalter took a significant step in the history of organized crime.

The problem was that Buchalter had plenty of strong-arm hoods, but few talented contract killers capable of carrying out the relatively complicated task of disposing of seven inconvenient members of humanity without arousing the entire city. To solve the problem, Buchalter opened negotiations with the Mafia, represented by one of its rising stars in Brooklyn, Albert Anastasia (successor to Toddo Marino as waterfront *capo*). Buchalter proposed, and Anastasia accepted, a plan for a joint organization of professional killers, using the top talents of both Jewish and Italian organized crime. Murder Incorporated was born.

The new organization represented a fusion of murder and corporate methods. With Buchalter as president and Anastasia as chief executive officer, Murder Incorporated put a staff of killers on annual twelve-thousand-dollar retainers. Each killing, jointly decided by Buchalter and Anastasia—who would rule on "requests" for murders from throughout organized crime—was assigned to a team of assassins. The assignment was called a "contract" (a meaning that has since passed into the language), and the actual killing was called a "hit" (another meaning Murder Incorporated contributed to the English language). Headquartered in East New York, Murder Incorporated was dominated by a corporate ethos, including a firm rule that a murder was to be committed only for "business reasons" and another that "civilians" (ordinary citizens not connected with crime) were not to be harmed in the course of carrying out a contract.

The killers retained by Murder Incorporated were the cream of the New York underworld's best hit men, among them Vito (Chicken Head) Gurino, who perfected his deadly aim by shooting the heads off live chickens, and Frank (The Dasher) Abbanando, so called because his gun misfired once in the course of trying to kill a man; the victim chased Abbanando around a building, but was lapped by the faster killer, who then shot him in the back of the head.

But the organization's star killer was Abraham (Kid Twist) Reles, a fat, five-foot two-inch hood with thick lips; a flat nose and long gangling arms completed a simianlike appearance. Reles, whose nickname derived from his obsessive munching of chocolate candy twists that he devoured by the boxful, specialized in the use of an icepick, an instrument he could jam into a victim's heart in a split second. A cold-blooded killer, Reles inspired fear on the streets of East New

York among people who were aware that he had killed, in broad daylight, two black men—one at a car wash for failing to spot a small smudge on the front fender of his car, and the other at a parking lot because he failed to move fast enough when Reles ordered him to fetch his car.

No wonder that East New York was terrified of Murder Incorporated, whose "employees" (as the organization insisted on calling them) swaggered around the streets, oblivious to the police, who in the main gave them a wide berth. There were actually nearly two hundred such "employees," ranging downward from the elite killers, to "fingermen," who plotted the movements of prospective victims; to "wheelmen," who stole, and switched the license plates of, cars used in "hits"; and to the lowest category, "evaporators," who were responsible for ensuring that all possible incriminating evidence disappeared—including the body of the victim.

How many people Murder Incorporated killed during the peak years of its existence, from 1935 to 1939, will never be known with any accuracy. Some estimates run up to three hundred victims, but only about a dozen murders—including that of Arthur (Dutch Schultz) Fliegenheimer, who made the error of defying Lucky Luciano—are known for certain. And those are known because of an extraordinary event that took place in 1940: Abe Reles suddenly decided to become a stool pigeon.

Reles had been arrested for one of the many casual murders he had committed, nonsanctioned killings he had done over and above his killings for Murder Incorporated. Facing the electric chair, perhaps unsurprisingly he agreed to tell all he knew about the organization that retained his services. The revelations were sensational (Buchalter and Shapiro went to the electric chair), but Reles never got to enjoy the immunity from further prosecution and a future life he was promised by Brooklyn District Attorney William O'Dwyer. On November 11, 1941, in what is still one of the most famous officially unsolved murder cases in American history, Reles was thrown from the seventh-floor window of a Coney Island hotel in which the district attorney's office had been hiding him. The execution took place despite a twenty-four-hour police guard.

Actually, Reles was quite aware he was about to be murdered. After he revealed the role in Murder Incorporated of Buchalter and his associates, he had gone on to begin talking about certain Mafia figures, notably Albert Anastasia. To his horror, Reles subsequently learned that the corrupt O'Dwyer immediately ran out and sold that information to Anastasia. It was then only a matter of time. A grateful Anastasia paid a hundred thousand dollars to O'Dwyer and two equally corrupt police officers; these latter two men and a police captain defenestrated Reles before he could reveal much else about the Mafia.

The death of Reles ended any further investigation into Murder Incorporated, but the memory of Kid Twist lingered for many years afterward in the Brooklyn branch of the Mafia. At least several nights a week, a mobster would lift his glass in some bar and propose a toast: "Here's to Abe Reles, a great canary. He could sing, but he couldn't fly."

The heritage of Murder Incorporated also lingered long afterward in East New York. It inspired a form of mad lawlessness that could not be experienced anyplace else in New York City, something very much like the reign of evil gunslingers who take over a town in a grade B western movie. Partly, that was because Brooklyn in general had come under the sway of Albert Anastasia, who was not for nothing known in the Mafia as "The Mad Hatter" and "The Executioner."

Anastasia took final control of the borough in 1951 by the simple expedient of murdering his boss, Vincent Mangano, the then-reigning Mafia chief in Brooklyn. This was a serious move, for Mangano was one of the original five bosses selected during Lucky Luciano's reorganization of the New York Mafia into five families some years before. But economic expediency overrode any possible retribution against Anastasia; The Mad Hatter was known as a gargantuan moneymaker for the Mafia, Mangano was perceived in the rest of the organization as weak, and so perhaps it was time for a change.

The secret of Anastasia's earning power was his control of

the docks, at that time the central entry point for almost all imports into the United States (and most exports leaving it). The forty thousand longshoremen who worked the three hundred deep-water ports along the waterfront were firmly under Anastasia's thumb, mainly because his brother, Anthony (Tough Tony) Anastasia, had taken control of the Italian-dominated union locals, eventually becoming president of the biggest, Local 1814 of the International Longshoremen's Association. The Anastasias, along with Albert's chief lieutenant, Guiseppe (Joe Adonis) Doto, turned the docks into outlaw territory. They also turned the waterfront into a giant money machine, with vast profits from extortion, gambling, loansharking, kickbacks, and thefts.

Anastasia lived like a feudal prince on an estate on the other side of New York Harbor in New Jersey, guarded by a seven-foot-high barbed-wire fence, a pack of vicious Dobermans, and a squad of bodyguards. The draconian security was to protect himself from any potential enemies in the Mafia, for he had little to fear in the way of problems with the authorities; he was known as a master corruptor, with police and local politicians in Brooklyn on his payroll. Indeed, Anastasia was known as the man who had corrupted the entire borough, converting it into a virtual pirate kingdom whose main industry was crime.

If it was true, as often whispered, that Anastasia was the "king of Brooklyn," then the borough was under the rule of an extremely unstable monarch. For all his business acumen, Anastasia was also a homicidal maniac with a violent temper, a man who liked killing for the sake of killing. He would order up "hits" for the slightest infractions, and when he once read a newspaper account of a local citizen who had recognized and turned in to police the famous bank robber Willie Sutton, he immediately ordered the good citizen murdered on the grounds that "I hate a rat, no matter who he is." Even Anastasia's brother, "Tough Tony," no slouch at violence and killing himself, trod very carefully around Albert. He could not be faulted for such caution: Albert liked to have murder victims hideously tortured before being killed, and insisted on later hearing every detail, including precisely which tortures were inflicted on which part of the victim's anatomy, the volume of the victim's screams, and how the victim had begged for the mercy of death. As a hobby, he personally participated in some of the murders.

When the twelve-year-old John Gotti began prowling the streets of his new neighborhood of East New York in 1952, he entered Anastasia's kingdom of crime. On every block, there were pool halls, betting joints, "hot shops" (fronts for stolen goods), and illegal gambling parlors. Goods stolen from the docks were for sale everywhere, and the fences usually didn't bother even to take the stuff out of the original shipping cartons. Local police in uniform ran an extensive "pad" (payments for police protection), openly walking into places and picking up envelopes of cash.

In the luncheonettes and candy stores that dotted every block, Mafia bookmakers ran their operations from pay phones without any fear of arrest. Numbers and policy (illegal lottery) bets were sold as commonly as newspapers. Other bookmakers and loan sharks operated right on the street corners in broad daylight.

In contrast to the more understated Mafia world across the river in Manhattan, East New York operated as a wide-open mob town. To the young boys of East New York who hung around those luncheonettes and candy stores, the local *Mafiosi* were larger-than-life heroes, the guys in sharp clothes who always seemed to be squiring around beautiful women (many of whom were showgirls attracted to the thrill of being in the same orbit as dangerous mobsters). On any given day, the luncheonettes were full of mobsters, including young toughs who laughingly boasted of their "enforcement work," the beatings inflicted on loan shark debtors behind in their payments, or the damage they wreaked on a small shopowner's store after he refused the installation of a vending machine from a Mafia-controlled outfit.

The young boys were dazzled by the world these men represented: the big bankrolls they pulled from their pockets and spent as though money meant nothing to them; the diamond pinkie rings they all wore, carefully letting the gem occasionally catch the light and impress anyone watching; their idle chatter about how some local hood, caught in flagrante delicto with the wife of a Mafia *don,* had suffered the standard punishment of having his penis severed and stuffed in his mouth; the rollicking gossip about how "Louie," or "Tony," or "Sal" had wet his pants in fear when some mob enforcers pressed a gun to his head; and the sleek, beautiful women, who would sit beside the hoods, allowing themselves to be caressed in public and treated like doormats ("Go get me some ice, cunt") by young *Mafiosi* demonstrating their power over women.

Above all, these mobsters represented wealth and power, the kind of power that let them do exactly what they wanted, whenever they wanted to do it. There was one local mobster, for example, who wanted to buy a profitable bar in the neighborhood. The owner refused the offer, noting he had no intention of selling his business. The hood returned the following night atop a horse and rode into the place. He chased all the customers out, clopped up to the bar, and ordered a drink for his horse ("Scotch and water, but easy on the ice, because it gives him the runs"). The bar owner got the point, and immediately sold the place.

The dazzling world of organized crime stood in sharp contrast to what boys like John Gotti were being taught in school. Thrift, hard work, and good citizenship were the virtues the teachers tried to drum into every student's head, but in a working-class community like East New York, many boys wondered what was the point. John Gotti's father had worked hard all his life, yet he didn't seem to have a nickel to show for it. Meanwhile, the "bad people" were the guys who had the nice cars, the women, and, most of all, the money. No boy knew what life in that world was really like, but from what they saw, it looked very easy.

However, in fact, life among the *amici* of Brooklyn was becoming very difficult—and dangerous.

The beginning of the troubles that ultimately would convulse the Brooklyn branch of the Mafia—and the entire New York Mafia, for that matter—can be traced to a single day in the winter of 1946. On February 9 of that year, Lucky Luciano was transported from his upstate New York prison cell to Brooklyn, where he was to board an ocean liner for a one-way trip to Italy.

Luciano's release from prison was the climax of a Faustian bargain between the United States government and organized crime in which the Mafia had agreed, during the war, to provide the eyes and ears for a counterintelligence effort along the New York waterfront to balk the anticipated efforts of Italian and German saboteurs against transport shipping. It was the biggest and most successful scam ever perpetrated by the *amici*, for as they were perfectly aware, there was no danger whatsoever: the presumed armies of enemy saboteurs did not exist. Further, the only danger to the war effort on the waterfront was the Mafia itself, which throughout the war years continued to plunder the waterfront—war supplies included.

In any event, the government's secret payback in this deal was the release on parole of Luciano, with the proviso that he settle permanently in Italy, and never darken American shores again. His departure was something of a major event in the New York Mafia, for Luciano—although he disdained the title of *capo di tutti capi*—was in fact the organizational genius who had created the modern New York Mafia. He was the man who held it together, and the only Mafia leader with the prestige—which he continued to exercise from his prison cell—to impose the *Pax Romana* that had prevented elements of his criminal organization from destroying each other in the name of ambition.

And now Luciano was off to permanent exile in Italy, where he would not be able to wield the on-scene influence he had in the United States. The entire high command of the New York Mafia, its individual members already jockeying for dominance, appeared dockside that cold winter morning in 1946 to bid farewell to the man they invariably called "Charley Lucky." A small army of reporters and photographers also arrived, but they quickly realized their presence was not welcome in this company: some very large longshoremen, all of them brandishing evil-looking cargo hooks with razor-sharp points, made it clear that the send-off was to be a private one. From a distance, the reporters watched as the leaders of the New York Mafia trooped aboard the ship to pay their respects to Charley Lucky: Albert Anastasia, Vito Genovese, Joseph Profaci, Joseph Bonanno, Frank Costello, and Joe Adonis. Also arriving to pay their respects were the less-recognizable, but fast-rising, *capos* in the organization, among them Carlo Gambino and Thomas Lucchese.

Luciano's ship had no sooner sailed out of New York Harbor when, just as he feared, his *dons* were at each other's throats. The worst offender was the overbearingly ambitious Vito Genovese, who not only wanted to become *capo di tutti capi*, but also was demanding that the New York Mafia move more aggressively into moneymaking ventures, especially the growing narcotics market. Further, Genovese, a Sicilian traditionalist, wanted the Mafia to sever the partnership Luciano had forged with the Jewish organized crime syndicate led by Meyer Lansky and Bugsy Siegel. These demands immediately put him at odds with Frank Costello, the Mafia chief of Manhattan, who, as Luciano's closest adherent, wielded great influence in the entire Mafia. An affable, cautious man, Costello was called "prime minister of the underworld" for his diplomatic arbitration of assorted Mafia disputes. He hated any violence, and in his quiet way had built the New York Mafia into unexcelled heights of power because of his assiduous courting of politicians and police. Indeed, Costello managed to get New York City's officialdom to adopt a virtual laissez-faire attitude toward Mafia activities—provided, as Costello understood, that the Mafia stayed away from narcotics and downplayed violence, the guaranteed ways to arouse public concern. Moreover, Costello liked the Jews, and thought the alliance with them was a smart move, of mutual profit to both sides. After all, Costello pointed out, it was the Jews who had taught the Italian Mafia the intricacies of infiltration of legitimate businesses and the finer points of labor racketeering.

Genovese was unimpressed. A violent man, he thought such attitudes were turning the Mafia into a bunch of sissies. To likeminded *Mafiosi*, he related malicious gossip about Costello, such as the tidbit that the "prime minister" was seeing a psychiatrist to overcome his "terrible feelings of inferiority" touched off by his lack of education and breeding, and his dese-dem-dose vocabulary when among the people of high finance and society. Genovese, rabidly anti-Semitic, also complained endlessly about the Jews. "Why don't we get rid of these goddam kikes?" he demanded at one meeting. "What are we doing with these little sheenies just off the boat?"

"Shut the fuck up, Vito," Costello snapped. "You're a fucking immigrant yourself."

Genovese did not forget that insult, and soon found a kindred spirit: Albert Anastasia of Brooklyn. Like Genovese, Anastasia feared that Costello's corporate style would eventually turn the Mafia into a mom-and-pop grocery store. Besides which, Anastasia also harbored deep ambitions, and saw the opportunity that an alliance of convenience with Genovese presented for those ambitions. By the beginning of 1957, the convergent ambitions of Genovese and Anastasia coalesced into a plan of action. What happened next was to throw the Mafia into turmoil for the next twenty years.

On the evening of May 2, 1957, Frank Costello was returning to the lobby of his hotel when a dimwitted hood named Vincent (The Chin) Gigante stepped out of the shadows and fired a pistol at Costello's head from point-blank range. Gigante, a former boxer whose prominent chin instantly suggested his nickname, never had much luck in his life—a glass jaw cut short his ring career—and now his skein of bad luck continued. His murder contract from Genovese was simple, since Costello had no bodyguards. All Gigante had to do was to get within inches of Costello, then pull the trigger. He managed to hit Costello squarely in the temple, but the bullet veered at the last millisecond; it entered the skin, then traversed around his head just under the skin, emerging at the starting point after making a complete circuit. Gigante, assuming Costello was surely dead, fled. Costello only had a slight, if exceedingly unusual, scalp wound.

It was an incredible botch, but Costello—who told police he had no idea who would try to kill an innocent businessman such as himself—got the message, and announced his retirement. (He was to die peacefully nearly twenty years later on his suburban Long Island estate. During his retirement, he still wielded great influence in the corridors of power; once, when his lawyer mentioned the impossibility of obtaining tickets for the smash Broadway musical *My Fair Lady* at any price, Costello nodded solemnly. The following morning, the lawyer's doorbell rang. A large man who bore a strong resemblance to a gorilla silently handed the lawyer an envelope, then walked away. Inside the envelope were four front-row tickets for that night's performance.)

The move against Costello caused grave unrest within the Mafia hierarchy, and to make matters worse, it was clear that Anastasia was going off the deep end. Increasingly paranoid about what might happen to him in the wake of the failed assassination of Costello, he began lashing out in an orgy of killing against all enemies, presumed or real. Even his closest associates and leading *capi* became frightened of him; no one was quite sure if he might soon join the collection of corpses then littering Brooklyn in the bloodbath. In towering rages, Anastasia made it clear he wanted more power and more money, and he was prepared to kill anybody who he thought insufficiently supportive of that goal. At this point, one of Anastasia's shrewdest *capi*, Carlo Gambino, decided that something would have to be done.

Under ordinary circumstances, overweening ambition and murder are normally not crimes within the world of the Mafia, so Gambino needed to find some serious violation of Mafia organizational rules sufficient to cause Anastasia's fellow bosses to dispose of him. Gambino found it: he discovered that Anastasia, increasingly obsessed about money, had taken to demanding a forty-thousand-dollar "fee" from every new inductee into his Mafia family.

This unforgivable lapse of Mafia protocol left even Genovese appalled. Consequently, Gambino turned to the most violent and efficient killers then working in the Mafia, the infamous Gallo brothers of Brooklyn—Joe (Crazy Joe), Larry (Kid Twist), and Albert (Kid Blast). On October 25, 1957, they walked into the barbershop of the Park Sheraton Hotel in Manhattan while Anastasia was seated in a barber chair and shot him dead.

Three weeks later, the Mafia's hierarchy met in the small upstate New York village of Appalachin to discuss this dramatic turn of events. Before the conclave was interrupted by a raid of the New York State Police—gravely embarrassing the participants—they heard, to the dismay of Gambino and others seeking to restore the *Pax Romana* of Luciano, Genovese and Bonanno each make separate pleas for the title of boss of all bosses. Even more troublesome were the two men's renewed attempts to take over all heroin trafficking for themselves.

Clearly, things were in a state of flux, and further trouble was certain.

News of Anastasia's assassination hit East New York like a thunderclap, for unaware of the intricacies of Mafia politics, most people there assumed that the mighty Anastasia was beyond such mortal fates. A period of uncertainty began. Who would replace Anastasia? How would things change? As it turned out, not much changed. Carlo Gambino was promoted to replace Anastasia, and underworld life went on pretty much as before, albeit under much less flamboyant direction from the distinctly nonflamboyant Gambino.

Among those preoccupied with the news of Anastasia's murder was a seventeen-year-old East New York street punk who considered Anastasia his great hero. The teenager had determined to be just like The Mad Hatter, and had begun emulating Anastasia's distinctive swagger, machine-gun style of speech, and malevolent glare directed at all other human beings. The teenager was John Gotti, and his arrival at this stage in his life may have been inevitable: for some years, he had admired the *amici* and their alluring lifestyle. Now, this child of the streets was consumed with the immediate ambition of becoming an apprentice in that world, with even larger ambitions to dominate it, like Anastasia.

Gotti became a child of the streets despite the best efforts of the New York City school system to prevent it. His academic record, already pockmarked with a lengthening list of citations for fighting other boys, arrived at his new school in East New York, P.S. 178, with the notation "Discipline Problem." That was an understatement: to the teachers of P.S. 178, he was a savage, with a temper that would erupt without warning. By the eighth grade, he was a full-scale problem, and school officials, unable to deal with his violent temper, suspended him after he nearly caved in another boy's skull.

He was also a truant, with an uncanny ability to avoid the truant officers who prowled the neighborhood, rounding up students who had either slipped away or simply not appeared at P.S. 178 that day at all. Warnings to Gotti's parents by school authorities about the possibility that their son might get left back a grade appeared to have no effect. The simple fact was that Gotti found the world of the streets, with the Mafia wiseguys and endless excitement in the pool halls and betting parlors, impossible to resist. School held no allure whatsoever for him; that was a world of stifling boredom. On the streets was constant action, and, best of all, the *borgata*.

He had left his baby *borgata* behind in Manhattan, but quickly joined a new, much tougher one in East New York. Entree to the gang, unimaginatively called by its members the "Fulton-Rockaway Boys" after the streets where most of them lived, was provided by Gotti's older brother Peter, a gang member.

In the era of *West Side Story,* the gangs that existed in virtually every New York City neighborhood were primarily concerned with "turf," the doctrine of defending a gang's territory—as defined by the gang—against rival gangs. Occasional "rumbles" (street battles between rival gangs) were held to decide such matters.

But as with so much else in East New York, the youth gangs there had a rougher edge. Gangs like the Fulton-Rockaway Boys were predominantly organizations of young thieves, and battles with rival gangs usually concerned divisions of spoils. In the course of prowling the streets, the gangs developed an intimate knowledge of where money could be had for the taking: the store with an inadequate security alarm that could be easily bypassed; the "stash" points where thieves stored hijacked goods and would not complain to police if some turned up missing; and shops with elderly owners not especially alert to shoplifting boys. The gangs also required some knowledge of Mafia politics, for crimes involving any "connected" operation could get boys into serious trouble with Mafia hoods whose criminal career was thievery, but who took special umbrage if anybody stole

from them. For that reason, gangs checked carefully to see
if a local gambling operation was "sanctioned" (Mafia-
approved). If not, the winner in a high-stakes card game
would be waylaid on his way home, or a local bookmaker
not under Mafia aegis would find his cash stash missing.

Gotti had been a member of the gang for only a short
while when he began to dominate it, his forceful personality
attracting a number of *goombata* who were to follow him for
decades to come. Chief among them was a short, squat boy
who first met the twelve-year-old Gotti when the Gottis
moved to East New York from Sheepshead Bay. Angelo Ruggiero, like Gotti, had a violent temper, and shared similar
ambitions about becoming a famous crook someday. Ruggiero was nicknamed "Quack-Quack" by other gang members, partly because of his odd, ducklike walk, but mostly
because his constant chatter reminded them of an agitated
duck clacking its bill. Ruggiero was never quiet, and he
seemed compelled to say something, *anything,* every waking
moment; no secrets existed in the Ruggiero household, for
Ruggiero was certain to have revealed them publicly at some
point.

"For Christ's sake, Ange, don't you ever stop talking?"
Gotti would say occasionally, in exasperation.

"No," Ruggiero would reply, and go on chattering.

Salvatore Ruggiero, Angelo's older brother, was also a
gang member and follower of Gotti. He was a sphinx compared to his brother (possibly because he had no hope of
getting a word in), preferring to invest his energies in a mad
quest for speed. Despite two serious injuries suffered in accidents on "borrowed" motorcycles, Salvatore loved anything
that he could propel at great velocity. A maniac behind the
wheel, he taught himself how to drive at the age of thirteen,
and liked to roar around deserted areas of Brooklyn in cars
that he somehow obtained under vague circumstances.

Another early *goombah* of Gotti in the gang was Anthony
Rampino, whose consuming passion was stickball. He was
always eager to get a game going, and demonstrated extreme
finickiness about his personal equipment for that unique urban
version of baseball: not just *any* broom handle would do, and
the pink-colored Spaulding rubber ball had to pass his careful

inspection before he would consent to its use in the game. With the exception of his ambition to become a successful thief, Rampino was preoccupied with few other concerns. A cadaverous-looking boy, he had huge hands and long arms that seemed to reach down past his knees, and an odd, rubbery-looking face. By the hour, he liked to contort that face into all kinds of horrible grimaces in front of a mirror; years of practice allowed him, at a second's notice, to shape his face into something like the Phantom of the Opera. He firmly believed that such faces could frighten any enemy. He was nicknamed "Roach" because of his vague resemblance to the insect; the name assumed a double meaning not too long afterward, when Rampino began developing a serious drug habit.

Other *goombata* in the gang—among them Anthony Gurino, a plumber's apprentice, and Michael (Mickey Boy) Paradiso, at age twelve already a professional burglar—were to play important roles later in Gotti's life, but he was especially close to Rampino and the Ruggiero brothers. His relationship with another gang member, his younger brother, Gene, was more complicated. For reasons no one could quite understand, there was an underlying tension between the two brothers, a tension missing in Gotti's relations with three other brothers also in the gang: Peter, Vincent, and Richard.

One reason might have been John Gotti's insistence that his brothers were uniformly and hopelessly stupid, an assertion Gene, for one, denied. It may have been a case of Gene's being more resentful of his brother John's overbearing manner, for John Gotti was quite right: his brothers *were* stupid. Peter was openly called "a complete retard" in the neighborhood, while Richie had some sort of strange fascination with grass (he would achieve his Nirvana some years later by working as a groundskeeper at Yankee Stadium). Vincent, the quietest of the Gotti boys, was already drifting into alcohol and drugs, and seemed to have little grasp of the world around him. As for Gene, he was noted for his inability to comprehend even the simplest statement addressed to him, and people dealing with him learned to speak slowly and repeatedly.

John Gotti himself was quite a different matter. By the age

of fifteen, already a gang leader, his personality was clearly defined: quick, shrewd, vicious, extremely ambitious, violent, and determined to dominate all those around him. Unlike most of his *goombata*, Gotti had a clear vision of his future, which was to become a Mafia kingpin in the mold of Albert Anastasia.

No other possibility seems to have crossed his mind. At the age of sixteen, having attended school long enough to fulfill the requirements of New York State's Mandatory School Attendance Law, he appeared at Franklin K. Lane Junior High School—which he had only fitfully attended, in any event—with a form signed by his parents. It attested that they concurred in his decision to quit school and go to work. With perhaps a sigh of relief, school officials struck Gotti's name from the rolls, and he walked out, smirking, never to return to any school.

He swaggered out of the building with a vaguely familiar walk, recognizable only to those who recalled actor Richard Widmark's famous portrayal of gangster Tommy Udo in *Kiss of Death*. Gotti, struck by that portrayal, had seen the movie six times. Shortly afterward, he adopted the persona as his own, walking and talking in a precise imitation of Widmark's gangster character, including Tommy Udo's chilling *heh-heh-heh* laugh.

By law, among the obligations Gotti faced for being permitted to leave school was gainful employment. Not much in the way of opportunity existed then—as now—for high-school dropouts, and Gotti was able to find only occasional work as a coat presser in a small garment factory in East New York, or as a trucker's helper. But Gotti devoted as little time as possible to such employment, for his real avocation remained the streets. There, he was trying to act the part of sixteen-year-old aspiring mobster. One fertile field he discovered almost immediately was the school he had just quit, Franklin K. Lane Junior High School, whose students liked to place bets. No Mafia bookie would have anything to do with kids, but Gotti was happy to accommodate them, charging anywhere from twenty-five to fifty cents per transaction for the privilege of handling their modest wagers.

The junior bookmaker seemed to spend the bulk of his

earnings on clothes, including some striking outfits that soon
made him the talk of the neighborhood. In the days when
the standard youth gang attire was dungarees and T-shirts
with sleeves rolled up to the shoulder, Gotti walked around
in an all-purple outfit with purple shoes. He also had an
all-green outfit (with green shoes) that made him look like
something out of Sherwood Forest, and another that featured
black pants, white shoes, and a bright orange shirt.

Those startling outfits made Gotti a singular figure as he
began to lead his *borgata* on expeditions to surrounding communities. These were primarily trips of exploration to make
contact with other gangs and get some sense of what opportunities existed outside the immediate neighborhood. First, the
Fulton-Rockaway Boys went east, to the further limits of East
New York, to make contact with a young mobster named
Leonard DiMaria, who ran an infamous mob hangout misleadingly named Helen's Candy Store.

The place was a candy store in name only; in fact, it was
one of the biggest hangouts in Brooklyn for a wide variety
of Mafia toughs, aspiring mobsters, bookmakers, and fences
of hijacked goods. No one could remember the last time
anyone actually had bought candy or a soda at the fountain
in what had become a den of thieves. Police who regularly
stopped by were struck by how everything suddenly fell
totally silent the moment a cop walked through the door.
Usually, the cops were looking for DiMaria, an active loan
shark and hijacker whose character was well known to them:
once, arrested on a minor burglary charge, DiMaria, apparently taking his cue from some movie about the Gestapo,
hurled himself out a precinct window—landing in the middle
of a shift change in the parking lot below. "You dumb shit,
Lenny!" a detective yelled after him. "It's only a six-month
charge!"

DiMaria also had a reputation as a cop-hater, on one occasion daring several cops twice his size to a fight. The cops
just laughed at him; one snapped, "Shut up, mutt," and
casually knocked him cold with a quick jab. Possibly, DiMaria recognized the same rampant aggressiveness in the sixteen-year-old gang leader and aspiring mobster named John
Gotti who arrived at Helen's Candy Store for a visit. What-

ever the reason, DiMaria took an instant liking to him, and Gotti's name was mentally filed away as somebody of possibly valuable use later.

A more significant encounter took place at DiMaria's pirate den, during which visit Gotti was introduced to a strapping young man with hands the size of ham hocks. Wilfred Johnson, whose mother was Italian, was known as "Indian" because of his Indian father; an aspiring strong-arm artist, he was noted for one incident when, assigned to impress upon a pizza store owner the desirability of making his loan shark payment on time, he put his fist through the solid plaster wall of the man's store. Gotti and Johnson were immediately drawn to each other, and an instant friendship was struck, a very strong one that would endure for nearly thirty years.

Gotti also led his *borgata* to southern Queens, where a meeting with the Rockaway Boys gang revealed that the gang was making very tidy profits from the Mafia. The gang was recruited by local hijackers to transfer loads off hijacked trucks to smaller trucks, plus other minor tasks, for which they were rewarded with hundred-dollar bills.

Similar profits were being earned, Gotti discovered, by another gang in Brooklyn, the Fulton-Pitkin group. When Gotti's East New York *borgata* was formed, he and fellow gang members occasionally would help the Fulton-Pitkin boys rumble with black gangs—such as the dreaded Mau Mau Chaplains—who had drifted over from the black ghettos. But only a few years later, the Fulton-Pitkin boys had no further interest in such rumbles; now, they were too busy making piles of money aiding local *Mafiosi* in various assignments for profit.

An even bigger eye-opener awaited Gotti when he traveled north, into the Queens community of Ozone Park, territory of a mixed Irish-Italian gang known as the Saints. One of the gang's leaders, Matthew Traynor, struck up an immediate friendship with Richie and Gene Gotti, who learned from Traynor that the Saints had been making a lot of money for quite some time. They had impressed a local Mafia soldier in Ozone Park when they showed up at a local mob-owned bowling alley one day and demanded extortion payments. When three hulking Mafia hoods stopped laughing at the sight of some teenage punks trying to shake them down, they chased the kids out into the parking lot. At that point, one of the Saints pulled out a fragmentation grenade he somehow had obtained, and heaved it at the three Mafia hoods. They ran for their lives, and the grenade blew an automobile to smithereens.

Declaring this event an embarrassing loss of face for the *amici*, the local Mafia chieftain called in Traynor and the Saints for a sitdown, during which he informed them of a "special arrangement." The Saints would not cause any further trouble by attempting to shake down bowling alleys or explode fragmentation grenades in parking lots. In return, Mafia hijackers would hire the boys to help unload hijacked loads and pay them several hundred dollars for each job. (The Saints happily agreed to this deal, not bothering to inform the *Mafioso* that not too long before, they had lowered Traynor, small for his age, through the skylight of a local bar to burglarize the place. In the back room, Traynor found seventy-eight thousand dollars, and realized he had stumbled across a Mafia gambling drop. The next day, the Saints watched as the *Mafioso* who owned the bar angrily stomped around, threatening to sever the testicles of whichever hood he was certain had ripped him off.)

Gotti needed some sort of important Mafia connection to score similar profits for his own *borgata*. That connection arrived in the person of Angelo Bruno, a soldier in East New York who specialized in gambling operations. Hearing of Gotti's own little gambling operation around the junior high school, Bruno was impressed. He enrolled Gotti as a junior apprentice for his own, much more extensive, gambling operations.

Bruno was further impressed as he watched Gotti at work. First of all, Gotti appeared to work harder than anybody else at the job; seemingly, he was flitting in and out of the pool halls and gambling dives around the clock to pick up bets, deliver winnings, and transmit, on behalf of loan sharks, disquieting messages that a customer's interest payment was late. That baleful glare of his conveyed his sponsor's growing displeasure, if necessary, and the implied threat that further lateness in a loan shark payment could result in serious difficulties from other, much larger, emissaries.

Gotti also had a photographic memory and abundant street smarts, along with a sound grasp of the subtle art of diplomacy in that world: just the right touch of condolence to a losing bettor (with encouragement to book some more bets), the proper level of congratulation to a winner, and the correct response to a gambler who wanted a further extension of his already stretched credit limit ("What am I, Santa Claus?").

Police in Brooklyn gradually became aware that Bruno's operation had been joined by a new operative, a young street punk who dressed in what one detective insisted were "real greaseball outfits." The cops had heard the world of gamblers in East New York buzzing about this character and his clothes, along with rumors that the kid was very sharp, but had an explosive temper.

It was his temper that earned Gotti his first notation on what would be a lengthy rap sheet. In May 1957, angered over the curt refusal by a young Mafia-connected guy to pay a gambling debt, Gotti boldly stalked into a local club, kicked aside the table on which the debtor and some of his friends were playing poker, then proceeded to beat him up. That set off a brawl, and when cops arrived, they arrested Gotti and others for disorderly conduct, the only charge they could think of filing at the moment (it was unthinkable in the world of the East New York Mafia for assault victims to complain to police).

The case was dismissed in court, but the real significance of the incident was that it did much to advance Gotti's reputation in the estimate of Angelo Bruno. As Bruno, a veteran *Mafioso* understood, his organization constantly needed to sustain itself by finding young men with the rare combination of brutality and smarts. In Gotti, Bruno became increasingly convinced, he had found that combination.

For his part, Gotti was very eager to impress Bruno, for the Mafia soldier was the required first step toward a larger goal: working for Bruno's boss, the Brooklyn Mafia *capo* assigned the East New York territory, the man who could not only find plenty of profitable work for Gotti, but enough work to keep Gotti's *borgata* busy, too.

The *capo's* name was Carmine Fatico, a former soldier for
Albert Anastasia, known in the Mafia by his nickname
"Charley Wagons" (a possible reference to all the trucks his
men were hijacking). A cautious man of strict Mafia protocol,
Fatico was not an easy *capo* to see, especially for a seventeen-year-old street gang leader. However, Bruno finally
arranged a meeting, and John Gotti, clad in one of his more
outrageous purple outfits, stood before a desk in the back
room of an East New York social club. Seated behind the
desk, Carmine Fatico, attired in his usual conservative business suit, stared at Gotti. Then he stared some more. Then
he scowled.

"You look like a fucking guinea," he said, finally.

Gotti was crushed: seemingly, he had blown his first big
opportunity. But appearances were deceiving in more ways
than one, for Fatico, a shrewd judge of men, had looked
deeper than the garish purple outfit. And he liked what he
saw.

3

Amici Nostra

You live by the gun and the knife, and you die by the gun and the knife.

—JOE VALACHI

TO WATCH Alphonse (Funzi) Tarricone move through life was to be reminded that whatever standards the Mafia demanded for its members, intellectual attainment was not among them. A supremely pragmatic organization, it preferred to judge *Mafiosi* on their ability to follow orders and make money.

Still, even by such loose intellectual standards, Tarricone was breathtakingly stupid, seemingly incapable of the simplest mental function. That deficiency was a source of frustration to his bosses, who had recruited him primarily because of his sheer physical presence: over six feet, seven inches tall, he weighed nearly three hundred pounds, with huge hands and arms. Given his size and frightening appearance, the Mafia had use for such a man, not surprisingly in the field of general strong-arm work, mostly collecting money from people unwilling to pay.

Careful briefing was required before Tarricone was sent out on such assignments, for he was likely as not to exert muscle against the wrong man, or to forget where the victim lived, or to lose his temper and unintentionally kill the victim in the process. But even with the most careful and detailed preparatory work, the odds were good that Tarricone still might foul up the assignment. When that happened, Tarricone would stand, shoulders slumped and head dipped in shame, as his *capo*, Dominic Cataldo of the Colombo Family, who was less than half his size, would subject him to a withering tongue-lashing that featured questions about Funzi's ancestry, the size of his brain, and the shame he had brought upon the organization. Following this verbal assault, during which the word *stupid* was often and prominently mentioned, Cataldo would stand on tiptoe, reach up as high as he could, and slap Tarricone in the face several times. Tarricone would not utter a word during this process, nor did the thought ever cross his small mind of raising one of those mammoth hands to protect himself; a single swat would have put Cataldo in the hospital for six months. Tarricone was a total Mafia loyalist who subscribed to a literal interpretation of the Mafia's unwritten discipline code as exercised by a *capo*, a rank Tarricone believed just below God.

Such stern discipline had done little to improve what passed for Funzi's deductive abilities—indeed, fearful of making a mistake, he began to think too much, only making things worse—and Cataldo was practically beside himself with frustration. Periodically loaned out to the crews of other Mafia families for strong-arm work that required someone of frightening bulk, Tarricone fouled up various assignments, including one in which he threw a loan shark debtor deficient in the repayment schedule out a window—an unaccountable lapse, since Funzi was supposed only to scare the man. Clearly, Funzi could not be permitted to carry out such assignments on his own.

Which is why, in the early spring of 1966, when an especially sensitive assignment arose, it was decided that Funzi would be accompanied by more intelligent minds. One of them was John Gotti, and the fact that he had been selected for the job reveals something about his criminal career to that point.

The assignment grew out of one of the Mafia's largest and most profitable operations, one so large it required the joint efforts of the Colombo and Gambino families. Colombo *capo* John (Sonny) Franzese ran the operation for the Colombos, while Carmine Fatico oversaw the Gambino interests. Beginning in 1962, Fatico and Franzese organized an auto-theft-to-order ring, in which thousands of luxury cars were stolen off the streets to fill specific orders from customers seeking to buy such cars at bargain-basement prices, and who were not especially concerned about the source. The operation represented a basic truth about the Mafia: as a criminal organization, it could not survive long without the cooperation of otherwise law-abiding citizens willing to do business with criminals to obtain something illegally. In this case, no customer could be unaware that he was buying a stolen car—obviously, a new Cadillac DeVille purchased for a mere two thousand dollars was either a hopeless lemon or had been stolen.

The cars were not lemons, for the Mafia guaranteed quality. Two of Fatico's soldiers, the brothers John and Charles Carneglia, ran a large chop shop that elevated auto theft to an assembly-line basis. A customer would request, say, a tan Cadillac, an order that would be transmitted from a contact man to Carneglia and other operatives via a thinly coded phone message ("The customer wants a brown, two-piece suit"). A crew of expert thieves, capable of breaking into, and hot-wiring the ignition of, any automobile in less than fifteen seconds, would be dispatched to find a Cadillac—a tan one, preferably, but any color would do. The stolen car, taken to Carneglia's shop, in a matter of hours would be repainted, if necessary, in the ordered color, its identification numbers altered, and the customer would be provided a forged registration, obtained by the ring from corrupted New York State Department of Motor Vehicles employees. The profits were enormous, because a Cadillac, sold for even two thousand dollars, represented high return on investment, considering the relatively modest overhead and the fact that the wholesale price of the merchandise was nothing.

Operations center for the enterprise was a large used-car lot in Queens, and it was there the problem that ultimately involved Tarricone and Gotti developed. The Mafia had a front man who ran the lot, cover for handling the growing volume of stolen cars, and early in 1966, he was told to sell one of Franzese's own personal cars. A customer expressed interest in the car, but the mob's man, for some odd reason, decided to warn him off. After explaining the car belonged to the infamous Colombo Family *capo* Sonny Franzese, he said, "Don't buy this car; it's probably got a bug in it."

Word of this flippancy reached Franzese, who was furious. The front man at the lot, he decreed, would have to undergo a major beating to atone for this insult. Tarricone was the logical choice for the job, but Franzese, aware of Funzi's inclination to foul up jobs when operating alone, asked his colleague, Gambino Family *capo* Carmine Fatico, for assistance. Fatico dispatched two of his junior hoods, men he felt demonstrated promise in the business of breaking heads. One of the men was Wilfred Johnson. The other was John Gotti.

A few days later, the man at the used-car lot was confronted with a sight that must have made his blood run cold: the huge bulks of Tarricone and Johnson, along with the smaller but ferocious-looking Gotti, had dropped in for a visit. What happened next was saved for posterity, because, unknown to all the participants, police investigating the stolen car racket had planted a bug inside the used-car lot's office. Police listening that morning heard only routine transactions until the three hoods arrived. Then they heard angry voices, which they deduced were those of Tarricone, Gotti, and Johnson, followed by the sound of cloth being ripped.

Now thoroughly alarmed, the police monitors realized that the three visitors were ripping off the man's clothes, preparatory to beating—or possibly killing—him. They heard the sounds of fists smashing into flesh and bone, screams, and pleas for mercy. "Take that, motherfucker!" Gotti yelled, as he began kicking the man in the testicles.

"Please don't hit me there no more," the victim sobbed, but Gotti kept kicking him as Tarricone and Johnson smashed their huge fists into the rest of his body. Next came the sounds of the man being dragged across the floor—probably by the standard Mafia method of grabbing his testicles, then pulling.

Horrified, the police were in a dilemma. If they intervened, that would almost certainly tip off the presence of their bug inside the office. On the other hand, they could not simply sit on their hands while the man was being beaten to within an inch of his life, or worse. One cop had a sudden inspiration: he called in a false alarm to the local fire department, whose approaching sirens caused Gotti, Tarricone, and Johnson to flee.

Puzzled firemen who arrived at the used-car lot found no fire, but they did encounter a naked and bleeding man who was attempting to put on some ripped clothes. He did not want to discuss the subject of fires, how he happened to be naked and bleeding in his own office, or anything else of interest. A day later, he fled, and has never been seen since. (The Carneglias and a dozen other men, including Franzese, were convicted of auto theft charges shortly thereafter; no charges were filed against Fatico, Gotti, Tarricone, and Johnson for lack of solid evidence.)

The beating represented the kind of assignment endemic to aspirants for higher Mafia positions. The Mafia is an equal opportunity employer: usually, everybody starts at the bottom, performing the assorted tasks higher-ranking *Mafiosi* do not (or cannot) dirty their hands on. Such tasks include the collection of debts, strong-arm work against malefactors, varied matters involving illegal gambling operations, and, ultimately, killings.

As in any other hierarchal organization, new Mafia recruits are put through their paces, fulfilling the most menial assignments to test their loyalty and ability. In turn, the new recruits exert every effort to impress their superiors, to demonstrate that they have the proper combination of qualities that deserve higher rank, most notably the ability to earn a lot of money for the organization. The ambitions of all recruits are fixated on the goal of being "made," the formal induction into the Mafia that provides the status of "respect and honor."

Like all new recruits, John Gotti sought, above all, to impress his *capo*, Carmine Fatico, for "Charley Wagons" was one of the most powerful *capi* in the entire Gambino organization. At first glance, Fatico did not convey the impression of powerful Mafia chieftain. A small, thin man just under five feet, five inches tall, he had what appeared to be a permanent worried expression. Along with his brother, Donato, known as "Danny Wags," he had served his Mafia apprenticeship for Albert Anastasia, who recognized the Faticos' abilities and finally gave them control of one of the Brooklyn Mafia's most lucrative territories, East New York.

There, Carmine set up shop in a storefront he converted into a social club. Unable immediately to come up with a name for the place, he called it, simply, "the club," a name that stuck. Very much a disciple of Anastasia and his reputation of stern discipline, Carmine and his brother ran a tight ship. Danny Wags, regarded as the lesser of the two brothers mentally, served as chief court factotum in the front section of the club, screening the various applicants and supplicants who came each day to the club seeking an audience with Charley Wagons. The *capo* himself sat behind a desk in a plainly furnished office at the back of the club, flanked by a praetorian guard of several hoods who would glare menacingly if any of the visitors dared raise his voice in the presence of *capo* Fatico.

Members of Fatico's crew, somewhere around one hundred twenty "made" soldiers and associates, were under strict and detailed instructions, and repeated failure to carry out instructions was a certain guarantee of eventual expulsion from the crew. Fatico was a prodigious money-earner, grossing about thirty million dollars a year, mostly from hijacking, illegal gambling, and loansharking. Like most successful *capi*, Charley Wagons had what the Mafia called a "hook," a single, immensely profitable criminal specialty, individually created and nurtured, one so spectacularly successful that it created a man's permanent reputation within the Mafia as a major "earner."

In Fatico's case, it was a simple insight: gay men in New York, one of the largest such communities in the United States, yearned for their own special brand of nightclubs and bars where they could socialize. But in the 1950s, homosexuality was a serious crime in New York, and the State Liquor Authority refused to grant liquor licenses to any place that "caters to a homosexual clientele." Fatico moved into that vacuum, creating a network of "private" bars and clubs aimed exclusively at gay customers. For that privilege, gay customers were outrageously overcharged for drinks and entertainment, and Fatico soon had a vast money machine operating. He also created one of the Mafia's favorite entertainments: *Mafiosi* in Fatico's favor would be permitted to visit the clubs and bars, there to witness such mind-boggling sights as drag queens, fist-fucking demonstrations, and hermaphrodites (known to Mafia wiseguys as ''chicks with dicks'') performing striptease routines. To the visiting wiseguys, it was like watching a carnival sideshow. (However, Fatico did not realize he was creating a social revolution: in 1969, gay men, tired of endless police harassment and ripoffs by the Mafia, rioted at one of Fatico's places, the Stonewall Inn in Greenwich Village. The riot ultimately led to the birth of the national gay rights movement and revision of New York statutes to decriminalize homosexuality.)

Fatico's profitable enterprises were reflected by his upward mobility, including an expensive suburban home on Long Island, and a winter place in Florida. His Long Island neighbors knew only that he was some sort of vague ''Brooklyn businessman,'' although they did wonder about the elaborate security precautions around his home, including a system of lights that lit up the house like a Christmas tree when anyone approached, and two German shepherd attack dogs who terrorized the local mailman.

Despite their molding under the tutelage of Anastasia, unlike The Executioner, the Faticos disdained any sign of flashiness. Both men were extremely conservative dressers, and save for Carmine's passion for handmade alligator-hide shoes, there was nothing to mark them as Mafia. Carmine was a devoted family man who insisted that all members of his immediate and extended family show up at his home for a family dinner every Sunday and holiday (an invitation very few of them dared refuse).

This low-profile approach had its advantages. Although Carmine had a record of twenty arrests and nine convictions, most of them were for minor offenses, and he had served very little actual time in jail. When arrested, he would adopt an act of total stupidity, speaking with the accent of a recently arrived Italian immigrant who had no idea of what the charges were all about. But the police had no illusions about who Fatico really was and the kind of violence this man, who looked like an ordinary businessman, was capable of ordering. They knew, for example, of the local punk who defied

Fatico by carrying out a robbery of a Mafia-sanctioned operation; when his body was found, police could not locate his
head. A subsequent autopsy revealed the hood had been so
savagely beaten that his head was smashed into his chest
cavity. Then there was the local numbers runner who didn't
turn in the proceeds: Fatico had him cruelly dispatched with
the "Italian rope trick," which involved two hoods holding
either end of a rope wrapped around the man's throat.
Depending on the strength and mood of the two men holding
the rope, a victim might linger for hours until granted the
mercy of death.

Fatico hoped the combination of his low-profile approach
and terrifying reputation for retribution would serve his crew
members as the proper role model for ambitious hoods to
emulate. He also meant that example to serve as inspiration
to his crew's minor leagues, composed of several dozen teenage boys who represented the top talent recruited from various street gangs. Their numbers, which had included Gotti,
were assigned the crew's most menial chores connected with
gambling operations and burglaries. The boys were tested
for possible future use as criminals by being dispatched on
burglary assignments based on inside information. Favorite
targets were places whose goods could be easily and
profitably fenced: television repair shops, clothing stores,
and supermarkets.

Gotti already had made an impression by efficient work in
the Fatico crew's gambling operations, but he demonstrated
less skill as a burglar. In late 1957, shortly after being
enlisted, he was arrested while stealing copper from a construction site. (He received a suspended sentence.) He later
was caught in another burglary, which earned only another
suspended sentence from a local court system whose leniency
toward criminals known to be associated with the crew of
Carmine Fatico was astonishing (or perhaps not, since most
local criminal court judges were known to have received their
jobs from a political clubhouse system underwritten by Mafia
money).

Similarly, Gotti received still another suspended sentence
after being caught in a gambling raid in 1959. His immediate
superior, soldier Angelo Bruno, and *capo* Carmine Fatico,

however, retained faith in his abilities, often mentioning how
the young man was marked for great things. But that didn't
put too much money in Gotti's pocket, and he was perpetu-
ally broke. To make things worse, Gotti had developed a
gambling habit, and was in hock to loan sharks all over
Brooklyn, largely because he was a very bad gambler, noted
for his ability to pick losers.

Gotti could have used some extra cash, for in 1960 he met
and fell in love with a petite, pretty, raven-haired girl from
Brooklyn. Victoria DiGiorgio was a high school dropout
whose choice of a steady boyfriend did not impress her parents. They met a young man who struck them as typical
Brooklyn Italian lowlife: greasy ducktail haircut, black leather
jacket, and swaggering air. Victoria's father, a builder, and
her mother, Russian-Jewish, hoped for something better, but
options disappeared in that era of very different social mores
when Victoria announced she was pregnant. A wedding was
hastily arranged, and a few months later, the couple, living
in a small East New York apartment, became the parents of
a baby girl, Angela.

Gotti began supplementing his meager criminal income
with a job as a trucker's helper (helpfully arranged by Fatico),
but the combination of low salary, paltry income from crime,
and a bad gambling habit soon put the couple in grave financial difficulty. At this point, Gotti discovered that whatever
else the former Victoria DiGiorgio was, she was not a typical
Mafia wife.

One concept dominated the lives of Mafia wives, whatever
their husbands' ranks in the organization: their husbands as
providers. A *Mafioso* left his home during the day, returned
that night or the next morning, and placed the cash on the
table. The Mafia wife was to use this money for food, rent,
and care of the children. She was never to ask any question
about the source of the money, nor was she to inquire about
her husband's hours, and where he had been all night. *Mafiosi*
seldom told their wives when they would be home, and most
of them had girlfriends who, under Mafia social protocol,
could be escorted to restaurants and nightclubs—but never to
the same places where wives were taken. (One grossly fat
Mafioso, following a night of wild sex with a young woman,

returned home the next morning. As he sat at the kitchen table, his wife silently and dutifully placed a bowl of corn flakes before him—into which his head fell as he died of a heart attack.)

For some Mafia wives of the successful *capos*, underbosses, and bosses, "provide" meant a pleasant existence: seven-hundred-thousand-dollar suburban mansions with Mercedes to drive, and an apparently unlimited amount of cash to buy anything the wives wanted. But most women who married *Mafiosi* only dreamed of such an existence. They tended, like Victoria DiGiorgio, to marry men in the lowest echelon. The majority of Mafia wives were the products of the strict and narrow atmosphere of tight Italian families who knew absolutely nothing of the world outside their own neighborhoods. Their lives were focused exclusively on the family and the home, circumscribed by what many Italian women called "the four Cs": cook, clean, children, church.

Among the Mafia's firmest unwritten rules was one specifying that no Mafia business was to be discussed at home. Another was that wives were not to venture beyond the tight circle of family and their husbands' friends. The wives were expected to suffer the years of irregular income, prison, and other hazards as their husbands slowly moved up from the lower ranks to the middle echelon and began earning decent money. That transformation might be accompanied by a move from a small, cramped apartment to a home in the suburbs, where the wives would become members of the Mafia's middle class, dreaming of the day when they would reach the top of the heap. There, they would be accorded the elaborate respect and courtesy shown to wives of bosses. Of course, the wives at such lofty heights would still do the cooking and housework, for security precautions prohibited the hiring of domestic servants who might be police or FBI undercover agents.

But Victoria Gotti was not about to play the role of dutiful Mafia wife. As she often reminded her husband, "I'm only *half* Italian." She did not need to add that the other half was Jewish, and Jewish wives are not noted for unquestioning obedience to their husbands. In truth, Gotti was henpecked; only his closest friends knew that the tough-talking, swag-

gering hood was often at a loss on how to deal with a wife
who clearly had a mind of her own. And when Victoria Gotti
did not get her way, she walked out. The couple was
estranged several times, and they were only drawn back
together because of a genuine and deep affection they had
for each other.

As a provider, Gotti did not have much to offer. Despite
the high regard in which he was held by the Faticos, Gotti
continued to demonstrate a consistent record of failure in the
criminal arts. In 1963, he was arrested with Sal Ruggiero in
a stolen Avis rental car, and two years later, he botched two
burglaries that earned him a six-month prison sentence, his
first incarceration of any significance. Prison cut off Gotti's
already inadequate income, and Victoria Gotti, facing the
daunting task of supporting their three children alone, took
the shameful step of applying for welfare. She took a step
even more embarrassing to her husband by suing him in
Domestic Relations Court for nonsupport.

His wife's actions caused a grave loss of face for Gotti
just as he was making a major push to become a big-time
mobster. One of the traditional marks of such success was
ownership of a bar that could be used as a mob hangout, so
Gotti bought a small Brooklyn bar that had seen better days
and turned it into a sort of Wild West saloon where he and
the small group of *goombata* who followed him could relax
among like-minded friends. Gotti's wife was furious when
she found out about it: there was hardly enough money in
the house to buy food for the three kids, yet her husband was
purchasing a bar and gambling as though he had Rockefeller's
income.

In gambler's parlance, Gotti was "betting on the come,"
in effect hocking his future to a conviction that somehow it
would all work out, that the proverbial card to fill the inside
straight would arrive in the next deal. To a certain extent, it
did. Carmine Fatico, still enamored of Gotti's potential, provided a big boost for his protégé's career when he devolved
upon him the Mafia's most important route to upward mobility: killing. Gotti, now working in partnership with his apparently devoted *goombah*, Wilfred Johnson, was assigned

several contract murders, including two black gamblers whom
Fatico suspected of embezzling gambling proceeds.

The significance of the murders was not only that they
were efficiently carried out, but also that such acts guaranteed
that a low-ranking crew member would come to the attention
of higher authority in the organization, in this case the powerful underboss of the Gambino family, Aniello Dellacroce—
and, of course, *Don* Carlo Gambino himself. Murders were
matters regarded most gravely within Mafia organizations,
and carefully controlled from the top. A man who carried out
orders to kill, and killed well, was someone whose name
would be mentioned with increasing frequency in the right
circles.

As a reward for such efficiency, Gotti was introduced by
Fatico to his crew's most profitable enterprise, truck
hijacking. The enterprise was a successor to what had been
the Mafia's most lucrative field of endeavor, along the New
York waterfront. But construction of Idlewild Airport—later
renamed in honor of the slain President Kennedy—promised
even greater riches. Sprawled across five thousand acres once
occupied by a marshland and a golf course, the airport gradually replaced the waterfront as the chief entry point for
imports into the United States. By the mid-1960s, nearly
thirty billion dollars' worth of goods moved each year
through a network of airline shipping companies.

As in the case of the waterfront, the Mafia quickly discovered the airport's weak point: labor. Shipping companies had
plenty of security to guard the Swiss watches, shipments of
cash and jewels, computer parts, designer clothes, and just
about everything produced by human hands, but once the
goods were loaded aboard delivery trucks, shipments worth
up to several million dollars were in the hands of the drivers.
And drivers could be bribed, or if they were heavy gamblers,
a large debt to a Mafia loan shark might induce them to leave
the keys in the ignition when they stopped somewhere for a
coffee break. Almost all the drivers were members of Teamsters Union locals taken over by the mob, which extorted
huge bribes from shipping companies to keep labor peace.

The real key to the Mafia's successful hijacking operations
at the airport—losses from hijackings ran somewhere around

wo billion dollars a year—was a network of mob-controlled
ences capable of matching a stolen shipment with crooked
businessmen who later sold the stuff at steep discount.
Again, as in other areas, the Mafia depended on the greed
of law-abiding citizens: otherwise-legitimate businessmen
buying up lots of Paris fashions at a fraction of their worth
could not have failed to know they were buying stolen
goods.) The fences were highly specialized, some handling
only stolen shipments of gourmet food, which they could
dispose of in less than an hour to restaurant owners willing
to cut a corner and make a little extra profit. The Mafia
fences generally paid about 30 to 50 percent of the value of
goods to the Mafia hijackers; by contrast, junkies got only
about 10 percent, on the theory that junkies were too stupid
to know the difference and, as junkies, deserved their fate,
anyway.

In introducing Gotti to the field of hijacking, Fatico
instructed him in the prevailing rules. Most important, the
thefts were organized on a businesslike system, with shipments pretargeted for maximum profit (such as designer
clothes and jewelry); often, a shipment would be stolen to
fulfill a fence's specific need, such as a sudden market for
five hundred cameras. Fatico abhorred nonsanctioned "cow-
boys," the guys who sought to get in on the racket by ran-
domly hijacking promising-looking truckloads; Fatico warned
that any crew member found to be "cowboying" without
sanction would be dealt with mercilessly, for such action
represented a violation of the fundamental principle behind
all Mafia hijacking operations: the bulk of the proceeds was
to be forwarded upward, to the family.

Hijacking had an immediate and beneficial effect on Gotti's
finances, but as he was aware, attrition was extremely high in
that field. Both the police and FBI had been exerting stronger
pressure against the hijackers, and although Fatico was able
to recruit new hijackers to replace the growing number of
those sent to prison, the word around the mob was that there
probably were better things to do than stealing from the
airport.

Nevertheless, Gotti plunged in. One technique he and his
brother Gene devised was the preparation of forged freight-

forwarding documents, which they would use to pick up valu
able shipments in their own truck. Their luck ran out in
1967, when they walked into the United Air Lines air freigh
terminal and presented phony documents that enabled them
to drive out with twenty thousand dollars' worth of clothing
and electronic equipment. Two weeks later, they pulled the
same routine, this time getting twenty-three cartons of expen
sive women's clothing. The police tracked them down, and
Gotti faced serious charges. Things went from bad to worse
and in the process Gotti was to suffer another severe persona
embarrassment.

Out on bail in the United Air Lines thefts, Gotti remained
active, becoming involved in the hijacking of two trucks on
the New Jersey Turnpike. Gotti, operating on a telephone
from his bar in Queens (called the Crystal Lounge), was
trying to get the trucks back to a drop in a warehouse near
the bar. Using the phone was a mistake, for the police had
a wiretap on it. They heard what could only be described as
a farce: the hijackers in New Jersey could not manage to start
one of the trucks, and an increasingly furious Gotti was trying
to instruct the men how to restart it. The connection between
Gotti's phone and a highway pay phone in New Jersey was
a bad one, and Gotti was screaming in rage and frustration.
He did manage to convey directions for the second truck to
rendezvous at a drop in Brooklyn—where police and FBI
agents were waiting. Several hours later, an undercover
police detective, calmly sipping coffee while on stakeout at
the warehouse, was astonished to hear the driver of the truck
(who apparently assumed the detective was a member of the
hijack crew) ask for his help as he backed the truck into the
warehouse. The detective obliged, then police and FBI agents
arrested everybody at the site, including Gotti. The other
stalled truck? It remained parked on the side of the highway
in New Jersey, the object of loud cursing by a hijacker still
trying to figure out how to get it working. Barely able to
stop laughing, the cops and FBI men found him kicking the
engine, as though that would somehow restart a multihun-
dred-horsepower diesel truck. He was arrested, along with
Gotti's *goombata* Angelo Ruggiero and Gene Gotti.

Fatico was unhappy about this comedy of errors, but there

wasn't much he could do about the airtight case that Gotti confronted. The New Jersey hijacking, which involved two states, was an interstate federal crime, and that was bad news; Gotti pled guilty, was sentenced to four years, and luckily got a concurrent sentence on state charges.

Gotti headed off to the federal penitentiary in Lewisburg, Pennsylvania. A forbidding place that was one of the toughest prisons in the entire federal system, Lewisburg was known as the Mafia's graduate school, the destination of many top mobsters who spent time there instructing younger up-and-coming men in the finer points of organized crime. Lewisburg was ruled behind the walls by an unofficial administration of *Mafiosi* who had a de facto working arrangement with the official prison administration to keep things calm and orderly—and therefore make life easier for the official administration.

The style for *Mafiosi* in prison had been set by Lucky Luciano years before. While incarcerated at New York's Clinton State Prison, Luciano had a cell with an electric stove, curtains on the cell door, and a pet canary. Dressed in unique prison uniform of silk shirt and highly polished shoes, Luciano held audiences in his cell and the exercise yard, and he was guarded around the clock by a ring of paid bodyguards. Each day, he would hold court, dispensing favors, advice, and orders; those granted the rare privilege of an audience with him could be seen actually backing away after finishing, as though just concluding a conversation with a monarch.

At the time of Gotti's arrival in Lewisburg in 1969, there were several hundred Mafia or Mafia-connected inmates, all of them gathered into an unofficial organization which ensured that any inmate with an Italian name received special treatment: nononerous work details, sufficient supply of cigarettes and candy, protection from black prison gangs, and, rarely, invitations to spend an evening at "Mafia Manor," a special section set aside for top-ranking *Mafiosi* to savor steaks and whiskey, all provided by corrupted guards.

The ruling leader of this clique was the most notorious mobster then at Lewisburg, Carmine (Lilo) Galante, a Bonanno Family killer and heroin trafficker serving a twenty-

year sentence for narcotics. A pure thug, Galante was totally
fearless: in a prison population predominantly black, he
would approach a long line of men waiting to use the pay
phone, cut to the front of the line, and bellow, "Get off the
fucking phone, nigger!" Even the black prison gangs were
afraid of him.

Galante met Gotti shortly after the aspiring Gambino Family mobster arrived at Lewisburg, and immediately sought to
recruit him. He was warned off by another prisoner, who
noted, "No, no, Lilo; Johnny's with Charley Wagons."
Translated, that meant Gotti was the property of Carmine
Fatico; thus, recruitment of a different family's man would
violate still another of those unwritten Mafia strictures.
Galante relented, but made sure that Gotti's prison existence
was as comfortable as possible. Given a work assignment
that required less than an hour a day to perform, Gotti spent
most of his time lifting weights and in lengthy discussions
with older *Mafiosi* about assorted intricacies of organized
crime. These discussions, Gotti noted, invariably seemed to
have a central focus: the persona, attitude, philosophy, outlook, and acumen of the man considered the greatest criminal
genius who ever lived, the one man whose very existence in
large measure determined all their futures—most especially
that of John Gotti.

This dominant figure, whose name was most often uttered
in tones of awed respect, was a nondescript old man who
occasionally shopped among the outdoor fruit stands of Little
Italy. Only the obsequiousness of shopkeepers revealed that
he was a man of any importance. Carlo Gambino would
accept these elaborate, fawning gestures of Old World respect
with his characteristic half smile and slight bow of the head.
He projected the air of benevolent patrician, accurately recaptured in the character of *Don* Vito Corleone of *The Godfather*, a thinly veiled portrait of himself, the *real* godfather.

People in that neighborhood would talk for weeks afterward how they had actually seen *Don* Carlo in person; had
actually spoken a few words of Sicilian with him; had actually accepted his money when he bought a few pieces of
fruit. Gambino was a figure of immense prestige to first-

generation Sicilian immigrants, who marveled how he had never forgotten his humble *paisan* roots, even after he became the virtual *capo di tutti capi* of the Mafia—the man, so it was whispered, whom even the United States government feared because he could pick up a telephone and bring to a halt every airport and waterfront in the country.

And yet, his admirers agreed, he remained the same old Carlo. Quiet, cautious, soft-spoken, and courtly, he was a small, thin man with a great beak of a nose in a puckish face; thinning gray hair and a slightly stooped walk completed that classic image of Sicilian culture, the kindly, old Italian uncle lovingly generous to children and unfailingly courteous—complete with tip of his hat—to women. Success had not changed his lifestyle: devoted to his wife of forty-five years, he was a family man of modest tastes who liked to read poetry for relaxation. He dressed with equal modesty, and the rumor around the Mafia was that *Don* Carlo had never spent more than a hundred dollars for a suit in his life.

At home in their modest Brooklyn row house (or in their equally modest summer house on Long Island), the Gambinos treated visitors with Old World courtesy. Even police detectives arriving at the Gambino home to serve warrants or grand jury subpoenas were offered Mrs. Gambino's homemade cookies and other Italian delicacies. (Once, FBI agents surveilling the Gambino vacation home on a blisteringly hot summer day were summoned by Mrs. Gambino to try her special, homemade lemonade. "Such nice boys," she said as the agents sipped the lemonade. "Someone should tell Mr. Hoover how his men suffer on days like this.")

The government and police view of this gentle old man, however, had a distinctly hard edge. Thick dossiers portrayed a murderer, labor racketeer, narcotics dealer, loan shark, and organized crime leader of noted distinction. The dry language of police and FBI reports conveyed the sense of a remarkable man: twenty-two-year-old stowaway to the United States in 1924; loyal soldier during the 1930s convulsion in the New York Mafia, when he narrowly escaped assassination; waterfront hood; *capo* under Anastasia; master intriguer who gradually took de facto control of the entire Mafia; and, finally,

organized crime czar and innovator said to have his hooks
into virtually every important industry in America.

Amateur psychologists among his law-enforcement adversaries always wondered why Gambino ever bothered to
become a criminal: blessed with an intuitively brilliant business sense, *Don* Carlo could have become a multimillionaire
businessman legitimately. Perhaps, but his touch was sure in
the underside of the American economy. During Prohibition,
he managed at one point to corner the market in distilled
alcohol, buying up the entire supply for fifteen dollars per
five-gallon tin. Gambino quietly waited as desperate bootleg-
gers drove the price up, then sold out his supply for fifty
dollars a tin. In World War II, he understood that many
Americans, however devoted to the war effort and in favor
of eradicating crime, also were willing to deal with criminals
who could provide supplies of such rationed items as tires,
gasoline, and sugar. To accommodate that market, Gambino
set up a huge black market using forged ration stamps; he
made over a million dollars in one deal alone.

Later, he perfected Mafia infiltration into legitimate business and labor unions, centering on his principle that there
was great profit to be made in the nexus between the worlds
of Mafia and non-Mafia. In that nexus, Gambino capitalized
on the willingness of some businessmen to hire the Mafia to
guarantee labor peace; on the eagerness by some unions to
make large profits on pension funds by allowing the Mafia
to invest them; and on the desire by some industries to fix
prices with the aid of the Mafia. It all made perfect sense to
Gambino, and he was therefore astounded to learn that a
prominent New York restaurateur announced he would rather
close his landmark restaurant than deal with a union known
to be under Gambino's control. With his characteristically
mild-mannered approach, Gambino (noted for his guiding
principle, ''I'll make an offer he can't refuse'') unsuccessfully tried to reason with the man: ''Where would this city
be if every businessman threw in the towel because of a little
unpleasantness?''

At the same time, the two dozen crews that constituted
Gambino's organization were busy in every traditional organized crime, ranging from illegal gambling to murder. Gam-

bino oversaw it all with careful attention to matters of personnel, insisting on the highest possible standards for the men he named *capo*. In the main, they tended to be reflections of Gambino himself: low profiles, huge money-earners, and strict disciplinarians.

Gambino had distaste for flashy mobsters who attracted too much attention, particularly such men as Ricardo (Richie the Boot) Boiardo, a leading light in the New Jersey Mafia. Boiardo lived in a thirty-room mansion on an estate that featured life-size statues of himself and members of his family on the grounds. In his spare time, he puttered around in his vegetable garden, which contained a huge sign that read "Godfather's Garden," presumably meant to deter local raccoons from eating his rows of sweet corn. Nearby was a crematorium in which Boiardo burned the bodies of his murder victims.

Gambino also openly criticized another New Jersey mobster, Anthony Campisi, whose crew murdered a bookmaker trying to muscle in on their territory. After the murder, the crew celebrated with a big champagne party, then appeared at the victim's funeral in pink suits to insult his family. Equally, Gambino had harsh words for some of the flashier mobsters of the New York Mafia, including John (Gentleman Johnny) Masiello, a major loan shark in the Genovese organization, who conducted business in a striking ensemble of electric blue and a huge diamond pinky ring.

Gambino always counseled modesty and a low profile, and his own career was a demonstration of the wisdom of that approach. For forty years, the police and the United States government tried to destroy Gambino, and never succeeded. Gambino last served any serious jail time in 1937, on a bootlegging charge, and after then evaded all efforts to nail him. No one in the law-enforcement establishment ever succeeded in finding the hundreds of millions of dollars Gambino earned, and while his *capi* and soldiers were arrested and jailed, their boss remained untouchable.

Nothing seemed to work: the FBI actually succeeded at one point in planting a bug inside Gambino's Brooklyn home, only to watch as *Don* Carlo adjourned to the porch or out into the street when he had important business to discuss with anyone. Cases prepared against Gambino usually collapsed before trial, most often because it was impossible to find a witness with sufficient suicidal tendencies to testify against him. Little mystery why: Gambino was the Mafia's chief "judge," presiding over many sitdowns that decided a man's fate. This gentle, soft-spoken old man was an avenging angel of savage ferocity, ordering up scores of murders to maintain Mafia discipline. (One miscreant, who committed the cardinal sin of attempting to seduce the wives of *Mafiosi* in prison, was ordered by Gambino to suffer a horrible end: he was slowly fed into a large meat grinder, limbs first, with his executioners commanded to prolong the agony as long as possible.)

John Gotti subscribed fully to the Gambino management style, except for the family godfather's firm policy that all aspirants be required to serve long apprenticeships. Gambino believed that men should not be "made" until they had thoroughly mastered all aspects of organized crime, and enforced the rule by periodically "closing the books"—ordering a moratorium on any further formal inductions until aspirants had mastered their craft to Gambino's satisfaction. The rule was enforced by holding an individual *capo* directly responsible for any failure of his crew member.

Gotti chafed under the Gambino edict, and following his release from prison on parole after serving three years, indicated his impatience to Fatico. Why, Gotti complained, would he be required to wait so long before even being considered for formal induction? By that point, he had already devoted fifteen years of his life to the organization; he had dutifully carried out every order, including killings, and had served his prison time loyally, without complaint. Yet, he appeared no closer to his immediate goal of being "made."

"You gotta be patient," Fatico counseled, and proceeded to begin his protégé's serious education in organized crime.

First, there was illegal gambling, and its attendant business of loansharking, the twin pillars of organized crime. The simplest (and most profitable) form of Mafia gambling operations was the numbers, or policy, game that predominated in the black ghettos. Basically a lottery, players selected one, two, or three digits from zero to nine to win, with odds thus ranging from ten to one, to a thousand to one. The winning number was determined by the last three digits of an established daily number that theoretically could not be "fixed," such as that day's total sales of U.S. Treasury stocks. Individual numbers tickets, sold in barbershops and candy stores, cost anywhere from a quarter to a dollar each. The profit, which was the difference between the total "play" (number of tickets sold) and payouts for winning numbers, if any, often was enormous.

Because such operations required sprawling organizations of runners, collectors, and bankers, the Mafia, with its talent for organization—and established disciplinary procedures—completely dominated the racket. Likewise, the Mafia also controlled another profitable illegal gambling operation, casinos hidden away in large apartments, storefronts, or warehouses. Some of these casinos could be quite elaborate, with roulette wheels, chemin de fer, and baccarat. Others were more austere, often an empty warehouse in which crap games for high stakes were played. All of them, however, worked on the same principle: the Mafia provided the capitalization, and was in effect the "house" against which the players played. The mathematical laws of probability established that such casinos would return huge profits to the house.

The third form of illegal gambling was the one most utilized by noncriminal Americans who liked to wager their money on sporting events, but found that the law allowed them only very limited opportunities to do so. Enter that staple of American culture, the friendly neighborhood bookmaker. Almost all bookmakers are affiliated in some form with the Mafia, for only the Mafia and its resources can accommodate every bookmaker's most pressing concern, the "layoff." Simply put, any bookmaker dreads the very real possibility that all his customers will have the same winning bet at the same time, thus wiping out his limited stake. To avert that problem, a bookmaker shifts some of his action to a Mafia-controlled bookmaking operation, which covers the bets, if necessary—in return for a cut of the profits. All bookmakers aim for the ideal, summarized, let's say, in the case of the New York Giants and the Denver Broncos playing in the Super Bowl: an equal number of bets on either team, therefore guaranteeing the bookmaker's profit, since he collects a 10 percent fee on every bet. Almost always, a layoff is needed to achieve that ideal balance.

Gambling operations are inevitably accompanied by loansharking, defined legally as the loaning of money at usurious interest rates; i.e., greater than 30 percent per annum. In its simplest form, such a loan of, say, a thousand dollars is repaid in thirteen weekly installments of one hundred dollars each. This is known within the Mafia as a "six for five" loan (five dollars borrowed on a Monday had to be repaid with six dollars the following Monday). Each unit of interest, usually defined in hundred-dollar amounts, is called a "point," and the entire interest burden—which always has to be paid before principal—is termed "juice," "vigorish," or, more commonly, "vig."

Typically, a relatively small loan of less than ten thousand dollars has a small vigorish, usually about five points. But, as Gotti learned, there are many variations. There are "knockdown" loans, usually of large size, to be repaid in four installments, and "special" loans among the *Mafiosi* themselves with reduced interest. Gamblers, a loan shark's best customers, often have special arrangements involving loans to repay other loans. Despite the often bewildering array of loans, one principle remains supreme: all loans are secured by the physical well-being, life, or property of the debtor. What makes the system work is the constant fear in which all debtors exist; so long as they believe that terrible retribution will be exacted for missing a payment, they will do *anything* to ensure timely repayment of a debt.

Mafia aspirants have to learn the subtle arts of loansharking: how to "put money on the street" properly; how to select the best customers; when to beware of making a large knockdown loan (the larger the loan, the greater the incentive to flee if payments cannot be made); how to apply pressure in the proper amounts at the right psychological moment. John Gotti turned out to be an extremely talented loan shark, for his deep understanding of the psychology of hopelessly addicted gamblers (he was one himself), and ability to project menace tended to make his customers very prompt payers.

Operations like loansharking and illegal gambling can be extremely profitable, but since a large share of the proceeds has to be forwarded upward in the family, street hoods like John Gotti understood they would never get rich permanently working the streets. Greater wealth awaited promotion into the Mafia's really lucrative rackets, the operations that enriched the middle and upper echelons of the Mafia hierarchy.

Among them was pornography, a classic demonstration of the Mafia's ability to profit from a technically illegal enterprise that many Americans nevertheless wanted, as demonstrated by the classic pornography film *Deep Throat*. The movie cost less than fifty thousand dollars to make, yet in five years earned over thirty million dollars. Legitimate film distribution companies would not distribute the film across state lines for fear of violating federal statutes, so the Mafia immediately moved in, handling the interstate distribution in return for hefty slices of the take. (And trumped the deal by quietly buying up so-called adult film theaters, where they charged outrageous prices.)

Carlo Gambino, via his lieutenant, Ettore (Terry) Zappi, was the Mafia's preeminent figure in the pornography trade. His business acumen in this area was sharp: when the videocassette revolution arrived, transforming the business overnight, Gambino immediately set up companies that handled the new business, which he soon dominated. Pornography producers who chose not to cooperate were treated to the distinctive Gambino touch. For example, the producers of the phenomenally successful porno movie *Behind the Green Door* refused to allow a Gambino distribution outfit to handle their movie; there was no way, they insisted, they would pay the Gambino company's stiff fees. Unlike other Mafia chieftains, who would have sent in hoods to break kneecaps, Gambino said nothing. But a few weeks later, the producers were appalled to discover that Gambino had undercut them by making hundreds of pirated versions of their movie, destroying the market. (Gambino was much more circumspect about his connection to the extremely profitable field of child pornography. His family dominated that trade, despite the reluctance of some Gambino chieftains; their normally quiescent wives were raising hell about being involved in a "filthy" business.)

Also out of reach for most street-level hoods in Gambino's organization were the profits from a vast variety of assorted rackets involving legitimate and quasi-legitimate businesses. Gambino, a premier criminal capitalist, plowed profits from street crime into cash-transaction businesses in which the proceeds of illegal activities could be hidden, and the new profits, in turn, could be skimmed. Favorites included garbage collection, vending machines, trucking, construction, garment manufacture, restaurants, and assorted restaurant supply companies. All of these specialized businesses were suited perfectly for Gambino's favorite ploy, the "vertical monopoly," in which he controlled the supplier to the business, the union local representing the business's workers, the business's largest customers, and, of course, the business itself. The potential for profit under such an arrangement, every monopolist's dream, was almost breathtaking.

Gambino had a number of important henchmen to effectuate such schemes, among them the remarkably talented Carmine (The Doctor) Lombardozzi, a high school dropout and former street hood who demonstrated the kind of original thinking that made him the Mafia's greatest white collar criminal. Lombardozzi's insight was that Wall Street brokerage firms were notably lax on how securities and stock certificates were handled—most often by underpaid clerks who drank too much, or used drugs, or had gambling addictions. Lombardozzi went to work, and in a process he called "putting them to sleep," he corrupted the clerks further and had them steal certificates, most of which were kept in vaults. That meant the banks usually didn't know the certificates were stolen. In a period of one year from 1969 to 1970, Lombardozzi contrived to steal fifty million dollars' worth of certificates.

But that was just the beginning. Lombardozzi used those stolen certificates to create a network of dummy companies with false assets, which then floated bloated stock; when enough money had been raised, he took the money and ran. (In one deal, he cleared over twenty million dollars.) Lombardozzi was also a prime mover in another favorite Gambino operation, the "bust-out." It involved getting a foot in the door of a marginally profitable company, usually via a loan-sharking debt. Lombardozzi and other mobsters would gradually take full control, establish a good credit rating, and at some point, order huge quantities of supplies for the company on credit. The supplies would be sold off at bargain-basement prices, then the mobsters would walk away from the company, leaving it an empty shell with no assets and huge bills from suppliers.

Gotti learned a great deal about these trade secrets from his mentor, Carmine Fatico, but there was one Gambino operation that Fatico could not discuss. Not because it didn't exist, but because it wasn't supposed to exist: narcotics.

Officially, among the *amici nostra* (our friends) of the Gambino Family, as they liked to call themselves, no one was supposed to deal in narcotics in any manner, shape, or form. Death was the instant penalty for anyone caught "doing drugs." The stern dictum was part of an elaborate disinformation effort by the American Mafia to convince everyone that as an organization, it was interested only in providing certain services which most Americans desired, but which an often-arbitrary legal system prevented them from obtaining. Mafia bosses continued to insist that they were in the business of "victimless crimes," and would never stoop to such terrible things as selling drugs. The Mafia continues to perpetuate this myth, and it has found its way into popular culture, most prominently in such works as *The Godfather*.

In fact, the Mafia almost from the first moment of its existence in this country dominated the drug traffic. It has concentrated on heroin, because the Mafia could control the laboratories that produce the stuff, along with the distribution networks that bring the drug into the streets. (Cocaine has too many production areas and variegated distribution points for any single organization to control the traffic.) Further, nothing produces profit like heroin: a kilo—2.2046 pounds— of uncut opium base bought in the Middle East or Southeast Asia costs about twelve thousand dollars; processed and finally reduced to 3.5 percent purity for street sale, that same kilo will earn over two million dollars.

Beginning in the early 1950s, the Mafia reorganized and renewed the heroin traffic, forming a partnership with the Corsican underworld, which controlled most of the sources of opium supply in the Middle East. The Mafia established processing laboratories in Sicily, staffed with the best French "cooks" (drug chemists). The famed "French Connection" was born, and it soon flooded the streets of urban America with the highest-quality heroin ever seen. The Mafia, reaping huge profits, was directly responsible for the manifold increase in the number of heroin addicts in the United States, from somewhere less than fifty thousand in the 1950s to nearly half a million several decades later.

The Mafia bosses tried to stay carefully in the background, avoiding direct involvement in the actual trade. Highly organized and efficient, the *Mafiosi* watched, in some amusement, as much less organized criminals tried to muscle in. One was Frank Matthews, a black ex-numbers runner from Brooklyn who decided that since heroin primarily was sold to blacks, then black organized crime should reap all the profits. He established his own connection with some renegade Corsicans, formed an organization of like-minded criminals, then set himself up in a Brooklyn apartment house protected by machine gun nests. He made a fortune in the process of becoming the most flamboyant dope kingpin in America, strutting through the black neighborhoods in gold chains and a floor-length sable coat, and roaring around in the streets in a Rolls-Royce or Mercedes, which he simply abandoned when the ashtray got full. His Christmas shopping tended to be simple: he wrapped up large bundles of cash in holiday wrapping paper, then handed them out to his friends.

Concerned about possible Mafia moves against him, Matthews sought to warn them away, snarling at one Gambino soldier, "Touch one of my people and I'll load my men into cars and we'll drive down Mulberry Street [in Little Italy] and shoot every wop we see." Gambino and the other Mafia bosses did not react to this challenge; convinced that such flamboyance was self-destructive and, more significantly, disorganized, they watched and waited. Sure enough, Matthews was arrested by federal drug agents, and his disorganized organization immediately fell apart (he fled before trial, forfeiting a million-dollar bail, but escaped with twenty million dollars in cash).

However, some Mafia bosses could not resist becoming more directly involved in the heroin traffic, and in the period 1956 to 1964, the Federal Bureau of Narcotics convicted 206 individual *Mafiosi* involved in heroin trafficking. It took the conviction in 1959 of a Mafia boss, Vito Genovese, for heroin trafficking to drive home the lesson of caution and strict control. As usual, Gambino had the organizational solution. The main components of his plan included, first, a shift away from the "French Connection," badly frayed by constant assaults from federal drug agents, and second, a system of cutouts, men who would conduct the actual high-level transactions on behalf of the entire Mafia, using Mafia investment capital. All the families would share in the profits, but individual members of families would not be allowed to deal in drugs, under pain of death. There was a sound reason for this latter stricture: heroin trafficking charges carry heavy prison time (about forty years), a great inducement for even a loyal *Mafioso* to become an informant in exchange for immunity. In the Mafia's view, Joe Valachi's road to perdition began when he was arrested for selling heroin.

The new heroin connection was in Sicily, where a tight web of family and clan relationships made such a business very secure. Many of the people involved in the new "Sicilian Connection" were related to Gambino by birth or marriage. Gambino had another innovation: because that narcotics deals were being made too openly, and were often detected by law enforcement surveillance teams, a more secure system would have to be devised. To that end, Gambino bought a Miami Beach tourist hotel. Major deals were discussed at the hotel in the more tolerant Miami atmosphere. To mislead possible surveillance, Gambino hired a group of women who posed as the wives or girlfriends of Mafia drug dealers when they were at the hotel; groups of single men attract attention, but couples at a tourist hotel tend to look like tourists.

And so, as Gotti understood, the whole question of narcotics and the Mafia amounted to a gigantic hypocrisy. He discovered that despite the official stern strictures, dealing in narcotics seemed to be endemic throughout the upper- and middle-management echelon of the Mafia. It was not long before he discovered that Carmine Fatico, for all his threats to his troops about the consequences of dealing in narcotics, was himself dabbling in heroin. For the moment, Gotti did not confront Fatico on this issue, for he grasped the essential truth of it all: the issue was not heroin-dealing itself, but *who* was profiting.

The mobster-in-training had been provided an important lesson, one he would not forget.

4

"A Hoodlum's Hoodlum"

As a wiseguy, you can lie, you can cheat, you can steal, you can kill people—legitimately. You can do any goddam thing you want, and nobody can say anything about it. Who wouldn't want to be a wise guy?
— BENJAMIN (LEFTY GUNS) RUGGIERO

FOR MOST OF THE MORNING that warm spring day in May 1972, Special Agents Patrick Colgan and Thomas D'Onofrio of the FBI had been checking all the familiar haunts, searching for the man they would have no trouble spotting. Frank (Buzzy) Carrone, with that slightly demented look, and the empty right socket where the eye had been gouged out, or shot out, or something, stood out in a crowd. It was like looking for Cyclops.

Buzzy might be easy to spot, but as the two FBI agents were aware, that solved only part of the problem. The real difficulty was Carrone as violent psychopath: he unfailingly packed a gun, a permanent appendage from the days when he was recruited into the crew of *capo* Carmine Fatico as a hijacker, and later when he began dabbling in bank robbery. A sufficient number of shaken bank tellers had told the FBI accounts about the bizarre-looking man with one eye and a gun, and now the time had come to pick up Carrone for a discussion of this matter.

Colgan and D'Onofrio cruised the streets of Queens, checking Carrone's known rat holes. Colgan was driving one of the Bureau's undercover vehicles, a decrepit, green compact car with brakes that only barely worked and an engine that sounded as though it might not make the next block. As an undercover car, it was a perfect disguise, although both agents wondered what would happen if they were to become involved in a high-speed chase.

And that, unfortunately, was precisely what happened. "That's him," D'Onofrio said, spotting Carrone leaving a building. As the two agents prepared to move, Carrone spotted them, some sixth sense apparently telling him that the two men in the wreck of a green car were FBI agents. He jumped in his car, and took off.

Colgan and D'Onofrio were after him, but a siren and a flashing red light only caused Carrone to speed up. Like a scene out of a chase movie, the two cars roared in and out of traffic. Accelerator pressed to the floor, Colgan was right on Carrone's tail when D'Onofrio noticed they were entering a school zone. The speedometer read 90 mph.

"For God's sake, slow down!" D'Onofrio shouted, as a school crossing guard shooed away small children about to cross the street.

"I can't!" Colgan shouted back.

"What are you talking about, you can't?"

"NO BRAKES!"

Carrone had opened a growing gap between them, but some distance ahead, there was the sound of crunching metal and glass as Carrone plowed into a woman's car. Reaching the scene, the two FBI agents saw that both cars appeared to be empty. Assuming that Carrone had taken the woman driver as a hostage and left the area, the agents, guns out, began scanning nearby buildings as a crowd gathered. Suddenly, someone in the crowd shouted, "Look in the front seat!"

That warning saved Colgan's life, for as he turned to look at Carrone's wrecked car, Carrone himself popped up from where he had been hiding under the steering wheel. He came up firing, four shots whizzing past Colgan's head. Both agents dived for cover while firing back at Carrone. There were screams of alarm as the watching crowd scattered in terror. With all those people running around, the agents had to hold off on firing any more shots. To their fury, by the time things calmed down, Carrone had managed to slip away in the confusion.

"Well, lucky for you the creep only has one eye and his aim is bad," Colgan's boss, FBI Supervisor John Good, summarized his agent's close call. Good was grateful that neither of his agents had been hit, but he was also angry, a white-hot anger that was about to make life extremely difficult for Fatico and his minions.

"No one, *no one* takes a shot at my agents," Good announced, and led equally angry agents into Fatico's lair. Fatico sought to calm Good, but he might just as well have tried putting out a forest fire with a glass of water. Nothing Fatico tried—Buzzy was a "cowboy," the crew long ago ceased having anything to do with him, he personally saw the soundness of Good's position, he quite understood the FBI's anger, he felt great anger himself at someone who would try to kill an FBI agent, and so forth—would mollify Good, who seemed to be hardly listening.

"We want Carrone, and we want him *now!*" Good yelled, making it clear that he held Fatico and the crew directly responsible for Carrone. To underscore the point, he and his agents began a campaign of pressure against Fatico, an old police technique called "rousting." Fatico's crew members found themselves confronting FBI agents day and night, and constantly being dragged in for questioning, all with the cooperation of uniformed police, who seemed to find an astonishing number of traffic violations on cars owned by Fatico and his people. For weeks on end, Fatico and company found their lives a living hell, a nightmare, Good made clear, that would not end until they gave up Buzzy Carrone.

Fatico would have loved to give up Carrone, the man who was causing him so much grief, but in truth he could not. Despite Good's conviction that he was hiding the one-eyed bank robber, Fatico had no idea where Carrone was, nor did anyone else in the crew. (Carrone in fact had fled to Massachusetts, where he was lying low for the moment.) Nevertheless, Fatico ordered his crew members to kill Carrone, if they could find him; meanwhile, they were to pass the word that Carrone's options had expired—either the FBI would track him down, or the Mafia would, and thus Carrone had a choice of fates at the hands of an infuriated FBI or an equally angry Mafia. That message was subtly conveyed to the FBI by one of Fatico's crew members, Gene Gotti, who as he was being led into the FBI's Manhattan headquarters for still another session of harassment, suddenly turned to Good and said, "Listen, John, we understand. You're doin' whatcha gotta do."

In other words, no hard feelings, because the Mafia was just as eager as the FBI to dispose of the man who was causing them so much grief. Word of the Mafia's eagerness for his demise finally reached Carrone at his hiding place in Massachusetts, plunging him into a deep state of fear. When his money ran out, Carrone held up a bank, but a silent alarm alerted a posse of Massachusetts State Police troopers. They chased the fleeing Carrone as he hid in some nearby woods. The troopers fanned out, trying to find him; one trooper, tiptoeing through some heavy underbrush, suddenly heard three loud clicks behind him. He turned, his gun out, and saw Carrone standing there, a gun pointed at the trooper's head. But Carrone was out of bullets. As the trooper leveled his own gun on him, Carrone, a man at the end of the road, begged him, "Do it."

But the trooper would not shoot a man with an empty gun, and arrested him. In prison, his head filled with whispers from other inmates that some bad Mafia people in New York were seeking to kill him right inside the jail, Carrone spent his days literally quaking with fear, convinced that at any moment one of Fatico's people would slip poison into his food, or waylay him in a darkened corner. His mood was not improved by a visit from some of Good's agents, who made it clear that they took the attempted murder of FBI agents very seriously, and were determined in some unspecified way to make Buzzy's life very uncomfortable. Unable to sleep, hardly eating, Carrone one day dropped dead of a heart attack. He was thirty-seven years old.

The problem with Carrone could not have come at a worse time for Fatico, for he was desperately eager to mollify the FBI—especially Good's squad—in some way, since the Bureau was causing him terrible business difficulties. The

FBI had mounted a renewed attack on airport hijackings, and while Fatico could absorb the increasing personnel losses, he was not prepared to withstand an FBI innovation, a direct assault against the network of fences that handled the swag. One by one, Good's squad knocked over the big fences, and Fatico was hurting badly. Without those fences, the goods his crew stole could not be disposed of efficiently. Income was down drastically.

Worse, some of the new men being recruited for hijacking operations demonstrated a notable lack of talent in that area. One of them, Salvatore Polisi, spotted a likely looking target one day and decided he would hijack the truck and bring it to Fatico as a means of impressing the *capo*.

Polisi jumped in front of the truck, gun in hand, and announced to the driver that he was hijacking it.

"You don't want this truck," the driver said.

"Shut up and get the fuck out," Polisi ordered, waving the gun at him.

The driver shrugged. "Okay, but I'm telling you, pal, you're making a big mistake." He got out of the truck as Polisi got in and drove away; in the process, Polisi did not notice that the driver, despite his experience, was smiling broadly.

Like a hunter returning with his trophy, Polisi proudly showed the truck to Fatico. Opening the rear doors to inspect whatever treasure lay inside, Polisi was confronted by the sight of several large boxes. He ripped one open, frowned, then ripped open another, and another. When he had finished opening all of them, he sheepishly showed his great prize: a shipment of half a million wire coat hangers.

Fatico stared. "What the fuck is this?" he asked, at last.

"Uh, maybe we could melt them down," Polisi suggested hopefully. Fatico turned on his heel and walked away.

There was no immediate answer to the crisis, but Fatico realized he would have to come up with a solution as soon as possible. He was operating now in a new and expanded territory, with extra personnel and the expenses of an entirely new setup. Additionally, he was under serious legal attack in suburban Suffolk County on Long Island, which was in the process of indicting him on charges of running a suburban branch of his loansharking operation in the county. Legal expenses were mounting.

Fatico had left East New York because, as he phrased it, "the fucking niggers and spics are moving in." The remark was somewhat disingenuous, for the Mafia itself was responsible for the dramatic change in East New York's demographics, from predominantly Jewish and Italian to predominantly black during a period of less than a year. In effect, the Mafia carried out a bust-out operation for an entire community.

It began in 1969, when the remnants of the old Jewish organized crime syndicate and the Mafia combined to pour profits from heroin and gambling into real estate fronts. Men working in the fronts then set about to buy hundreds of one- and two-family homes at rock-bottom prices by informing their owners that "the niggers are coming; you better sell now while you can." To underscore the point, hoods hired blacks who were ostentatiously walked around neighborhoods as though they were scouting places to buy.

In the real estate trade, the technique is called "block-busting," and thousands of panicked homeowners sold out at low prices. There was a further refinement: the real estate fronts rounded up poor blacks, informed them they could now achieve their dream of actually owning their own homes, and presented them with phony Federal Housing Administration applications which attested to the applicant's economic suitability to pay off a mortgage. When most of them defaulted—the federal government, which guaranteed the mortgages, took the loss—the real estate fronts would buy up the houses at public auction, and start the process all over again.

Fatico and his organization followed the flight out of East New York. He headed north, into the predominantly Italian community of Ozone Park, a middle-class area of neat, small homes, owned mostly by second-generation Italian graduates of the ghettos of Manhattan and the Bronx. In terms of Mafia territory, Ozone Park was in the jurisdiction of Gambino soldier Andrew (Fat Andy) Ruggiano, a mountain of a man who specialized in cigarette bootlegging; he had warehouses of stolen, untaxed cigarettes peddled to certain outlets that put a forged tax stamp on them, then pocketed the seventeen cents per pack tax the State of New York was supposed to have received.

Ruggiano, old and ailing, was eased into semiretirement by reassignment to Florida, and Fatico was assigned the territory. Ruggiano had spent most of his working day at the wickedly named Our Friends Social Club in Ozone Park, but the place had "too many old greaseballs" (as Fatico put it), and the new *capo* of Ozone Park decided he wanted a new social club.

He settled on two vacant adjoining storefronts facing 101st Avenue, and had one of them redone in minimalist Mafia interior decoration: several card tables, a counter, a coffee machine in the front, and a spare office in the back containing a desk and a few chairs. The only wall decoration was a television set. The second, smaller, storefront was set aside as a storage area; it contained two pay phones near the front door.

John Gotti accompanied Fatico from East New York, and was among the first patrons of the crew's new social club. For some odd reason, which he did not explain, Fatico named the place the Bergin Hunt and Fish Club. Gotti spent the rest of his time at his favorite Brooklyn dives, including the Bamboo Lounge and Gefkins Bar, notorious joints known as the kinds of places that no non-Mafia person usually entered unless he was selling stolen goods. Among such customers were mailmen with drug habits who stole credit cards out of the mail, then sold them to certain steady patrons who paid cash immediately, with no questions asked.

Gotti, usually trailed by a group of young punks who looked to him as a leader, also liked to hang out at an infamous Ozone Park dive, the 101st Bar. Strictly Mafia, the 101st was a curious place. There was no cash register, and patrons were expected to throw fifty or sixty dollars on the bar occasionally as a rough approximation of their tabs. Those failing to perform this ritual would be informed by a very large bartender with no neck, "You owe fifty dollars."

An oblong-shaped joint, the 101st was packed every night with Mafia punks and their girlfriends. Strict protocol prohibited the bringing of women to Mafia social clubs, so women

would be escorted to dives like the 101st; men who brought
in whores had sexual relations with them atop the pool tables,
or took them into the supply room in back for more private
encounters.

At the Bergin, meanwhile, Fatico began to organize his
newly expanded crew, which now included members of Ruggiano's group. It was a variegated collection, including some
graduates of the old Ozone Park street gang, the Saints—
among them Matthew Traynor, who had now become a bank
robber—and *Mafiosi* of varying talent. By far, the most interesting was a veteran hijacker named Salvatore (Sally) DeVita,
whose nickname underscored an interesting fact: he was the
only known transvestite Mafia hood in existence.

An incredibly ugly man, DeVita nevertheless spent much
of his time attempting to perfect the art of women's makeup
or trying on one of the many lady's outfits and shoes that
crowded his closet. DeVita made no secret of his inclinations,
but withstood only a certain amount of teasing. He would
tolerate the joshing of fellow hijackers when, having just
stolen a truckload of designer dresses, they would ask,
"Sally, would you like us to put aside the nice blue one for
you?" Other times, Sally would demonstrate less tolerance;
it was wise at such points not to push him too hard, because
when DeVita wore dresses, he invariably carried a pistol
underneath.

Despite his best efforts, however, DeVita always managed
to look like a Mafia hood underneath all the makeup and
fancy clothes. One night, a local hood entered the men's
room at the 101st, and encountered DeVita, dressed to the
nines, making a last-minute adjustment in the mirror. Obviously, DeVita had exerted a lot of effort: a beautiful blond
wig, face in rouge, mascara, and lipstick; a stunning Oscar
de la Renta dress; stockings; and expensive high-heel shoes
and a five-hundred-dollar handbag; all rounded off with stra-
tegically placed padding.

"Oh, hello, Sal," the hood said, without thinking. He
instantly realized his mistake: DeVita looked crushed at being
recognized. DeVita refused to speak to his fellow hood for
months afterward.

DeVita was one of the regulars who congregated at the

new Bergin Hunt and Fish Club, headquarters of the reconstituted Fatico crew. The crew had a sort of pecking order, with the more noted (and better-earning) members often lording it over the lesser-knowns. The top roost was occupied by the brothers John and Charles Carneglia, chop shop owners and hijackers; another brother team, Nick and Blaise Corozzo, specialists in disposing of stolen property; Leonard DiMaria, loan shark; Anthony (Tony Roach) Rampino, killer and strong-arm artist; Angelo Ruggiero and his brother Salvatore, loan sharks and hijackers; William (Willie) Batista, noted for his ability to hot-wire a truck in seconds; Michael (Mickey Boy) Paradiso, hijacker; William (Foxy) Jerothe, hijacker; Frank (Frankie the Beard) Guidice, gambler; Phillip (Philly Broadway) Cestaro, bookmaker; Anthony (Tony Lee) Guerrieri, gambler; and Wilfred (Willie Boy) Johnson, enforcer.

Also on the top roost were the Gotti brothers, John and Gene. Older brother Peter was on a much lower rung: following his father, he had worked in the Sanitation Department for some years, but retired on disability after injuring his head (leading to many jokes in the Bergin about how the accident occurred to the one part of his anatomy certain to sustain no lasting damage). In deference to John, Peter was given a job as a sort of general manager of the Bergin. A similar job had to be found for the fourth brother in the crew, Richie, whose grasp of the criminal arts was very shaky. In one of his more inept episodes, he and a confederate attempted to hold up a high-stakes poker game in a Manhattan hotel room. Brandishing sawed-off shotguns, they demanded that the players turn over their money. Hardly bothering to look up from their cards, the players told them to go to hell. Flustered, Richie did not know what to do at that point, whereupon the players began throwing poker chips at the robbers, finally chasing them down a hallway. At his brother John's urging, Richie subsequently was given a job as general manager of the Our Friends Social Club, where the majority of its elderly members—a few of them connected with the Mafia—considered him a "nice Italian boy."

The Bergin was opened at 8 A.M. every day. It did not really start to come alive until late morning, when several of its "members" began to drift in. Some had racing forms, and tried to handicap the day's races; others discussed assorted scores to be made, or previously successful ones. They referred to each other, usually, only by nickname: "Nicky Nose," "Joe Pineapples," "Anthony Tits," "Frankie Dap," "Johnny Cabbage," "Mickey the Pig." (Because there is a relatively limited range of first names among Italian-American males—traditionally, sons are named after one of the Twelve Apostles—the Mafia adopted the practice of differentiating among many similar first names by using nicknames, usually keyed to a physical deformity or prominent event in someone's life.)

Sometime around noon, some of the more noted crew members would arrive, and later still, the *capo*. While the crew chief conducted his business in the back room, the men in the front simply hung around, waiting to be called for various assignments. A few paced constantly in little circles, an old prison habit they could not break. Others played cards, while the pay phones were in constant use by men working on gambling operations. The talk around the club was dotted with references to "dimes" (thousand-dollar bets) or "nickels" (five-hundred-dollar bets). Upstairs, in a vacant apartment over the club, Gene Gotti helped run a large-scale sports betting operation.

John Gotti, known as an addicted gambler, spent a lot of his time playing ferocious card games, mostly a game known as "box gin" (three games at a time), for stakes of a penny a point and a dollar a game. Given the intensity with which he played the game, anyone would have thought the stakes were considerably higher, but Gotti not only hated to lose, he was determined to beat the odds. Most often, he did not, and was known as an easy mark in any card game. To his eternal fury, his brother Gene, whom Gotti considered inferior in every possible respect, was an amazingly lucky gambler. He loved to irk John by describing how he had triumphed on a nine-to-one shot at the racetrack—at a time when John Gotti, according to murmurs around the Bergin, "couldn't win a bet on the color of his own underwear."

Ironically, despite his hopelessness as a gambler, Gotti was unsurpassed in his grasp of the intricacies of illegal gambling operations. Fatico, who clearly treated Gotti as his personal favorite, gave him management authority over the crew's gambling network, with instructions to revitalize it as a means of replacing lost income from hijacking operations.

Gotti quickly infused the crew's gambling network with new energy, and income began to increase. This was no simple task, for the network was fraught with difficult management problems. Many of them arose in one of Fatico's most profitable gambling operations, a network of illegal casinos in locations throughout Queens. For one thing, such casinos invariably required some form of police protection, which involved dealing with corrupt cops who sometimes had the habit of attempting to extort more money if they thought the casinos were very profitable. Then there was the problem of staff: casinos of even modest size required all kinds of workers, including "stickmen" (who operated the craps tables) and card dealers, who had to be watched carefully so they did not set up an arrangement with gamblers to jointly clean out the house. Illegal casinos tended to attract a rough trade, so the toughest hoods had to be hired to keep control of some of the more rambunctious patrons, such as the one who always arrived at the door carrying a submachine gun (to protect his winnings, he claimed), and the man who liked to announce his presence by throwing a large meat cleaver into the wall.

Other gambling operations of the crew also came with management headaches. A large-scale illegal dice game, which usually attracted the most degenerate gamblers of all, inevitably involved loans (and loans on top of loans) to players, in turn requiring collectors for the loans. Additionally, a number of push-button poker machines were sited in bars all over Queens, and while they were immensely profitable (up to three thousand dollars a week), the machines had to be monitored for possible skimming by bar owners, who in turn had to be occasionally reminded how the presence of such machines in their establishments was very good for their health. Meanwhile, a flourishing numbers operation required a large number of personnel and constant oversight, as did an equally profitable illegal sports betting operation, with its wire rooms (apartments outfitted with banks of telephones to handle bets) and collection points.

Gotti was a tireless executive in managing these operations, an increasingly striking figure who not only seemed to have mastered all the finer points of an extremely complicated business, but also maintained tight control with stern discipline. An executive who did not mind getting his hands dirty, Gotti personally would solve intractable personnel problems, usually by threats, occasionally by beating up a miscreant. His growing reputation was often sufficient to induce cooperation; a man who was refusing to pay a large gambling debt, or some other transgression, would become cooperative when told that "Johnny Boy"—Gotti's nickname in the Fatico crew—was about to arrive for a visit. To his contemporaries, Gotti was becoming someone clearly marked for greater things. As Carmine Fiore, one of the low-level hoods attached to the Fatico crew, said admiringly, "What you got there is a hoodlum's hoodlum."

That reputation was especially useful in addressing the gambling operations' most persistent problem, the often-complex division of gambling territories among the various crews and families. Such arrangements were scrupulously observed at the higher management levels, but at the lower levels, there were recurring efforts by small-time hoods to muscle in on somebody else's territory. It required all of Gotti's sinister reputation to nip these violations in the bud. In one instance, he and his chief henchman, Willie Boy Johnson, walked into a storefront gambling operation in Queens that was "nonsanctioned" and in the territory of a local bookmaker who was paying tribute to the Fatico crew for the privilege of the local franchise.

"You can't operate here," Gotti snapped to the invaders, an injunction underscored when Johnson casually picked up a heavy desk and threw it into the street. Then, with one hand, he ripped a pay telephone off the wall and heaved it through the storefront window. Their minds suddenly set right by this display of executive decisiveness, the miscreants abjectly apologized, wondered aloud how they could have made such a silly mistake, and announced their intention of atoning by paying several thousand dollars to Fatico "as a sign of our respect."

The question of sanctity of territory was paramount,

because no one wanted any kind of intra-Mafia war to break out. Not in the New York Mafia, which by 1972, had had its collective fill of such wars—wars, as Carlo Gambino never tired of pointing out, nobody ever seemed to win. *Don* Carlo was something of an expert on that subject.

For all its elaborate rules, rigid structure, and clear divisions of territory, the Mafia was always plagued by the one factor it could not control: human greed. It was an ironic situation, for greed has always been the supreme impetus for the Mafia.

Still, despite Gambino's everlasting injunctions that there were enough riches for all without recourse to such insanities as territorial wars or moves to gain even larger slices of the pie, the Mafia was periodically convulsed by such problems. One occurred in Gambino's backyard of Brooklyn not too long after the murder of Anastasia.

Although Gambino assumed that Anastasia's demise in 1957, his own rise to leadership, and an elaborate series of arrangements to keep the peace forestalled any further disruptions, in fact one occurred almost as The Executioner's body was being laid to rest. The Gallo brothers, the killers of Anastasia, assumed that a grateful Mafia would cut them in for a greater share of the spoils for their small (twenty-man) crew. But their superior, Joseph Profaci, reigning head of what became known as the Colombo Family, had no intention of sharing anything, least of all money. An unbelievably cheap man, Profaci was a multimillionaire, with vast income from assorted rackets and his own legitimate business, which was a virtual monopoly over all the olive oil sold in New York City. A family man and devout churchgoer, Profaci nevertheless had a reputation for ferocity; once, when a local junkie stole gems from the crowned head of the Madonna in Profaci's parish church, the man known in the Mafia as the "olive oil king" had the thief tortured for hours, then strangled to death with a set of rosary beads.

Despite pleas from Gambino that he keep the peace by giving the Gallos slices of lucrative Profaci operations, Profaci refused, accentuating his contempt by attempting to have Larry Gallo strangled to death (an incident reprised in *The*

Godfather). The Gallos retaliated by murdering one of Profaci's key aides, Josepn (Joe Jelly) Gioelli, an execution they announced by dumping Gioelli's overcoat on Profaci's doorstep. The coat contained a large fish, an unmistakable clue to Gioelli's fate and a clear reference to the old Sicilian Mafia saying, "Tonight, he sleeps with the fishes."

And so the "Gallo War," as it became known, was on. To Gambino's dismay, it preoccupied the entire Brooklyn Mafia, a senseless bloodbath that claimed twenty lives before finally ending in 1962 when Profaci died of cancer. His successor, Joseph Colombo, promised the Gallo crew a greater share of the spoils, and that would have appeared to be the end of it. Gambino had sponsored Colombo for higher rank, convincing the Profaci organization that it would be a wise move, despite Colombo's young age (forty-one) and pronounced lack of extensive experience in the criminal arts. But on the asset side of the ledger was his relative anonymity to police and the FBI, talent for diplomacy, and insistence that Mafia melodramas ultimately hurt the organization as a whole. (A more important, but unstated, reason for Gambino's sponsorship was Colombo's selfless act of disloyalty in informing Gambino that Joseph Bonanno had tried to enlist him in a plot to kill *Don* Carlo and make the man known as "Joe Bananas" ruler of the New York Mafia.) The sponsorship of Colombo was one of Gambino's few major miscalculations, for his protégé turned out to cause more trouble than Profaci and the Gallos ever did. The problem was that Colombo had the brains of a grasshopper, and was muleheaded, besides. In 1970, to Gambino's growing uneasiness, Colombo—angered over his son's arrest by the FBI in a theft case—decided to go on the offensive. He created an organization called the Italian-American Civil Rights League, which as its first order of business began noisy protests against "stereotyping" of Italian-Americans by various authorities with the label of "Mafia." To everyone's surprise, the league was initially successful: references to "Mafia" were excised from *The Godfather* movie, and U. S. Attorney General John Mitchell ordered that the terms "Mafia" and *La Cosa Nostra* be removed from the Justice Department's official lexicon. Frank Sinatra performed at a gala league fund-raiser, and this cruel hoax on millions of Italian-Americans seemed destined to be a major political force.

But, as Gambino realized, the league was actually a disaster for the Mafia. Organizationally, the Mafia functioned best in a condition of deepest secrecy, its hand as invisible as possible. Excessive attention always had been the Mafia's worst enemy. Besides, Gambino argued, Colombo's tactic of putting pickets around FBI headquarters in Manhattan, while guaranteed to garner front-page publicity for the league, also had the effect of making the FBI very angry. And the FBI was not an organization that Gambino wanted to have in a foul mood; among other things, the Bureau might discover that the league finances, swelled by contributions from Italian-Americans all over the country, amounted to a giant skimming operation. Colombo was stealing the proceeds and paying shares to other Mafia bosses, including Gambino himself. And given Colombo's lack of smarts, there existed a reasonable certainty that he would foul it up.

The foul-up occurred one winter morning in 1970 when Colombo and one of his *capi*, Rocco Miraglia, sat in Miraglia's car in Brooklyn discussing business. Miraglia arrogantly had parked his car in the space reserved for a State Supreme Court judge at the Brooklyn courthouse. Engrossed in the business discussion, they did not notice the approach of two FBI agents who suddenly materialized with an arrest warrant for Miraglia, alleging he had committed perjury before a federal grand jury.

The agents grabbed Miraglia from the car, at the same time seizing from him a black attaché case he was carrying. Suddenly, a panic-stricken Colombo began shouting, "That's mine! That's mine!" He attempted to grab the case, only to be shoved back inside the car by one of the agents.

The commotion attracted the attention of two uniformed police officers, who, after the standard inquiry ("What seems to be the trouble here?"), checked the FBI agents' credentials and arrest warrant. One of the cops began writing in a black notebook.

"Sir, you're illegally parked," he said. "I'll have to give you a summons." Nothing so enrages criminals as calm police officiousness, and Colombo almost went into orbit.

*"YOU'RE WRITING A FUCKING TICKET, AND THESE
FUCKING FBI SCUMBAGS ARE STEALING MY PROP-
ERTY! I WANT TO FILE A CHARGE AGAINST THESE
COCKSUCKERS! WHY THE FUCK AREN'T YOU DOING
ANYTHING ABOUT THEM STEALING MY BRIEFCASE?"*

"Sir," replied the cop, not even bothering to look up as
he wrote out the parking ticket, "these gentlemen are special
agents of the FBI, have identified themselves to our satisfaction as such, and appear to have a valid federal arrest warrant.
Please address any complaints you might have to the United
States Attorney's office for this district."

Colombo was beside himself with rage. *"I DON'T
BELIEVE THIS SHIT!"* he screamed. *"WHAT THE FUCK
KIND OF COPS DO WE HAVE IN THIS CITY? HERE'S
THE FBI, STEALING MY PROPERTY, AND YOU'RE NOT
GONNA DO ANYTHING ABOUT IT?"*

"Have a nice day, sir," the cop said, handing him a ticket.

Enraged, Colombo headed for the office of Denis Dillon,
then head of the Justice Department's Eastern District Organized Crime Strike Force, headquartered in the nearby federal
courthouse in Brooklyn. Colombo burst into Dillon's office,
demanding the FBI return his briefcase. Dillon, stalling for
the time he believed sufficient for the FBI to photocopy whatever was inside the briefcase, fenced with Colombo for a
while. When the briefcase reappeared, Dillon discovered it
contained lists of names with amounts of money written next
to them. Among the more interesting was one for "Carl,"
with a figure of thirty thousand dollars. Clearly, "Carl" was
Gambino, and the thirty thousand dollars was his cut of
league proceeds.

Astonishingly, Colombo admitted that "Carl" indeed
referred to Gambino, but denied the figure listed was any
kind of split: "Oh, that's money Carlo raised selling tickets
for the league." FBI agents and Dillon laughed uproariously,
for the idea of Carlo Gambino personally selling tickets, like
the people who peddle church raffles on the street corner,
was truly hysterical.

Gambino did not think the matter so funny. Furious, he
later berated Colombo as a moron, noting that although the

federales would not be able to make a case (the briefcase was technically illegally seized evidence), it had been a very close call; the great *Don* Carlo himself had come within a hairsbreadth of being nailed, all because of the stupidity of Joe Colombo. It did not ease Gambino's growing disenchantment with him, nor did Colombo's persistence in continuing with the league, despite *Don* Carlo's firm advice not to do so. Thus, Gambino was not about to stand in the way when the leader of the Gallo crew, Joseph (Crazy Joe) Gallo, released from prison on parole, arranged to have Colombo shot during an outdoor rally for the league in 1971.

And yet, that was not the end of the madness. Gallo went insane: not having done enough to earn the enmity of the Colombo Family, he walked into a Long Island nightclub partially owned by Sonny Franzese, the infamous Colombo *capo.* "Get out, this joint is mine," Gallo said. He followed that move with an even more unpardonable transgression, arranging for the burglary of a Greenwich Village bakery known to be a favorite of mobsters. The bakery was not connected with the Mafia, but its owners lamented their uninsured loss to people in a position to exact a certain form of justice for the crime. Some time later, Gallo was murdered in front of his family in a Little Italy restaurant.

There were other, similar, headaches afflicting the Mafia. Joe Bonanno, the organization's chief megalomaniac, continued to follow his obsession of becoming *capo di tutti capi,* an ambition the rest of the ruling commission firmly squelched. Bonanno then turned his rage on his own family, naming his halfwit son, Salvatore (known as "Bill"), as *consigliere* of the Bonanno organization, and igniting a bloody struggle within the family. Known as the "Banana War," it consumed a dozen lives to no purpose.

Equally pointless were the depredations of another maniac, the violent hood Carmine (Lilo) Galante. By 1974, he had served twelve years of a twenty-year sentence for narcotics trafficking, somehow being convicted in a trial that featured the jury foreman being pushed down a flight of stairs, one of Galante's codefendants throwing a chair at the prosecutor, and another codefendant leaping into the jury box and beating up jurors who dared to find him guilty. Galante also harbored ambitions of becoming supreme boss of the entire Mafia, and upon his parole, dynamited the bronze doors off Frank Costello's tomb as symbolic demonstration of his intentions.

Needless to say, Gambino was appalled, but for the moment, there was no easy solution at hand for the Galante problem. That would come later.

In terms of John Gotti's criminal career, all these disruptions did him harm, for while he was not directly involved, the turmoil diverted attention away from the day-to-day operations of the Mafia. There, in the front trenches, Gotti was making a name for himself, but recognition at higher levels—the essential prerequisite for a man to get "made"—was not forthcoming. Simply put, there was too much static in the air for the accomplishments of a street hood to receive due notice.

Again, Gotti wondered aloud just what he had to do to win formal induction; Fatico had gone out of his way to congratulate him on his stewardship of the crew's gambling operations, yet he was no closer, seemingly, to his goal of becoming a real wiseguy. But then, in a remarkable stroke of luck for Gotti, there occurred an event that was to transform his entire career. It was an event in which Gotti was not only to perform in a way guaranteed to be noticed at the highest level of the family, it had the bonus of being personal—to Carlo Gambino, of all people.

The chain of events began in May 1972, when Emanuel (Manny) Gambino, one of *Don* Carlo's sons, was kidnapped. The kidnapping was carried out by a wild bunch of Irish gangsters from Manhattan's West Side, who had discovered the profitable sideline of abducting bookmakers, loan sharks, and assorted associates allied with the Gambino organization, and holding them until a hundred-thousand-dollar ransom was paid. Usually, the men were released following negotiations in which a portion of the demanded ransom was paid. The gang, under the nominal leadership of a hood named James McBratney, then decided to expand their horizons and snatch a bigger (and more profitable) target, one of Carlo Gambino's own sons.

McBratney was already engaged on a course certain to earn the wrath of Gambino, and in kidnapping *Don* Carlo's son, he guaranteed a future filled with peril. But like a small boy kicking over a hornet's nest, McBratney seemed to have no idea that kidnapping the son of a man in Gambino's position was a certain way to get into very serious trouble. The Gambino organization bided its time, over a period of several months negotiating a payment of about one hundred thousand dollars for Manny Gambino's return, but they ransomed a corpse: Manny Gambino's body was found in January 1973. McBratney had not only taken the money, he had murdered the kidnapped Gambino, for reasons which remained obscure. The result was inevitable: Gambino Sr. ordered that McBratney was to die, as slowly and horribly as possible.

By this time, it was spring of 1973. The murder order was passed to Gambino's chief aide in this area, the family underboss, Aniello Dellacroce, who in turn consulted Fatico on the best men for the job. Fatico put together a special three-man squad: John Gotti, Gotti's closest *goombah*, Angelo Ruggiero, and Ralph (Ralphie Wigs) Galione, a hijacker and occasional hit man whose ill-fitting toupee had led to an inevitable nickname.

The plan was to kidnap McBratney and bring him to a site where inventive minds could dispose of him in a manner befitting his terrible crime. On May 22, 1973, the trio tracked down McBratney to a bar in Staten Island. Flourishing phony police badges, the three men told McBratney he was under arrest and was to come with them. Not fooled, McBratney resisted. As he struggled with Gotti and Ruggiero, Galione brandished a gun on the bar's patrons, warning them to keep back. One drunk insisted on intervening, and when Galione pushed him, the gun went off accidentally. Panicked, Galione then pumped three bullets into McBratney, and the three men fled. McBratney died immediately.

As mob executions went, it was not a classic piece of art. Nevertheless, it had the desired result, and a grateful Gambino was ready to help when the police, armed with eyewitness descriptions, went looking for Galione and his two friends. Galione turned out to be beyond justice—he was shot to death outside his apartment, probably by angry friends of

McBratney—and Ruggiero and Gotti went into hiding. An FBI informant told the Bureau where to look, and several months after the killing, Ruggiero was arrested. Gotti was picked up in a Brooklyn bar by his old FBI nemesis, Supervisor John Good, who arrived with a posse of twenty heavily armed agents (the McBratney shooting technically was a violation of Gotti's federal parole).

"Jesus, John," Gotti exclaimed as Good and his FBI posse pounced on him. "What the hell is all this for?"

"Because you're a murderer," Good replied.

Gotti was the very picture of wide-eyed innocence: "Who, me?"

Gotti would need something more substantial than that to combat the murder case the State of New York now filed against him, for in truth, it was a "dead case," as defense lawyers like to say, a case so airtight, there really was little point in going to trial. Which is why certain subsequent events in the New York judicial system were decidedly odd.

First, Gambino hired attorney Roy Cohn to represent Gotti and Ruggiero. Cohn had a reputation for mysterious powers of control over certain segments of the New York City judicial establishment, and once again demonstrated them. Via Dellacroce, Gambino ordered Gotti and Ruggiero to plead guilty. Gotti was distinctly unhappy about this order: after all, Galione was dead, John Gotti had not actually shot anyone, and there was thus a reasonable possibility that sufficient doubt could be introduced for a jury to deadlock, or acquit. But Dellacroce said no: "Carlo says you take the fall, and that's it."

Embittered, Gotti held his temper in check and followed orders—and discovered that Gambino knew exactly what he was doing. To Gotti's astonishment, the Staten Island District Attorney's Office agreed on a plea bargain, under which Ruggiero and Gotti would plead to a reduced charge of attempted manslaughter, with a four-year prison sentence. Furthermore, the D.A.'s office unaccountably failed to classify either Gotti or Ruggiero as a "persistent offender," which under New York State law meant a very stiff prison sentence. If John Gotti was anything at that point, he certainly was a "persistent offender." The deal was incredible, but not especially surprising in the history of the Staten Island District Attorney's Office, which had a notably lax record in dealing with organized crime defendants.

In any event, Gotti and Ruggiero went off to the state prison at Green Haven in August 1975. Predictably, both men were well taken care of by the prison's Mafia establishment: Gotti was assigned a job as a porter, a task which took all of one hour a day. The rest of his time was spent socializing or lifting weights, precisely the same way he had spent his previous prison sentence.

He was also busy corrupting: several prison guards got three hundred dollars each to take Gotti on trips back to Queens for conjugal visits with his wife and to have supper in one of the Italian restaurants he favored. At the same time, it was arranged that a fellow hood Gotti met and befriended in prison, Arnold (Zeke) Squiteri, would be permitted similar visits to his home in the Bronx. Additionally, the guards were put up at a local motel with prostitutes to play with while Squiteri and his mob associates met elsewhere to discuss business. Since Squiteri was a heroin trafficker, those business conversations had to do with narcotics, a fact that would assume some importance in Gotti's life later.

But for the moment, Gotti was not exactly undergoing a terrible penal servitude. After less than two years in jail, he was paroled. The chief parole condition of gainful employment was provided by an old boyhood friend, Anthony Gurino, by 1977 a plumbing and heating contractor. According to Gurino, Gotti was hired as a twenty-five-thousand-dollar-a-year "salesman" for Gurino's firm, although there was no record of Gotti having any special expertise in heating and plumbing systems.

A short while after Gotti's parole in July 1977, Dellacroce solemnly informed Gotti that his patience, loyalty, and talents were now to be rewarded: he would be "made." Sometime later that summer, Gotti and eight other deserving associates of the expanded Fatico crew, including Angelo Ruggiero, were inducted into the Mafia. No one, aside from the participants, knows exactly how it happened, but there were some important traditions common to all such occasions.

Accompanied by his sponsor—usually a crew chief—the

initiate was taken to a private room, customarily in the back of a Mafia-owned restaurant. He confronted the upper echelon of his Mafia family, who stood around a table, on which rested a gun and a knife, covered by a paper tissue. The family *consigliere* in attendance pointed at the gun and the knife and intoned, "This is the gun you live by, and this is the knife you die by."

The *consigliere* took a needle and pricked one finger of the initiate's hand. The blood was wiped with the tissue, which was then set afire inside the cupped hands of the initiate, who repeated this phrase twice: "If I should betray *La Cosa Nostra,* I should burn like this paper." Following that, the initiate joined hands with the *Mafiosi* in attendance, who chanted, "Now you are born over again. You are a new man from now on." The *consigliere* concluded the ceremony by repeating certain Mafia "rules," violation of which would bring death, among them having sexual relations with the wife of another *Mafiosi,* or raising hands against a fellow made man. (This part of the ceremony varied widely from family to family, with each organization emphasizing certain injunctions it felt the most important. Initiates of the Genovese Family, for example, were commanded, for some mysterious reason, "No government bonds.")

Gotti had returned to a Mafia family bereft of its progenitor: Carlo Gambino died peacefully at his home in 1976, his death announced in the *New York Daily News* classic man-bites-dog headline, CARLO GAMBINO DIES IN BED. Before his death, Gambino had carefully determined his succession, selecting one of his *capi* (and son-in-law), Paul Castellano, to succeed him. The news came as a shock to the underboss, Aniello Dellacroce, who assumed he was the natural next in line. But Castellano, a Mafia diplomat in Gambino's mold, mollified Dellacroce by awarding him direct and total control over some of the family's most profitable crews, the Fatico group among them.

Dellacroce's initial audit of the Fatico crew's operations did not inspire great confidence. Although the gambling network was extremely profitable, illegal gambling operations require a huge overhead, swallowing up large percentages of the gross. Mafia crews tended to use gambling profits as

"work" money, i.e., putting that cash back onto the street
to capitalize the much more profitable enterprises of hijacking
and loansharking. But hijacking by Fatico's crew had been
nearly brought to a halt by the FBI's assault on the fences,
and Fatico was under severe legal attack aimed at his highly
profitable Long Island loansharking operations. (He later went
to prison for four years.) While that attack was under way,
the profits were drying up. Then, too, Carmine Fatico had
begun falling prey to a number of old man's illnesses, and
his brother was hit with hijacking charges (in 1979, Danny
Wags was sentenced to a three-year prison term.)

All in all, not an especially promising outlook, and Dellacroce began to search around for a long-term solution;
clearly, Carmine Fatico and his brother were no longer up to
the demands that the job of *capo* imposed. During the past
several years, Dellacroce had heard much from the Faticos
about their protégé, John Gotti, and now the underboss began
to devolve more and more responsibility on the *Mafioso* only
so recently inducted.

With Dellacroce's blessing, Gotti moved rapidly into the
leadership vacuum of the crew, and was de facto acting crew
chief almost before everybody else quite realized what had
happened. It was Gotti who now sat at the nondescript desk
in the back room of the Bergin, issuing orders and holding
audiences. Among the steady parade into that room one day
were several local teenage gang leaders whose violent confrontations had aroused the ire of some residents of Ozone
Park. Following an old immigrant tradition, instead of going
to the police, they complained to Gotti. The gang leaders
were read the Mafia equivalent of the riot act, and Gotti
ordered them to stop fighting in the local neighborhood. "I
want you to understand," he said, glaring at them, "there's
only one tough guy around here, and that's me."

Maybe, for by this point, Gotti had an established reputation as a violent man of monumental temper who occasionally
would beat up people in the Bergin's back room with his
own hands. The men who knew Gotti best, his *goombata*
who had been with him for twenty years, saw this kind of
thuggery as characteristic of the man: a *capo* was not supposed to dirty his hands with such tasks, yet Gotti could

never seem to outgrow his roots as a street punk. To them, Gotti's sudden elevation was a fluke. As one of his oldest *goombata*, Tony Roach Rampino, sneeringly observed to some of his friends, "Shit, I'd be big too if I'da killed the Irishman for Carlo Gambino."

Not even Gotti's new trappings as a middle-class mobster convinced them that their old *goombah* had changed his stripes, that he wasn't still the same street hood they all remembered. Gotti had moved into a nice home in the Queens community of Howard Beach, known as "the Mafia's bedroom" because of all the middle-echelon mobsters who moved there. Yet, this new resident of one of Queens's most distinctly upper-middle-class neighborhoods immediately reverted to type the first time he was confronted with a routine neighborhood problem. A neighbor consistently failed to cover his garbage cans properly, causing a bad odor. He was approached by his new neighbor, John Gotti, who threatened to break his legs if the garbage cans were left uncovered. Similarly, Gotti's newfound taste for fancy clothes, including thousand-dollar suits, also betrayed his roots; as his *goombata* noted, each time Gotti fancied a new suit, he simply selected one from a stolen shipment.

To be a street hood was no sin in Dellacroce's eyes, so long as he was a *profit-making* street hood. Gotti was, but as both he and Dellacroce realized, neither the underboss, the acting *capo*, nor the rest of the crew were going to get rich solely on gambling and loansharking. Something of much greater profit potential was required.

Gotti found it, an enterprise that returned modest investments ten-thousandfold, and promised a veritable fountain of money for Dellacroce and everyone else involved. It would be provided by two of Gotti's oldest *goombata*, the brothers Sal and Angelo Ruggiero. They called this magical source of cash *babania*.

By 1975, thanks to several severe injuries, Sal Ruggiero was cured of his addiction to high speed. Then, too, he had very little time for such pursuits, for Sal was a very busy millionaire "businessman" (as he preferred to call himself). His business was heroin (called *babania* in Sicilian slang), dealing in multi-kilo arrangements that made him one of the biggest dealers in New York.

Despite his long friendship with Gotti, Sal did not seem consumed with the same ambition to become a major Mafia powerhouse as did his brother, Angelo, and their mutual friend. Instead, he appeared content to stay on the fringes of the Fatico organization as some sort of vague associate, although no one seemed quite certain what he did. The vagueness was deliberate, for Sal Ruggiero by 1970 was deeply involved in heroin trafficking, and by Mafia rules, that was strictly forbidden. So the fiction had to be maintained: Ruggiero moved heroin while officially neither Carmine Fatico, nor John Gotti, nor Carlo Gambino knew anything about it. All the while, Fatico accepted a share of the heroin sales' proceeds from Sal, with the facade further maintained by both men's bland insistence that the money was the result of some successful hijackings.

Sal Ruggiero's heroin pipeline was known as the "Pleasant Avenue Connection," and it was along that deceptively named street in East Harlem that the Mafia "unofficially" controlled the importation and sale of almost all the heroin in the United States. Pleasant Avenue was the center of the last enclave of southern Italians in East Harlem, rapidly being subsumed by blacks and Puerto Ricans moving into the tenements vacated by Italians who had moved up the next step of the immigrant ladder, to neighborhoods in Brooklyn and Queens. By 1970, the street, with its old-neighborhood look of tenements, luncheonettes, and mom-and-pop stores, was a bustling wholesale market for heroin.

Some of those tenement apartments contained heroin "cut houses," small laboratories in stifling rooms with no air conditioning and the windows sealed tight. Under armed guard, women worked naked cutting quarter-kilos of heroin into small quantities, mixing it with milk sugar, and packaging it into small "nickel" (five-dollar) plastic bags at a fraction of the original purity. Down in the street, *Mafiosi* lounging in front of small social clubs directed "movers," young kids who were paid up to two thousand dollars a week to move packages of pure heroin from one car trunk to another while their bosses exchanged attaché cases packed with hundreds of thousands of dollars. Occasionally, drastic discipline would be meted out to one of the young "movers" who got the idea of taking some of the heroin for himself: one such thief was found with his hands cut off and an exploded cherry bomb jammed up what remained of his rectum.

Much of this "Pleasant Avenue Connection" took place fairly openly, for it operated in partnership with corrupt cops of an elite police organization known as the Special Investigations Unit. The SIU, whose misdeeds were chronicled in *Prince of the City,* cooperated with the Mafia in an arrangement that created a heroin epidemic in the black and Puerto Rican neighborhoods. The effects could be seen everywhere: addicts passed out cold on the sidewalks, nodding out in high schools, lying in pools of vomit in the lobbies of apartment buildings. The addicts and street dealers almost never dealt directly with the Mafia, whose members despised blacks; instead, Jewish drug dealers, who did not mind dealing with blacks and Puerto Ricans, were retained to act as middlemen.

The "Pleasant Avenue Connection" ended in 1973, when a secret unit of honest cops and federal agents bypassed the SIU—which was supposed to be arresting high-level street dealers—and arrested eighty-six traffickers, including one *Mafioso* picked up as he left a Pleasant Avenue social club carrying a box stuffed with one million dollars in fifty- and one-hundred-dollar bills. Asked what he was doing with the money, he replied, "I was going out to buy a newspaper."

Also arrested was the connection's leading Jewish middleman, Herbert Sperling, an animal who had beaten to death one of his associates so viciously, medical examiners could identify the body only from the teeth found in the victim's stomach. Sperling liked to conduct business on a midtown Manhattan sidewalk; federal drug agents drilled a pinhole in a mailbox that Sperling leaned on while talking, and a tiny microphone picked up Sperling discussing narcotics deals. Arrested outside his Long Island home while exiting his rented Mercedes, Sperling was asked by agents why the car had an ax under the front seat and two pistols in the glove compartment. "Damned if I know," Sperling replied. "And you can be fucking sure that I'll never rent no car from Avis again." Convicted after a brief trial, Sperling was asked by the judge if he had anything to say. "Yes, your honor," Sperling said. "If you think I'm going to beg for mercy, you've got another think coming. You're all a bunch of fascist cocksuckers! You can go to hell! Fuck you, fuck you, fuck you, fuck you . . ."

While Sperling's defense attorney buried his head in his hands and prosecutors stared, open-mouthed, Sperling repeated "fuck you" for another twenty minutes. Finally, exhausted, he sat down.

"Are you quite finished?" the judge asked, calmly. "Mr. Sperling, you are going to jail for the rest of your natural life." He sentenced Sperling to life plus thirty years, banged down his gavel, and walked out of the courtroom.

Sal Ruggiero, who had kept himself in the shadows, was not arrested during the great roundup of the "Pleasant Avenue Connection" for lack of firm evidence, but drug agents began to target him. The focus of their suspicions was the Bergin, his chief hangout. Early in 1972, they constructed a work shack of the type used by railroad maintenance workers, and placed it on a railroad overpass near the club that afforded a clear view of the front entrance. The idea was to staff it with surveillance equipment, but before the agents could get it manned, Sal and his brother, Angelo, along with Tony Roach Rampino, climbed up the overpass and burned down the shack.

It was only a temporary setback, and the drug agents soon were boring in with renewed vigor. Sal began to feel the heat, and following an indictment for income tax evasion, he realized it was only a matter of time before he faced another for heroin trafficking. At this point, the Ruggieros and John Gotti devised the "Bergin Connection."

Reduced to its essentials, the plan called for Sal to go into hiding under deep cover, using a half-million-dollar cash stash he had kept for just such a purpose. While in hiding under a new identity, he would set up an entirely new drug operation centered in New York. John Gotti would serve as overall chairman of the enterprise, with Gene Gotti as chief executive officer, and two other members of the Bergin crew known to have excellent narcotics connections—John Carneglia and his brother, Charley—working as on-site supervisors.

Coordinating supervisor would be Angelo Ruggiero, who would work as liaison via telephone and mail drop with his brother, Sal. Mark Reiter, a Lower East Side punk who had been originally recruited by Carneglia as a loan shark and car thief, was enlisted by the ring to deal directly with black street dealers.

A number of *Mafiosi* entered into a partnership with the Gotti narcotics ring. Among the more interesting was a personal friend of John Gotti, a three-hundred-pound soldier of the Bonanno Family named Joe Massina. A notorious heroin trafficker known to have excellent connections among fellow traffickers in Montreal, he was one of the more popular mobsters: although known as a tough man, Massina in private was a rollicking gladhander who liked to entertain his friends at lavish dinners, tell the latest jokes, and take people out on his large boat, which featured massive displays of food, drinks—and cocaine, for those so inclined. In earlier days, he was a successful loan shark known for his reluctance to beat up debtors who didn't pay; instead, his favorite trick was to have their cars torched, on the theory that most of his customers were the kind of people more deeply attached to their vehicles than any human being. To the amusement of his mob friends, Massina's psyche seemed to be dominated by concerns over his weight, which he said prevented him from having sexual relations with women; on an endless diet, he brightened up when fellow mobsters would politely remark on how much weight he seemed to have lost.

Other *Mafiosi* involved in the ring were less engaging characters, but each one had a particular, specialized connection of some sort convenient for unloading kilos of heroin. They included: Joseph (Joe Butch) Corrao of Manhattan, a veteran mobster and dope dealer with connections in upstate New York; Richard (Red Bird) Gomes of Queens, with large-scale connections in the hashish trade; Peter (Little Pete) Tambone of Manhattan, another veteran mobster with narcotics sales connections throughout the city; Arnold (Zeke) Squiteri of New Jersey, a friend and former cellmate of John Gotti, and a man with big connections in Detroit; Squiteri's associate, Alphonse Sisca; Oreste (Ernie Boy) Abbamonte, a veteran Mafia narcotics trafficker; and Eddie Lino, a small-time narcotics trafficker who nevertheless had important connections to many black dealers.

The operating principle of the ring was to maintain tight security, work middle-level deals of several dozen kilos at a time, and at all costs, keep the involvement of *Mafiosi* from the eyes and ears of Gambino Family boss Paul Castellano. As part of that plan, Mark Reiter was formally (and loudly) banned from the Bergin by John Gotti on the grounds that he was a narcotics dealer. As Gotti hoped, gossip about his order reached Castellano, creating the impression that Gotti was vigilant against any open involvement of the Mafia with narcotics dealers.

Meanwhile, the ring flourished, and the Fatico crew's money worries were over. Indeed, some of them were swimming in money: Carneglia bought some real estate for ninety thousand dollars, the purchase price handed over in cash contained in two shopping bags. Angelo Ruggiero, who often complained about a lack of money, suddenly was flush, bragging to friends that he now had a stash of four hundred thousand dollars in cash. Sal Ruggiero, in hiding, bought a home in Pennsylvania, several cars, a boat, and was laundering his cash in extensive investments in Florida. Mark Reiter bought two boats for seventy thousand dollars and a two-hundred-thousand-dollar home, all with cash.

Underboss Dellacroce accepted his cut of this vast, sudden wealth, straightfacedly accepting Gotti's explanation that it was the result of hijackings, robberies, and gambling. Dellacroce, no fool, knew that explanation was a lie, but said nothing—at least for the time being.

And yet, while the money poured in, Gotti was bothered by a persistent worry: despite all the elaborate precautions, the operation had a central weak spot that the authorities someday might exploit. That weakness was the mouth of Angelo Ruggiero. As he had done for many years, apparently since the time he took his first breath, Angelo talked nonstop; the man simply could not shut up. Worse, from Gotti's standpoint, was Angelo's habit of openly talking about drug deals involving "me and Johnny Boy." On several occasions, Gotti had to upbraid him sharply, in one instance warning him to stop talking openly about "packages"—a common underworld term for shipments of narcotics—being moved by Gotti's friends. The warnings did no good; Angelo continued to chatter away. In exasperation, Gotti said to his *goombah* at one point, "Someday, your mouth is gonna do us all in."

Gotti was more prophetic than he knew.

5

The Little Lamb
of the Cross

You got to think like a Sicilian.
—CHARLES (LUCKY) LUCIANO

"SO WHAT DO WE DO if we have to take a shit?" Detective Victor Ruggiero of the New York City Police Department asked pointedly, if somewhat inelegantly, as his cursory reconnaissance of the apartment revealed lack of a bathroom.

"Here, you don't shit," his boss, Detective John Gurnee, replied. With that, Gurnee put the cigar back in his mouth and lit the end, the certain sign that the discussion was now concluded. He stared, deadpan, at Ruggiero, and no one in the room could be quite certain whether he was serious.

Ruggiero and two other NYPD detectives assigned to the Manhattan District Attorney's Squad—Frank Imundi and James Mullen—looked around the small apartment with dismay. The place in which they were to spend the next several months of their lives appeared as though it had been built sometime around the Stone Age: tiny and cramped, it had a kitchen in which even the cockroaches felt crowded, a nearly infinitesimal bedroom, no air conditioning, and no bathroom. (Like many of the tenement apartments built in Manhattan before World War I, there was a bathroom out in the hall, meant to serve all the apartments on one floor.)

But the creaky, old apartment on the third floor had one specific feature of interest, an irresistible lure that had drawn the detectives to the tenement squatting on one of the narrow streets in the lower Manhattan neighborhood known as Little Italy. It was an otherwise nondescript front window whose view across Mulberry Street included a storefront on the opposite side of the street. That storefront housed the Ravenite Social Club.

And the Ravenite Social Club was what the detectives had come to see. Or, more accurately, "surveil," to use the police officialese: who came and went to that old storefront with the green trim and big windows, what was said within earshot outside the club, and generally anything of interest.

This most numbingly mundane of all mundane investigative tasks was targeted against the very nerve center of the Gambino Family operations, the place where one of the world's most lucrative criminal enterprises made its decisions, formulated its deals, and, on occasion, ruled who would live and who would die. It was the working headquarters for the underboss of the Gambino Family, Aniello Dellacroce, the man who made many of those decisions. Seated at a round table in a back room of the club, surrounded by a phalanx of hoods who unhesitatingly would kill anyone he deemed deserving of elimination, Dellacroce presided over his empire like a feudal baron. In his Ravenite office, periodically "swept" for electronic eavesdropping devices, his person protected by the palace guard, Dellacroce felt secure.

For police with a consuming interest in what was transpiring at the Ravenite, there was only one way to get it: the old-fashioned way. A good vantage point would have to be found, and then, for days, weeks, and months, police detectives would watch and listen. The primary objective was the collection of intelligence, the key ingredient in all organized crime investigations: the various associations, partnerships, patterns of movement, and other data that revealed the changing dimensions and shifts of direction in the various crews and families. But there was a secondary—and in some ways, much more important—objective: whatever criminal activity they observed or overheard was the essential foundation for a court order the district attorney's office would seek for the installation of electronic bugs inside the Ravenite itself. The raw data the detectives hoped to collect would serve as the "reasonable cause" basis for the application.

In the early spring of 1979, the police had found that vantage point. For the next several months, they spied on the Ravenite with binoculars, video camera, microphones, and still camera. Called Operation Acorn, it was to have consequences far beyond a routine police surveillance operation directed against organized crime. And, ironically, some of those consequences directly affected a man who was not a target of the operation at all: John Gotti.

The main target of Operation Acorn was Dellacroce, whose full name, translated from the Italian, meant "little lamb of the cross." If ever a man had a totally inappropriate name, Dellacroce was that man, for he was in fact a vicious, sadistic killer and pure thug. There were not many grace notes in a personality that was wholly concerned with violence and crime, and even FBI agents and police detectives—who normally try to keep a detached view of the men they are trying to put into prison—grew to hate thoroughly one of the most despicable criminals they had ever encountered.

Born in Little Italy, Dellacroce had deep roots in America's oldest Italian immigrant community. He drifted into crime as a young boy, and by the age of eighteen was a full-fledged Mafia hood, specializing in strong-arm work and killing. One of those rare men who really enjoy killing, Dellacroce was among the Mafia's most fearsome enforcers. He had a startling pair of bulging eyes that he liked to fix on a prospective victim, much like a snake attempting to hypnotize its prey; the victim would then be told how Dellacroce proposed to dispose of him. All the while, Dellacroce stared into his eyes, relishing the terror they showed as the Little Lamb of the Cross specified, in great detail, how he would shoot the man first in the knees, to cause great pain, then in the stomach (with wrenching detail on how the bullet would tear apart the intestines), and, finally, if the executioner was feeling in a good mood, a final shot in the face.

Unsurprisingly, such cold-blooded sadism attracted the attention of Albert Anastasia, for whose organization Dellacroce went to work as a killer and enforcer. In the late 1940s, when Anastasia had a piece of the action in the Mafia-operated casinos of Havana, Cuba, Dellacroce was sent there

occasionally to enforce discipline for casino employees. Del‑
lacroce demonstrated a drastic approach to the recurring prob‑
lem of dealers conspiring with customers to rig a game: the
offending dealer would be ordered to report to the casino
manager's office, told he had been caught cheating the
casino, and instructed to put his right hand on a desk. Where‑
upon, one of the men in the office would smash it with a
sledgehammer.

Among Dellacroce's fellow hoods in the Anastasia organi‑
zation was Carlo Gambino. The two men despised each other,
and when Anastasia was disposed of, a furious Dellacroce—
fanatically loyal to Anastasia—vowed revenge. Gambino
struck first, arranging for the murder of Armand Rava, one
of Dellacroce's closest associates. Gambino then used one
of his characteristic ploys, informing Dellacroce that further
bloodshed was pointless and "bad for business." A deal was
worked out, under which Dellacroce would be named
underboss (second in command) of the organization and given
some lucrative operations. Among them was a post as highly
paid "adviser" to a major New Jersey wholesale food distrib‑
utor whose entire inventory consisted of material hijacked by
the Mafia from delivery trucks of competing wholesalers.
He was also awarded lucrative gambling and loansharking
territories controlled by Gambino in Florida.

Curiously, despite the reputation for double-cross in the
Mafia world, the Gambino-Dellacroce arrangement stuck, and
the two men actually became quite close. In the process,
they produced something of a schizophrenic Mafia family:
Gambino represented the business side, with its emphasis on
business operations and labor unions, while Dellacroce was
the family's archangel of darkness. It was Dellacroce who
handled most of the disciplinary proceedings, and often func‑
tioned as Gambino's representative around the country on
various sitdowns involving murder contracts. At such times,
he frequently moved about disguised as a Catholic priest,
"Father Timothy O'Neill," complete with clerical garb and
pious expression.

In private, Dellacroce was an animal. Occasionally, he
would have dinner at the house of his closest friend, Michael
(Mike Talley) Caiazza, a Brooklyn baker who also functioned

as a *Mafioso* and chief chauffeur for Dellacroce. To the disgust of Caiazza's wife, Dellacroce would fart and belch loudly through the meal, talk with his mouth full, and generally act like a pig. During conversations, if Caiazza mentioned the name of someone Dellacroce did not like, he would scream, "I'll kill that motherfucking cocksucker! I'll cut his fucking balls off!"

Dellacroce's behavior among other *Mafiosi* was just as brutal, and almost everybody was afraid of him. In that circle, he was known as "Neil," "The Pollak," or "The Tall Guy." Whatever the nickname, he was a rigid Mafia traditionalist, who insisted on the most elaborate shows of respect from subordinates. Above all, he was a man of direct action: after ascending to the post of underboss, he decided to set up headquarters at the Ravenite Social Club. His first day there, he stalked into the place and personally ripped out the club's only pay phone and threw it into the street, berating club members for talking gambling and other sensitive subjects over a phone probably tapped by police.

That was only the first step in an elaborate security net Dellacroce drew around the Ravenite. Founded in 1926 by local Mafiosi as the Alto Knights Social Club (after an old street gang), it later became a hangout for Lucky Luciano, among others, a quiet place on a quiet street where they could sip espresso and discuss business. In 1957, when Carlo Gambino took power, he renamed the place Ravenite, in honor of his favorite poem, Poe's "The Raven." But Gambino stopped hanging out at the place when he discovered that the police were demonstrating a growing interest in activities at the club, especially the day when he spotted two detectives in a car down the street taking photographs of everyone entering or leaving.

Warned about the developing police interest, Dellacroce set up an extensive early-warning system, using something much more efficient than electronic alarms or infrared detectors: the people of Little Italy. Born and bred in the neighborhood, he understood its people and exactly how to go about recruiting them.

Dellacroce became the generous godfather of Mulberry Street, handing out two hundred or five hundred dollars to people experiencing some bad luck, and he demonstrated lavish generosity at Christmastime. He told neighborhood residents about his "open door" policy: if anyone had a problem, they were to come directly to the Ravenite, and he would get it resolved. One elderly lady took him at his word: she came to see the underboss one day, in between sobs telling him how her husband had been beaten up by a local punk who took all his money. Dellacroce was the very picture of sympathy, stroking her hands, looking at her with those bulging eyes, softly and kindly reassuring her, as a priest would. Her husband would have his money back; she had his word on that as "a man of respect." She should go home now; soon he would have the matter resolved.

When she left, Dellacroce turned to his ever-present palace guard of hoods. "Find this fucking punk and take care of him," he ordered. A short while later, the terrified thief found himself being beaten savagely by several hoods. The next day, Dellacroce personally returned the stolen money, every cent of it, to the woman—who immediately fell to her knees and kissed his hand.

As Dellacroce intended, stories of such exploits spread rapidly among the old immigrant families in the neighborhood. They were eager to repay such kindness, and the underboss knew precisely the terms: they were to let him know immediately of any strangers lurking in the neighborhood, any cars that didn't seem to belong there, any strangers asking questions—in short, even the slightest ripple they noticed on the calm surface of Mulberry Street. The result was an efficient intelligence network that missed nothing, a guarantee that the moment a police detective set foot on Mulberry Street, there would be somebody to run into the Ravenite and tell Dellacroce about it.

That kind of tight security allowed Dellacroce to do just about anything he wanted at the Ravenite. He could dispatch some hoods to beat up two black men who were talking too loudly for his taste as they strolled past the club. He could decide who must die, such as the two suspected police informants he had murdered and their bodies dumped in the parking lot of a police precinct as a warning to police that they should not bother trying to convert any of his people into informants. He could preside as supreme judge over a Mafia court held at his round table in the back room. One such session was convened when two young hoods fought over a girl in Little Italy, and one of them suddenly pulled out a gun and shot the other. Infuriated over this disturbance in the local serenity, Dellacroce summoned the father of the boy with the gun.

"Where did your son get this gun that he carries around in the street, shooting people?" Dellacroce demanded.

"I can't remember," the nervous father replied.

Dellacroce's face turned bright red, and he slammed his hand on the table. "If I come across the table and take your eyes out, will you remember?"

"Oh, now I remember," the father, terrified, managed to stammer. "It was in a drawer in my house."

Above all, his security net allowed Dellacroce to run his criminal enterprise without fear of interference. He could have various *capi* drop by the Ravenite for discussions of sundry matters, and such essential business transactions as loan payments, gambling arrangements, and the movement of packages could take place openly, sometimes right in front of the club.

In sum, Dellacroce created a real criminals' lair at the Ravenite, complete with his special rules: men were to dress well while at the club, no drunkenness would be permitted on the premises, and uniformed police who patrolled the neighborhood were to be treated with elaborate courtesy at all times. Most important, things were to be kept *quiet* around the Ravenite; too much noise would attract undue attention. Such measures had contributed to a remarkable statistic: in a forty-year criminal career up to 1972, Dellacroce had been jailed a total of twelve months. In that year, he was finally nailed on a criminal tax evasion charge. But, as was the case with most Mafia bosses, prison was merely a minor inconvenience to business as usual: from his prison cell, Dellacroce continued as underboss, among other executive actions deciding how the Fatico crew should be reorganized in the light of Charley Wagons's legal difficulties on Long Island. He was also able to arrange for the murder of a loan shark working in his Florida operation who was discovered talking to the FBI.

Dellacroce's reputation as an "untouchable" was a source of continuing irritation to the entire law enforcement establishment, especially the Manhattan District Attorney's Office. In late 1977, following Dellacroce's release from prison and renewed family business at the Ravenite, the decision was made: it was time to put the Little Lamb of the Cross and his den of thieves out of business.

So Operation Acorn was born. At first, it appeared the operation would be a total failure, as had so many others that attempted to penetrate the web of security and its jungle telegraph warning system around Dellacroce and the Ravenite. Then Aniello Dellacroce's worst enemy arrived.

A large, strapping man, Detective John Gurnee had body language that indicated a certain aggressiveness: often in a hurry, on such occasions he walked with his upper body thrust slightly forward, a cigar about the size of a small torpedo in his mouth. The effect was like watching a navy destroyer plow through the seas at top speed. He had spent much of his career in the police department's Intelligence Division, specializing in organized crime intelligence. The division was among the department's most secrecy-shrouded operations; for years, instead of working out of police headquarters, it was based in a midtown Manhattan office building under cover of some vague-sounding commercial firm. Concentrated in the division were some of the department's best electronics experts, surveillance specialists, and undercover detectives.

Even in a division full of singular characters, Gurnee stood out. A born intelligence operative, Gurnee early in his career was noted for his near-photographic memory, obsession with secrecy (even his wife had no idea of what he did on the job), and constant tinkering with the paraphernalia of espionage. A devoted student of such things as tiny drills capable of making holes in thick cement for miniature microphones, Gurnee was most noted for his specialty of cameras. He never went anywhere without one, and although other detectives snickered—some of them began calling him "the tourist"—Gurnee over the years built a rogue's gallery to end all rogue's galleries. He photographed every single *Mafioso* he encountered, in the process accumulating a wall's worth of filing cabinets filled with a photographic history of the entire New York Mafia. Moreover, he seemed to know by heart the location of every picture; asked by another detective or FBI agent if he could identify some obscure, low-ranking Mafia associate, Gurnee would dive into his treasure trove and instantly emerge with the man's picture. From memory, he would then expound on the man's personal history, arrest record, known associates, and the rest of his dossier.

An uncommonly gifted detective, Gurnee became a striking figure in the underground war between the police and the Mafia. It was a war of surveillance and countersurveillance against men who devoted their lives to remaining as deeply as possible in the shadows, who were careful not to have their pictures taken even at family weddings, who did not use the telephone for even the most innocuous conversations, who were conscious every moment that the words they spoke might someday come back to haunt them, who would leave their homes in blizzards and downpours to walk the streets and conduct sensitive conversations with fellow criminals, and who devoted years to wrapping themselves in a cocoon of intermediaries and early-warning systems designed to ensure that they would never be held responsible for their own actions.

On the other side of the trenches, it required the best efforts of Gurnee and similarly talented detectives to penetrate this screen. Much of their work was what they called "grind," the maddeningly dull hours spent in surveillances through the one-way windows of unheated vans, monitoring often-unproductive telephone taps, and taking long-lens pictures of "people of interest" outside Mafia social clubs. Even with modern technology, there was no easier alternative to these traditional investigative techniques, although Gurnee and other detectives would occasionally introduce a few new wrinkles—such as sending several uniformed patrolmen to pretend they were writing tickets for the cars of *Mafiosi* parked outside the social clubs; when the mobsters ran out

to complain, they would enter a camera's field of vision.
Gurnee was among the most innovative in such operations,
and there were stories around the Intelligence Division about
how he had once directed a surveillance team in a supposedly
impenetrable building from the one place *Mafiosi* never
thought he'd be, the bottom of an elevator shaft; and how, on
another occasion, he managed to obtain some very interesting
photographs—snapped with one of his apparently limitless
collection of telephoto lenses while he perched atop a water
tower a half mile away.

Gurnee began to acquire a reputation among the *Mafiosi*
as a man to watch out for, and Dellacroce, who regarded
him as a personal nemesis, referred to Gurnee privately as
"that Irish cocksucker." Gurnee was unfazed by such insults,
for his feeling about Dellacroce was mutual. Like other cops,
Gurnee loathed the underboss, a foul-mouthed, repulsive
killer who they felt belonged behind bars the rest of his life.

Operation Acorn was designed to help accomplish just that,
but from the moment of its inception in 1978, the operation
clearly was going nowhere. Dellacroce's security network
was alert, and managed to spot undercover detectives almost
immediately. Further enraging the cops, Dellacroce decided
to play rough: when two undercover detectives were spotted
hiding in the trunks of cars to eavesdrop on conversations in
front of the Ravenite, one of Dellacroce's hoods opened a
fire hydrant, flooding the street and forcing the detectives
from their hiding places. Italian-speaking detectives had tried
to rent apartments near the Ravenite for observation sites, but
suspicious local landlords wouldn't rent to them. Electronic
bugging experts who cased the Ravenite took one look at
the hoods who always seemed to be around the place, the
neighborhood "watchers" in surrounding apartment buildings, and the large German shepherd watchdog who lived
inside the club, and pronounced it a very tough nut, indeed—
perhaps even impossible, given all that security.

The dismal record of failure brought a call for help to
Gurnee's division, and he was assigned to Operation Acorn
to "direct and assist." Immediately, Gurnee ruled that the
approach to that point was hopeless, and after studying the
problem for some time, devised an entirely new plan.

First, there was the matter of the all-important observation site. Although most real estate in Little Italy was still in the hands of Italians, Gurnee discovered that at least one building on Mulberry Street was owned by a Chinese businessman. Even better, that five-story tenement apartment building was almost directly across the street from the Ravenite. The businessman was subsequently approached by a tall, fair man who described himself as a fellow businessman, and who, for some unknown reason, wanted to rent one particular vacant apartment that faced Mulberry Street. The first month's rent and a security deposit were paid by a money order from an upstate corporation the landlord had never heard of.

Having achieved the first important penetration of Dellacroce's security screen, Gurnee now developed the rest of his plan. First, he decreed, detectives would arrive at the observation post at 5 A.M., before the neighborhood stirred, and would not leave the apartment—not even to go to the bathroom, he insisted firmly— until 10 P.M., when they could slip away under cover of darkness. Second, the apartment would be sealed tight, with the window facing the Ravenite opened just far enough to admit the lenses of video and still cameras, and the curtains drawn to cover as much as possible. The other detectives rolled their eyes heavenward when they heard that instruction: with the warm weather coming, they could just imagine the hotbox they'd be working in, not even permitted a fan (which would have disrupted the parabolic microphone of his own design Gurnee emplaced to pick up conversations outside the Ravenite).

Gurnee prepared a photo montage of all the *Mafiosi* he thought would appear at the Ravenite at some point or other, and taped it above the window as a guide for detectives trying to identify men who came into their line of vision. And with that, the newly revitalized Operation Acorn was under way in the early spring of 1979.

Almost immediately, they struck paydirt. Completely unaware of the surveillance post only eighty feet away, *Mafiosi* lingered in front of the Ravenite in the warm spring sunshine and discussed business. There was Armond (Buddy) Dellacroce, the underboss's son and aspiring mobster, telling a local hood named Louis Palmieri about some important

swag he thought worth ten thousand dollars. "Bullshit,"
Palmieri replied. "Sometimes you deserve a smack in the
head." There was Lenny DiMaria, the veteran East New
York loan shark, boasting to another local mobster, "I put
fifty thousand dollars out [on the street] last week." There
was DiMaria in animated conversation with Aniello Dellacroce, who expressed worry about a huge loan that apparently
was going sour. "The nut [interest] is thirty thou?" Dellacroce asked. DiMaria, hastening to reassure him, said,
"Don't worry, the guy will make good; no problem."

And on and on it went, the chatter of a major criminal
organization discussing the day-to-day problems of loansharking, illegal gambling, hijacking, and a hundred other felonies.
It was more than enough for a court order to wiretap the
Ravenite itself, which, as Gurnee understood, was where the
tricky part came in.

Just after 3 A.M. on a hot night in June, Gurnee, accompanied by two expert lockpickers from the Intelligence Division—men proud of their reputation as capable of picking
any lock in the entire City of New York in only a matter of
seconds—went to work on the Ravenite. The lockpickers
picked the locks in no time flat, but as Gurnee, carrying
bugging equipment he hoped to install inside the club,
entered the place, he immediately encountered the German
shepherd watchdog. To Gurnee's dismay, the dog, called
"Duke" by the Ravenite regulars, was much larger than he
thought; Gurnee noticed that when Duke stood on his hind
legs, he could look at the detective, over six feet tall, right
in the eyes. Duke, barking loudly and thrashing around, was
making a racket. Gurnee tried to calm him down, but to no
avail. It was time to abort.

"There's only one solution," Gurnee told the other detectives back at the observation post. "I'll have to go in there
myself, and somehow take care of the dog." The detectives
nodded solemnly in agreement with this plan; having seen
the monstrous size of Duke, Gurnee was perfectly welcome
to try it solo. "Good, John," said one detective. "You do
the dog."

"Of course," noted Gurnee, who habitually analyzed anything he encountered, "the important fact is that Duke is

obviously not attack-trained. Believe me, if he were, I'd be a meatball right now." At that point he was struck by a sudden inspiration.

The next day, he made two requests. One was to his wife, a skilled cook: could she make up a batch of her best meatballs? The second was to the police department's veterinarian: could he provide some animal tranquilizer pills, sufficient to put a large guard dog to sleep? Fearful of hurting his wife's feelings, Gurnee pointedly did not tell her that he put tranquilizer pills in six of her carefully prepared meatballs, and at 3:30 A.M. the following morning, he slipped back inside the Ravenite and gave them to Duke. The dog eagerly ate the meatballs, then just stood there, tail wagging, expecting more. Gurnee waited awhile for the dog to fall asleep, but Duke, still happily wagging his tail, loudly barked, demanding that Gurnee give him more of those delicious meatballs. Gurnee had to abort again.

"You gave him six pills?" The police veterinarian was incredulous when Gurnee told him the dog was still wide awake. "My God, John, six pills will knock out a herd of elephants!"

Perhaps so; even Duke the wonder dog seemed to be feeling the effects. The morning after his tranquilized snack, Gurnee and the other detectives, observing from their perch, saw one of the local Ravenite hoods carry out his assigned morning task: taking Duke for a walk. Duke, whose walk usually consisted of a leash-straining jaunt down the street, this morning seemed a little on the sluggish side. The detectives watched as the dog halted at a fire hydrant and, lifting his right rear leg, prepared to relieve himself. As in slow motion, the leg hovered unsteadily in the "up" position, and then Duke slowly keeled over on his side and fell into a deep sleep.

"Get the fuck up, Duke!" his handler yelled, but Duke was completely out. "Fucking mutt," the hood complained, as he lifted the huge dog and somehow managed to manhandle him back inside the Ravenite.

The incident involving the dog still had not alerted the Ravenite security net, but two nights later, when Gurnee was back inside the club, having succeeded in putting Duke to

sleep with still another tranquilizer-laced batch of his wife's
best meatballs, something went wrong. Gurnee heard a noise,
and spotted a half-dozen men outside with baseball bats. He
had two choices at this point: alert his backup force via the
walkie-talkie he carried, in which case they would activate
the rescue plan, under which several detectives in patrolman
uniforms would swoop down on the club, and arrest the "burglar" inside, taking him away in handcuffs. The second
option was to escape, somehow.

Gurnee decided on the second option, concluding that the
first would prematurely alert the perennially suspicious
Ravenite crew to the presence of some kind of police operation. He headed toward the back of the club, but spotting
another man with a baseball bat, suddenly veered toward a
flight of stairs. Taking them three at a time, he reached the
second floor, where he encountered a woman and her son,
worriedly muttering something about *policia* downstairs.
Gurnee, thinking fast, on the spot became the boy's friendly
protector, offering to take him down the stairs for a look.
"Everything will be all right," he assured the woman.

Fortunately for Gurnee, things were in a state of chaos
downstairs, with a platoon of hoods running around with
baseball bats. In the confusion, Gurnee and the boy melted
into the crowd outside. Then Gurnee slipped away, later
radioing the other detectives, who were frantically searching
for him.

Gurnee had made a narrow escape, but Dellacroce, suspicions aroused, assumed that the abortive "burglary" was
actually a police break-in to plant a bug. And there was no
doubt in his mind that his personal nemesis, Detective John
Gurnee, was involved in some way. "That Irish cocksucker
is out there someplace; find him!" he commanded his troops.

Operating on the presumption that the police had an observation post in one of the buildings near the club, several
Ravenite hoods began checking every possible observation
site along Mulberry Street. Gradually, they focused on the
apartment directly across the street from the Ravenite, the
one that never seemed to be occupied. Early one evening,
Gurnee and the other detectives froze, hardly daring to
breathe as they listened to two hoods sniffing outside the

apartment. Guns were slowly drawn as the detectives heard the hoods rattle the lock of the apartment door, followed by murmured plans to set the window curtains afire. As the police detectives in low whispers decided who would shoot whom if the hoods tried to break into the apartment, the crisis passed. The hoods finally moved on, apparently convinced that since they detected no sign of life inside the apartment, it was probably vacant.

Undeterred, later that night Gurnee and the detectives, in a predawn break-in that finally went off without a hitch, got into the Ravenite. Gurnee drilled a pinhole through the floor right under the table at which Dellacroce customarily sat, and concealed a tiny bug.

The bug was not productive, for Dellacroce, now convinced that the club was bugged, virtually stopped talking business inside. So did everybody else, but that provided the observation post with a bonus, for the police targets all began to stroll the street outside the club to discuss business—often right in range of the post's cameras and microphone.

Gurnee had a field day with his cameras, and the pictures he took raised a number of interesting questions. Most intriguingly, there was the presence of John Gotti and Angelo Ruggiero from the Bergin crew, and their close consultations with Dellacroce. Neither Gotti nor Ruggiero was a crew chief, so what were they doing out of their territory and in deep discussions with the underboss, Dellacroce? Even more interesting, Gurnee snapped pictures of Gotti in extended discussions with Peter (Little Pete) Tambone, a noted heroin trafficker; considering the Gambino Family's stern prohibition against narcotics dealing by its soldiers, why would Gotti be spending so much time with a dope dealer?

Gurnee and the other detectives were puzzled by much of what they were seeing and hearing, for they lacked the essential Rosetta Stone that would have told them they were witnessing the beginning of a shift of power in the Gambino Family, one that would have profound consequences on a number of lives. What they did not know at that point was that John Gotti had begun to occupy something of a fulcrum point in the family's internal structure.

To paraphrase Orwell, all *Mafiosi* are equal, but some

Mafiosi are more equal than others. By 1979, Gotti, despite
his official rank of mere soldier, clearly was preeminent
among the Gambino Family soldiers in the eyes of Dellacroce, who had devolved upon him growing responsibilities.
In fact, already there were whispers that Gotti actually had
a shot at becoming underboss when Dellacroce passed from
the scene, either because of age (he was in his late sixties),
or because of illness: he had been diagnosed with cancer, a
disease that would kill him six years later.

Even to suggest the possibility of Gotti becoming
underboss was remarkable, given the fact that he had only
become formally inducted a relatively short two years before.
But there were three reasons for the bond between Gotti and
Dellacroce. First, Gotti was earning a lot of money for Dellacroce, as was Angelo Ruggiero, a distant relation of the
underboss. Second, Dellacroce, a pure street hood who had
never quite outgrown his roots, saw in Gotti another street
hood very much in his own image. Third, Gotti, a shrewd
Mafia politician, assiduously courted the underboss, flattering
him at every opportunity, lavishly agreeing with the old
man's constant complaints about the new Mafia as a pale
imitation of the old. (Privately, to Ruggiero, Gotti mocked
the old man's obsession with old Mafia ways and insistence
on elaborate shows of respect as "all that *Cosa Nostra* shit.")

The Dellacroce-Gotti bond was solidified further in the
summer of 1979, when Gotti solved a difficult legal problem
for the underboss. The problem went under the name of
Anthony Plate, a hood who served as a partner of Dellacroce
in his Florida loansharking business. Both men were indicted
in Miami on federal racketeering charges, among them, as
the government delicately phrased it, "extortionate extension
of credit." In less formal terms, this meant that Plate had
jumped onto the desk of one businessman debtor, spat in his
face, and threatened to take chunks out of his flesh unless he
paid up immediately.

Plate did everything but carry around a neon sign on his
back reading "mobster," and Dellacroce greatly feared the
possibility that a jury, seeing them sitting together at the
defense table, would convict them both on Plate's sinister
appearance alone. In truth, the case against Dellacroce was

not especially strong, and as Danny Wags Fatico explained to Willie Boy Johnson one night in the Bergin, "If Neil [Dellacroce] would go to trial without this guy, he could beat the case, but he's gonna be next to him, and the jury is going to find them both guilty."

Dellacroce huddled with Gotti to figure a solution, and the standard Mafia one was devised: Anthony Plate would be murdered. "We're going to call Tony in for a strategy session," Gotti joked, but it was no joke to Plate. One morning in August, he walked out of his Miami Beach hotel and was never seen again. A few days later, Gotti, Willie Boy Johnson, and Angelo Ruggiero, having dropped out of sight for some time, returned and walked into the Bergin with deep suntans.

The murder of Plate solidified Gotti's bond with a grateful Dellacroce (whose trial ended in a hung jury), and at the same time enhanced his reputation at the Bergin as one very tough leader. That reputation, in turn, was most convenient each week when Gotti dispatched men of the lower ranks out into Queens and Brooklyn to collect his loan shark payments. The fact that the emissary was from Gotti almost always was sufficient to guarantee that the main customers for such loans—the owners of small delicatessens, Greek diners, and grocery stores—would have the envelopes with cash ready.

Gotti liked to underscore his reputation with constant boasting about his toughness, occasionally announcing to everyone in the Bergin, "I like to go and crack fucking heads, and I'll put them in the dumpster!" Not all members of the Bergin crew were impressed by Gotti's strutting routine, and some of them began to call him "cump" or "nigger" behind his back. They were careful that such nicknames should never reach his ears, for Gotti was known as a hard taskmaster with a violent temper, apt to scream in rage at even his closest *goombata*. "You dirty fuck!" Gotti shouted at Tony Roach Rampino one night after Rampino sought to leave the club and go home. "You don't go home until I tell you to!"

Another of Gotti's closest *goombata*, Willie Boy Johnson, got similar treatment when Gotti discovered that Johnson had taken some money out of an illegal gambling casino: "Motherfucker! You don't take *any* fucking money. I'll fucking kill you!''

Even the slightest infractions would ignite Gotti's fuse, such as the day when he thought that a low-ranking soldier in the Bergin crew, Anthony Moscatiello, was deliberately insulting him by not returning his phone call immediately.

"Listen," Gotti snarled when he got Moscatiello on the phone, "I called your fucking house five times yesterday. Now, if your wife thinks you are a fucking dunsky, or if she's a fucking dunsky, and you're gonna disregard my fucking phone calls, I'll blow you and that fucking house up!''

Moscatiello sought to mollify Gotti, but was cut off: "This is not a game! My fucking time is valuable! And . . . if I hear anybody else calls you and you don't respond within five days, I'll fucking kill you!''

Gotti was even angrier over what seemed to be a much more trivial incident: he had gone to a restaurant one night, and noticed that Michael Coiro, lawyer for the Bergin crew (he was later convicted on racketeering charges), did not immediately rise from his table and pay his respects to Gotti. The next day, Coiro was summoned to an audience in the Bergin back room. The moment he entered the Bergin, Gotti began screaming at him: "When I found you, you were a fifty-dollar ambulance chaser! You are a piece of shit! You're supposed to *run* when you see me! You sit there . . . you don't even get up to say hello to me! I'll kill you!''

Although the Bergin crew listening to this furious tirade assumed Gotti would kill the lawyer right there, elaborate and fawning apologies by Coiro—"I'm sorry, Johnny, please forgive me"—finally cooled Gotti's temper, and Coiro was allowed to leave the club alive.

Despite his elevated rank as acting *capo*, Gotti still liked to do strong-arm work himself. When a Queens caterer and acquaintance of Gotti complained that three non-Bergin hoods had tried to muscle into his business, in the process slapping him around and threatening to put a grenade in his mouth, Gotti had the three offenders brought to him for a meeting in the Bergin.

Gotti glared at them, then launched into a tirade: "Did you go by a catering place on Rockaway Boulevard and did you slap a guy there, with his wife and kids there, and did you tell him you are going to stick a grenade in his mouth? How would you like it if I stick a grenade in your fat ass and pull the pin? I don't want you to leave here alive!''

Terrified, the three hoods begged for mercy. Again, only an elaborate and repeated apology—"Sorry, John, we didn't know, we didn't know"—finally cooled Gotti's volcano, and they, too, were permitted to live.

The monumental displays of temper were among several changes in style and atmosphere Gotti brought to Bergin as he supplanted Fatico as crew chief (albeit with temporary rank). Although some crew members privately complained about Gotti's outbursts and his imperious treatment of some of them, they also conceded that the Bergin was a somewhat looser place than during the Fatico regime, when things were considerably more structured. Unlike during the Fatico days, when the crew chief insisted on a rigid division between the middle echelon and the lower ranks, Gotti mixed easily with the crew's lowest-ranking soldiers, the street hoods striving for higher rank. He instituted a regular weekly dinner at the Bergin, a come-one-come-all affair underwritten by Gotti's throwing several hundred dollars at someone and ordering him to go to a local Italian restaurant, and return with huge meals of spaghetti, sausage, and other Italian staples. The dinner would continue until the predawn hours, while a relaxed Gotti told funny Mafia stories and everyone generally had a good time.

One of the stories often told at such occasions concerned Gene Gotti—a frequent butt of jokes—and the local school bus company he and Angelo Ruggiero secretly owned. One night, a junkie unaware of that fact broke into the bus company's office, threw everything he could find into a school bus, then crashed the bus through a fence, and took off. It was 3 A.M.

Hearing of this theft, Gene Gotti ordered several of the Bergin hoods to find "this cocksucking lice punk" and bring him back to the Bergin for proper discipline. Finding the thief was easy enough—a school bus on the street at 3 A.M. tends to stick out—and he was hauled into the Bergin to

await the arrival of Gene Gotti. By this time, he realized his
gross error, and began shaking like a leaf as he listened to
the hoods speculate on what terrible punishment Gene might
order.

"You know," said one hood, laying it on thick, "the last
time Genie caught some guy stealing, he used that electric
drill trick."

"Oh, Christ no, he didn't!" another hood replied, right on
cue.

"Yeah, you know, where he takes the drill [bit], and he
heats it up over the fire until it gets red hot, then he puts it
in the drill. You shoulda heard that poor guy when they start
to work that drill up his ass."

Further speculations that Gene might not use such a technique, and would instead opt for even more horrible methods,
reduced the thief to a total wreck. All the while, he did not
notice that the Bergin hoods could barely restrain themselves
from laughing. He began sobbing loudly as Gene Gotti
entered the Bergin.

"You know," Gene said, "I don't mind you being a
thief—I'm a thief. I don't mind you stealing, *but you can't
rob from us!*" And with that, Gene let the robber go; the
man, hardly believing his miraculous deliverance, managed
to run out of the Bergin on rubbery legs while behind him,
Gene Gotti and the Bergin crew dissolved in laughter.

The years 1979 to 1983 can be regarded as the golden
years for John Gotti and his *goombata*, for everything seemed
to be going right. Gotti was the favorite of Dellacroce, who
in turn had praised his protégé to Paul Castellano, boss of
the entire Gambino organization. Castellano was impressed,
mostly because of the large amounts of money Gotti was
sending upward in the organization chart. (Gotti omitted mentioning that the bulk of those profits came from narcotics.)
To demonstrate their appreciation, Dellacroce and Castellano
bought Gotti a Lincoln town car, with combination locks
calibrated to his birthday. In 1980, Castellano made an even
more important demonstration of his esteem, formally
appointing Gotti as *capo* to replace the ailing Carmine Fatico.
The appointment underscored the judgment of the boss and

underboss that Gotti and his Bergin crew were the best of the twenty-three crews then operating in the Gambino Family.

But there was one cloud on this golden horizon: Gotti's gambling habit, which threatened to run out of control as he got his hands on some really big money for the first time in his criminal career. His losses were staggering: an illegal casino in Little Italy, bankrolled with one hundred twenty thousand dollars put up by the Gotti brothers, Angelo Ruggiero, and a new friend of John Gotti, a Brooklyn *Mafioso* named Frank DeCicco, promised good profits. It was too good to last: John Gotti began to bet against his own house, and after a few nights, he was in hock for fifty-five thousand dollars. Furious, Ruggiero called Gene Gotti to complain.

"He lost thirty [thousand] dollars last night!" Ruggiero began. When Gene professed not to know whom he was talking about, a bitter Ruggiero elaborated: "That fucking hardon, you know, the guy that your mother shit out." When Gene heard how much money his brother had lost, he could hardly believe it.

"We were on top sixty balloons [thousands]!" he said, stunned. "I left there one-thirty [A.M.], we were on top sixty balloons! We didn't need him in the fucking game! What, is he kidding somebody, or what, this guy?" Following a tirade against his brother, Gene then asked, "What, is he abusing his position, or what?"

A very good question, because as his *goombata* watched John Gotti's gambling losses mount, they could only assume those losses would come out of the crew's profits in some way. Among those most concerned about this possibility was Ruggiero, who would check in with Gotti each Sunday during the football season to determine the extent of the damage. Some football Sundays were worse than others, including the day Ruggiero called to ask how Gotti was doing with his bets.

"I bet the Buffalo Bills six dimes [thousands]," Gotti replied, "[and] they're getting killed, ten-nothing. I bet New England [Patriots] for six dimes; I'm getting killed with New England. I bet six dimes on Chicago [Bears]; they're losing. I bet three dimes on K.C. [Kansas City Chiefs]. They're winning; maybe they'll lose, too, these motherfuckers!"

Sensing the approach of an explosion of Gotti temper, Ruggiero tried to change the subject, but Gotti was in full tilt: "The Washington Redskins. I bet them for six dimes. Maybe they'll lose, too, against the [New York] Giants. Ah, Christ on the fucking cross! Right now, I'd give my fucking life just to have Buffalo win one!"

During this disquisition, Ruggiero calculated that Gotti had bet thirty thousand dollars, with little hope of winning. At one point in the 1981 football season, Ruggiero discovered that Gotti had lost two hundred thousand dollars—and the season wasn't even half over. "The man is fucking nuts," Ruggiero complained to other members in the crew.

There were few illusions among the Bergin crew about where Gotti was getting the bulk of his money. Despite periodic efforts by Gotti to hide it, just about everybody seemed to know that he was a narcotics dealer, with brother Gene, Angelo Ruggiero, and John Carneglia as chief partners. A blind man could not have failed to see what was happening: Arnold (Zeke) Squiteri, the New Jersey–based heroin trafficker, was spending a lot of time around the Bergin, and seemed to be close to Gotti. When he thought crew members were listening, the *capo* would refer to Squiteri as "a fucking junk pusher," yet Squiteri would advise members of the crew, "If you give money to Johnny, never say it was from a dope deal; say you won it at the track."

The crew was also aware that when Squiteri went to prison for murdering a Puerto Rican dope dealer, John Gotti traveled to the Bronx for an urgent sitdown with several local hoods who had tried to shake down Squiteri's wife. Gotti threatened to kill them if they didn't stop, but one hood said, "For Christ's sake, John, you're defending a dope dealer. Jesus, if everybody in this room who deals dope were to drop dead right now, I'd be the only one left alive." He stared straight at Gotti as he said it, but Gotti simply ignored the remark.

For those paying attention to the kind of people wandering into the Bergin, there were other clues. One important one was Mark Reiter, the Lower East Side punk who was the Gottis' chief liaison with blacks. Reiter's formal banishing from the Bergin in 1972 was a sham, other crew members discovered, a loud piece of theatricality designed to lull

Castellano into believing that Gotti would not "do drugs," for Reiter was subsequently seen in close consultations with Angelo Ruggiero and John Carneglia. As the word on the street reported, Reiter—usually called "Jewboy" by the Gottis and Ruggiero—was dealing in millions of dollars' worth of heroin for his business partners. The deals were with black wholesalers, who wanted as much as they could get of the dope world's "Tiffany of junk," the high-quality Sicilian heroin that was the purest stuff in the world—and only the Mafia had access to it.

How much of this eventually reached the ears of Castellano is not known. What is clear is that beginning in 1981, Castellano began to have second thoughts about the *capo* he had so quickly promoted. Possibly, what changed his mind was Gotti's heroin dealings, but a more likely possibility is that Castellano suddenly sensed that his ambitious *capo* would not be satisfied with that job or even that of underboss of the family; John Gotti intended nothing less than becoming boss. And if Paul Castellano was in the way, it did not require much imagination to deduce what a man with Gotti's reputation for violence would do.

There were accumulating clues to Gotti's higher ambitions. For example, Castellano heard that Gotti and his crew at the Bergin had taken to calling the family boss "the Pope," a derisive reference to Castellano's standoffishness. On a more personal level, Castellano also heard Gotti was spreading scurrilous gossip about him, including the rumor that he was impotent and had plastic surgically implanted in his penis to achieve erections.

Much of this gossip was spread during another development Castellano found disturbing, Gotti's ardent courtship of other family *capi*. Although Gotti was careful not to criticize Castellano's stewardship too openly, the contrast could not have been sharper. On one hand: Gotti, the energetic young *capo* with a vision of the future. On the other: Castellano, old and tired, out of touch with his street crews, seemingly concerned only with his legitimate businesses.

An important clue to Gotti's ambitions could be divined in one of his more interesting courtships, directed at a Brooklyn hood named Frank DeCicco. Under ordinary circumstances,

Gotti would not have paid much attention to DeCicco, who had never demonstrated the potential for criminal greatness, but he had one resounding asset to his credit: he was from the Bath Beach section of Brooklyn. This unremarkable fact was of consequence, for that made DeCicco part of what was known as the ''Bath Beach Mafia'' within the larger Mafia; Castellano and other bosses from Bath Beach tended to bestow favor upon those similarly blessed to have been born in that Brooklyn water-front community. DeCicco became a protégé of Castellano's, and the undistinguished Brooklyn street hood was elevated to an executive post in the Mafia-dominated Cement Workers Union. In that job, he functioned as a bagman for the payoffs from the rigging of construction projects to Castellano.

It seemed secure, but DeCicco had enough street hood shrewdness to wonder about his future. Castellano was old, Dellacroce was dying, and thus Frank DeCicco's future would be uncertain when both men passed from the scene; without Castellano, DeCicco would have no patron. When John Gotti struck up a friendship with him and discussed the future of the Gambino Family in the context of Castellano's demise—initially, in purely general terms—DeCicco was an avid listener. There were other conversations, and slowly, carefully, a fatal bargain began to take shape.

Some of those conversations took place on the sidewalk outside the Ravenite Social Club during the summer of 1979. They were memorialized by Operation Acorn's eavesdropping devices just across the street. As with a number of odd convergences they witnessed at the Ravenite that summer, the police were puzzled by this sudden friendship between Frank DeCicco and John Gotti.

It would take some time before all these convergences—including the curious new relationship between Gotti and DeCicco—made sense; months of sifting and analysis would be required before the pieces of the jigsaw puzzle fit together. Before that, there were two pressing issues to be resolved.

One was an astonishing event that occurred on July 12. Sometime that early afternoon, Gurnee—at home on a day off—heard a police radio bulletin that Bonanno Family boss

Lilo Galante had been just shot to death at a Brooklyn restaurant. Acting on a hunch, Gurnee immediately contacted the police observation post on Mulberry Street and ordered, "Activate all cameras." A short while later, the police cameras recorded the sight of two Bonanno Family *capi*—Anthony (Sonny Red) Indelicato and Philip Giaccone—arriving at the Ravenite in a tan Lincoln. Subsequently, they were joined by Steve Canone, the Bonanno Family *consigliere*. Considering that the Ravenite was strictly Gambino territory, the presence of Bonanno *Mafiosi* clearly indicated that something was up.

As the police cameras rolled, the men on the sidewalk below were joined by a sweaty and agitated Anthony Bruno Indelicato, son of the Bonanno Family *capo*. They patted his shoulders and congratulated him. "This shit has got to stop," the younger Indelicato said, in reference to what for the moment was unclear. Subsequently, Aniello Dellacroce arrived, and adjourned inside the Ravenite for a conference with Canone.

Now, everything suddenly made sense: the murder was a Commission-approved job to restore equilibrium in the Bonanno family and dispose of the homicidal maniac Galante. The young Indelicato, one of the hit men, had fled the scene, and, as prearranged, arrived at the mob summit conference to receive his congratulations (and, as it turned out, his reward: immediate promotion to *capo*). The meeting between Dellacroce—still the chief Gambino representative in the matter of terminal Mafia discipline—and Canone was to review the future realignment of the Bonanno organization.

What the police captured on videotape is the only known recording of at least part of a Mafia murder conspiracy. Those several feet of film would prove very costly to all involved, for, added to other evidence, they would form the crux of racketeering charges in several courtrooms. Among those affected was Dellacroce, who found himself indicted on charges of racketeering, including the accusation that he had arranged for the murder of Carmine (Lilo) Galante.

Dellacroce would never stand trial on these charges. Gravely ill as cancer destroyed his body, he stopped going to the Ravenite, and spent his days in a sickbed at his home.

At his bedside several times a week were John Gotti and Angelo Ruggiero, warming their hands beside the ebbing flame. As Dellacroce was aware, Gotti's ambitions were causing grave unease in Paul Castellano; already, he had indicated to Dellacroce that he would probably not appoint Gotti as the new underboss once the Little Lamb of the Cross departed this earth. Dellacroce had pushed Gotti's name, but Castellano was increasingly nervous about "Johnny Boy."

Like an old sea lion slowly awakening to the danger posed by the young male stealing his harem, Castellano realized that he would have to begin clipping Gotti's wings. He issued an even stronger edict on narcotics, ruling that any member of the family made after 1962 was strictly prohibited from any involvement in narcotics— under pain of death. He followed that up by pressuring the ruling Commission to issue a firm Mafia-wide ban that would also carry an instant death penalty. The new edict was aimed directly at Gotti and Angelo Ruggiero—along with Dellacroce, who, Castellano began to suspect, had been secretly sanctioning (and profiting by) Gotti's narcotics operation.

Castellano hoped that these and a number of other moves would brake the sudden, ambitious ascent of Gotti. Judging by appearances, however, Gotti seemed blithely unconcerned. He also seemed unconcerned by a second consequence of Gurnee's Ravenite operation, a grand jury subpoena inviting him and ten other habitués of the Ravenite to discuss certain aspects of organized crime, as revealed by Operation Acorn.

Gotti approached his grand jury appearance with all the concern of a man brushing away a piece of lint from his clothing. Waiting outside the grand jury room to be called, he strutted around in a new thousand-dollar suit. Noticing a police detective eyeing the suit admiringly, Gotti strode closer to him so that he could more properly appreciate its fine tailoring.

"That's a very nice suit, John," the detective said politely.

"Yeah?" Gotti sneered. "Well, I got it from a hijack load. Go solve the case."

Inside the grand jury room, Gotti's temper flared when grand jurors, apparently confused by the multiple witnesses, persisted in calling him "Mr. DiMaria," but he held himself in check long enough to spend several hours fencing with them, the crux of his testimony being that, yes, he knew Angelo Ruggiero very well, but he didn't know anything about organized crime. The grand jury finally gave up, and Gotti walked out.

Returning to the Bergin, he found a certain restiveness; many crew members were aware that Castellano no longer looked with great favor on their boss. This could have nasty consequences, for Castellano, however remote and out of touch with the realities of the street, was still a very powerful boss capable of exacting a terrible penalty against overambitious people under his command.

Gotti pooh-poohed all such talk. Even if Castellano ever took direct action to stamp out what he perceived as an incipient rebellion, John Gotti and the Bergin crew would be able to surmount any challenge. The Bergin crew, he assured them, was the mightiest and best in the entire Mafia; nobody would be able to defeat them.

"Listen," Gotti said, "we're the toughest fucking guys in the fucking world!"

Perhaps, but Gotti assumed that the men under his command—most especially the circle of *goombata* who had loyally followed him to this point—would not even consider the possibility of betraying him.

In that assumption, John Gotti was terribly wrong.

6

Goombah in
High Steel

*You know what the problem is? My brother wants to
be Mr. Nice Guy.*

—GENE GOTTI

JUST BEFORE DUSK on a fall evening in 1969, they spotted him crossing the busy street in the Bay Ridge section of
Brooklyn, that unmistakable bulk dodging the rush hour traffic, his distinctive hooded eyes under narrow, sloped forehead
scanning the parked cars for the nondescript sedan he was
seeking.

Wilfred (Willie Boy) Johnson, spotting the car parked
along the street, opened the rear door and slipped into the
back seat. He immediately went on the attack.

"What the fuck is this?" he snapped at the two men in
the front seat. "I didn't agree to meet with two guys."

FBI Special Agents Martin Boland and Bernard Welsh
exchanged a glance: veteran street agents and close working
partners, they could convey much in a glance. "I think I'll
go for a walk now," Welsh said, leaving the car.

Welsh's departure did not seem to improve Johnson's
mood. "You guys come here just to break my balls," he
complained.

"No," Boland replied, calmly. "We just want to talk to
you."

Johnson snorted. "Yeah? Then how come there are two

of you? We got nothin' to talk about. You fucking guys just want to hassle me, like the others."

"We're not the others," Boland said, "and we're not here to hassle you. And if you don't want to talk to two of us, then you can just talk to me. Got it straight?" Johnson stared at Boland for a full moment, carefully appraising the rich New York accent (Boland was a native of Brooklyn), and the distinctive cocky, wiseass air that most marked a man as a product of the New York streets. Johnson, a graduate of those same mean streets, began to relax.

With the deceptively casual air of two men chatting in a barbershop while waiting to get their hair cut, the FBI agent and the criminal fenced with each other for some time as darkness began to settle over Brooklyn. At no time in the conversation was the word *informant* (or the more perjorative versions *snitch, stool pigeon,* and *rat*) mentioned, yet that was the real topic of conversation. Boland was sitting in a car in Brooklyn with one of the most notorious thugs of the Mafia crew of Carmine Fatico for the express purpose of achieving the seemingly impossible: convert this hulking Mafia hood and total Mafia loyalist into an informant.

And yet, as both Welsh and Boland were aware, for all his reputation within the Fatico crew as a "stand-up guy," Willie Boy Johnson's loyalty had been strained just about to the breaking point. Out of prison in 1969 after a three-year sentence for armed robbery, Johnson, in fact, was in something of a white-hot fury. He dutifully had gone behind bars although he had nothing to do with the crime; at Fatico's urging, he had taken the fall—with the understanding that his wife and two small children would be taken care of while he sat in prison and loyally did his time. But, as Johnson discovered, not a dime went to his wife, who was forced to go on welfare to feed their children.

The FBI, ever alert for such discontents, became aware of Johnson's disenchantment sometime during 1967, when Special Agent John O'Keefe interviewed him in prison about some unsolved bank robberies the FBI suspected might have been committed by Brooklyn hoods Johnson knew. Johnson was not particularly helpful, but as O'Keefe noted, he was clearly angered about the breach of promise by Fatico con-

cerning treatment of his family. And the mere fact that Johnson, the unquestionably loyal Mafia worker ant, had
cooperated to a degree with an FBI agent meant that he had
taken that first, tenuous step, the most significant one.

O'Keefe's observation found its way into the great clockwork of the FBI Criminal Division files, and by the time
Johnson was released from prison, Edward Pistey, one of the
FBI supervising agents working on organized crime cases,
decided it was time for a move. Welsh and Boland were
dispatched to make contact.

The choice of the two agents for this task was a good
one: both men were native New Yorkers with the distinctive
rhythms and insights of New York street life, along with
an intimate knowledge of the Mafia world, all the essential
ingredients for dealing with a man like Johnson, among the
purest examples extant of Mafia street hood. As such, Johnson was not about to deal with anyone unattuned to his world.

The first contacts by Boland and Welsh were deliberately
low-key. Boland called Johnson on the telephone several
times, mentioning how he and Welsh had heard of Johnson's
"problem" while he was in prison. Boland expressed sympathy for Willie Boy's situation, adding, "You know, Willie,
at times like this, it would be nice to have a friend." Johnson
replied noncommittally, but as the two FBI agents noted, he
didn't hang up on them. Eventually, he agreed to a face-to-
face meeting with Boland.

During that subsequent meeting in Brooklyn, with its subtle
air of exploratory surgery under the guise of casual conversation, Boland searched for the keys that made Willie Boy
Johnson tick. The most important, Boland quickly discovered, was resentment: infuriated that his unquestioning loyalty
to Fatico and the Mafia had been abused—in the process
hurting his wife, to whom he was devoted—Willie Boy was
determined to wreak vengeance against the organization he
held directly responsible for the humiliation of his wife. Why
Fatico so foolishly reneged on his promise to Johnson was a
mystery, but the important fact was that as a result, Willie
Boy was prepared to hurt Fatico as much as he could. During
that first conversation, Boland also detected bitterness har-

bored by Johnson against some other *Mafiosi*, among them Angelo Ruggiero and, surprisingly, John Gotti.

Like all such men in his position, Johnson, however angry, was not about to cooperate until he received a good-faith gesture from the other side. Usually, such a gesture involves some sort of ongoing criminal charge, and sure enough, Willie Boy mentioned to Boland his pending legal problem: a counterfeiting charge against him in the federal Eastern District of New York, which includes Brooklyn, Queens, and Long Island. Johnson resented the charge, claiming to Boland that he wasn't really as involved as the U.S. Secret Service claimed. But, Johnson added, since the federal government was traditionally (and not unreasonably) obsessed with cases involving the counterfeiting of its money, there was little likelihood of getting any kind of break. Further, the charge was being prosecuted by the Eastern District's Organized Crime Strike Force, notoriously merciless with Mafia defendants.

Boland, spotting an opening, moved in for the kill. He knew Denis Dillon, then head of the Strike Force, very well; there was at least the reasonable possibility he might be able to work something out. "I'll look into it," Boland told Johnson. "If I can help you, can we talk again?"

Johnson shrugged. "Maybe," he said, and the meeting was over.

The next day, Boland went to see Dillon, who conceded that Johnson was right: the case against him, part of a larger counterfeiting conspiracy case involving a number of defendants, was not really that strong. Dillon was prepared to deal if Boland, among the FBI agents he most respected, thought the move might pay dividends.

"Maybe," Boland replied. "I just have a feeling that this guy can help us."

"Just a feeling," Dillon repeated, turning the matter over in his mind. In other words, the FBI was now asking him to take a very serious step—in an area of criminal law regarded most sternly by the federal government—based solely on the hopeful hunch of an FBI agent. Dillon considered this matter for a while, and made his decision: even the possibility of developing an informant inside the Mafia was a rare enough event to warrant the risk. To the disquiet of the Secret Service, Dillon quashed the charges against Willie Boy Johnson.

A few days later, Johnson received a letter from Dillon formally announcing the prosecutor's decision, a communication that pointedly did not mention why. "Thank you very much," a clearly impressed Johnson told Boland. "I'm very grateful. You're a man of your word. Let's talk."

And with that, Willie Boy Johnson became BQ-5558-TE in the FBI files, "BQ" signifying that the case emanated from the Bureau's branch office in Queens, a satellite of the main Manhattan headquarters, and "TE" meaning "top echelon," the FBI's rare designation for the cream of informants, the men regarded as "pure gold." If any informant deserved that designation, it was Willie Boy Johnson, because from the first moment, his information was detailed, specific, and right on the mark. Over the next sixteen years, he was, intermittently, one of the most valuable and revealing informants inside the Mafia that the FBI ever had.

In terms of effects, Willie Boy had tremendous impact; like a rock thrown into a pond, his revelations created ripples that spread in many directions. He gravely injured the Mafia—apparently his chief motive—and before he was finally finished, he would bring a number of high-flying Mafia careers to earth. And among the Mafia careers on which Johnson would have drastic impact was that of John Gotti.

In retrospect, it is difficult to imagine a more unlikely development than Willie Boy Johnson becoming an informant, for if there was one characteristic that best summarized his criminal career, it was unswerving loyalty.

Johnson's career began when he was only nine years old; arrested for stealing money out of a store's cash register, Johnson kept on stealing, and by the time he was twenty-nine years old, in 1964, he already had spent nearly half his life behind bars. A few years before, his intimidating physical presence (six feet, five inches tall, nearly three hundred pounds), propensity toward violence, and strong sense of loyalty made him a perfect recruit for the Mafia.

However, regardless of his loyalty while in service to the organization, Willie Boy could never receive formal benediction as a made man, since he was only half Italian. Johnson had no special ambition toward formal induction; for him, the Mafia represented the family he never had. Indeed, compared to the family in which Willie Boy grew up, the atmosphere of pirate crew he encountered in the Mafia crew of Carmine Fatico seemed positively warm.

Johnson was born into a special world along the Brooklyn waterfront, where a number of American Indians lived. They were New York City's strangest immigrants, Native Americans who had emigrated from reservations throughout the state. These descendants of the tribes who sold Manhattan Island for twenty-four dollars some three hundred years before were lured to the city by high wages paid for a remarkable physiological fact: American Indians have an uncanny sense of balance, far greater than any other racial group. The attribute was ideal for one of the most critical and difficult-to-fill jobs in the New York construction boom: so-called high-steel workers, the men who set in place, then welded, the steel girder frameworks of bridges and skyscrapers. The chore of working on steel beams only a few inches wide hundreds of feet above the streets without benefit of any safety devices, a prospect that would strike terror in the hearts of most men, was for the Indian steelworkers the equivalent of taking a walk to the corner grocery store.

John Johnson, Willie Boy's father, was one of those high-steel workers. But he symbolized the flip side of the Indians' natural gift: Indians have great difficulty processing alcohol (federal law prohibits the sale of alcohol on Indian reservations). Like many of his fellow Indians, Johnson not only couldn't handle alcohol, he was hopelessly addicted to it. Most of his evenings were spent in such infamous waterfront dives as the Wigwam and Tepee, places that catered strictly to a clientele of Indian construction workers. Their behavior in such places tended to underscore the wisdom of the federal law concerning sale of alcohol to Indians. By unofficial edict, cops in Brooklyn rarely entered bars like the Wigwam or Tepee without a force of at least six of their biggest men. Even with only two drinks, some Indians would get riotously drunk, at which point they tended toward pugnaciousness, daring anyone around them to a fight—especially any man in a blue uniform who happened to be in the vicinity.

When drunk, John Johnson would stagger home, and proceed to beat his Italian wife and their five children, including the husky little boy named Wilfred. As a result, the children hated their father, and Willie Boy's mother would periodically desert the family, eventually returning to find that nothing had changed: her husband was still a drunk, likely as not having blown his entire weekly paycheck on booze, and the children were still battered and bruised, virtual wild animals who spent most of their time in the streets.

Willie Boy's childhood was a nightmare of abuse, and by the time he started school, he was already out of control. Violent and in a constant rage, at the age of twelve he fell (or was pushed) off the roof of a school building during a fight; the resulting head injuries gave him blinding headaches that plagued him the rest of his life and tended to make him even more violent. By 1949, he was the leader of a rough street gang in East New York, where his reputation for pure thuggery led to recruitment by the local Mafia as an apprentice enforcer.

Johnson's initial specialty was pizza parlors, a large percentage of which had been capitalized by Mafia loan shark money. When the owners, already squeezed by high prices for mozzarella (a product almost entirely controlled by the Mafia) were late on their loan payments, most often they could expect a visit from Willie Boy Johnson, dressed in the prevailing hood uniform of dungarees, white T-shirt, and black leather jacket. Johnson began to acquire a reputation as a good strong-arm man, but was considered somewhat dimwitted (his I.Q. had been measured at 93), and he was adjudged not really capable of higher criminal achievement.

Like many other East New York thugs, Willie Boy hung out at Helen's Candy Store, the place where he first encountered John Gotti, the teenage gang leader, in 1957. Willie Boy never explained what sparked the immediate and deep friendship that began at that moment between those two products of the streets. Willie Boy was then twenty-two, in and out of jail, working part-time as a sausage-stuffer, a street punk with no apparent future; Gotti was a seventeen-year-old high-school dropout and aspiring hood who also did not appear to have a glittering future. Yet, the two of them were instant *goombata*. Possibly, they recognized in each other that terrible rage at the world they shared, or perhaps Willie Boy somehow saw in John Gotti the promise of future criminal greatness, and decided to hitch his wagon to that star. Whatever the cause, the relationship from the beginning was dominated by Gotti; for nearly the next thirty years, the older strong-arm hood would remain the young street punk's most loyal disciple.

As such, Willie Boy never grew much as a criminal beyond his early strong-arm days. When Gotti became *capo* of the Fatico crew, Willie Boy was still assigned enforcement work, the kind of duties that led to him being called "the terminator" by other members of the crew. If there was a real dirty job to be done, it was virtually certain that Willie Boy would get the assignment. The other crew members could never quite get over the incongruity of Willie Boy smashing his big fists into a victim—the same fists that contained the tattoo "true love" spelled out across eight of his fingers. For purposes of a steady income, Willie Boy was given sanction to run a modest-sized gambling operation in Brooklyn, but had the misfortune occasionally to be stuck with *goombah* John Gotti's bets— bets that Gotti would imperiously refuse to pay if he didn't feel like it.

There were any number of inconsistencies in Willie Boy's life, among them the fact that despite his background, he was a happily married man, devoted to the Italian woman he married in his early twenties. Unlike almost all of his fellow Mafia hoods, Johnson was never seen even looking at another woman. His wife, in turn, was equally devoted to him, through the years of jail, occasional spells as a welfare case, and the uncertainties of her husband's criminal career. Devoutly religious, she was a prominent member of her Catholic parish, deeply involved in charity work, and a member of the church choir. Her husband, in another triumph over his background, was a virtual teetotaler.

Among the more curious about these aspects of Willie Boy Johnson's life was his FBI handler, Special Agent Martin Boland. But Johnson firmly rebuffed even the most innocent questions about his personal life. "What the fuck do you wanna know that for?" he would say, making it clear he was not about to discuss anything concerning his family or his background. Boland dropped any further probing into these areas, and concentrated on what his informant had to say about the Mafia. In that area of discussion, Willie Boy Johnson was nothing short of sensational.

Very early on, the FBI realized that although Johnson had plenty of knowledge of specific criminal acts, his real value was beyond the conventional informant relationship of you-tell-me-who's-committing-a-crime-and-we'll-go-and-arrest-them. Willie Boy was what both the FBI and the Mafia called a "floater," a man assigned to a specific crew, yet loaned out to other crews for various assignments because of a particular specialty—in Willie Boy's case, strong-arm work. That meant Willie Boy had a panoramic view of the entire New York Mafia, which convinced the FBI that his worth as an informant was related to intelligence on organized crime. Johnson could provide priceless access to the one great commodity always in short supply: specific and detailed insight into who was who, who said what, who did what, and who went where. True, crimes could be solved by Willie Boy's information, but the solutions might prove short-sighted: FBI agents swooping down on a recently hijacked load, or anticipating some kind of major score, inevitably would point to the existence of a major informant inside a Mafia organization. Then, it was only a matter of time before a process of elimination—literally and figuratively—would pinpoint the leak.

Given Willie Boy's value as an intelligence source, Boland handled him as would a spymaster his prize mole. Under a highly secure system evolved by Boland, he would call Johnson at home and say simply, "Call me back in five." Johnson would go to a pay phone and call a prearranged number, which Boland periodically changed. Both men would rendezvous at one of several sites in Brooklyn Boland selected as being free of known *Mafiosi*. There, Johnson would slip into Boland's car and the two men would talk.

Almost always, Willie Boy did not volunteer information, but would answer direct questions. Boland had a lot of them, some submitted by various organized crime squads in the FBI, others from such agencies as the federal Drug Enforcement Administration. None of these agencies knew about Willie Boy Johnson; all they knew was that Boland was contact agent for a highly valuable source with extensive knowledge of Mafia current events.

Invariably, as the FBI and other agencies discovered, Willie Boy's information was rock-solid, and he lit up many dark corners. There was the day, for example, when Boland asked him about Paul (Paulie) Vario, Sr., an important *capo* in the Lucchese Family, who was running extensive hijack operations at Kennedy Airport. The FBI squad targeted against Vario and his band of thieves heard that Vario's operations center was a Brooklyn bar. Boland, relaying the squad's question, asked Willie Boy, "Is that where Paulie hangs out?"

"No, Paulie hangs out at the trailer most times," Willie Boy replied.

"Trailer? What trailer?" a puzzled Boland said. "Tell me about the trailer."

Johnson proceeded to drop a bombshell into the FBI's lap: Vario, fearful of wiretaps, was conducting his criminal business from inside a trailer parked on the grounds of a large Brooklyn junkyard he owned. He considered the arrangement so secure that he openly discussed Mafia business inside the trailer with visiting *capi* from other families, and used two unlisted telephones in the trailer to dispatch orders. Johnson not only provided that piece of priceless intelligence, but went on to give Boland the numbers of the two phones, and then drew a detailed sketch of the trailer's floor plan, showing precisely where Vario sat when he presided over discussions of Mafia business.

Equipped with that detailed information, the FBI had no trouble securing a court wiretap order, the affidavit for which quoted a confidential informant known only as BQ-5558-TE as the source of its inside knowledge on what criminal activity was occurring in the nondescript junkyard trailer. An FBI-installed bug subsequently picked up an astonishing range of incriminating conversations in that trailer. Known as the "gold bug" because of its value, the FBI eavesdropping ultimately would destroy Vario's organization. (Johnson trumped that episode by revealing to the FBI that some members of Vario's crew had carried out the eight-million-dollar robbery of Lufthansa Air Cargo in 1978, the largest cash robbery in American history, setting off a furious search by the Mafia for a suspected informant when the FBI began closing in. In the process, fourteen persons connected in some way with the crime were murdered by the Mafia during this mad hunt.)

Johnson also provided several interesting revelations about his own crew. Shown a DEA surveillance photograph of some Mafia heroin dealers hanging around the East Harlem street that gave birth to the "Pleasant Avenue Connection," he was asked by Boland if he could identify one young hood whose identity the DEA had not been able to deduce.

"Sal Ruggiero," Johnson replied, unhesitatingly, and went on to explain that Sal, Angelo Ruggiero's brother, was the key man in the multimillion-dollar heroin operation with tentacles into the Bergin. Johnson added a shocker: "He's been giving Danny and Carmine [Fatico] a lot of money, you know, out of respect."

Both the FBI and the DEA instantly grasped the significance of this revelation: that *capo* Fatico, in violation of the Gambino Family's prohibition against narcotics dealing, was directly involved. And since Fatico was an extremely cautious *capo*, it was a reasonable assumption that he was cutting in his boss, Aniello Dellacroce, for a piece of the action. Given Fatico's personality, there was no way he would take the risk of becoming involved in heroin without approval from Dellacroce. That insight, ignited by Johnson's information, was the real beginning of a long chain of events that finally was to rock the Fatico organization to its foundation.

Before that could happen, Johnson caused some immediate problems for John Gotti and Sal Ruggiero's brother, Angelo. Unusually enough, he volunteered the information without any prompting: Angelo and John, he revealed, were involved in the shooting of James McBratney, the kidnapper of Emanuel Gambino. Further, Johnson revealed where both men were hiding out. Later, he revealed, also without prompting, that Angelo and John had murdered Florida mobster Anthony Plate at the behest of Aniello Dellacroce. (This revelation

John Gotti, left, and Gene Gotti in police mug shots during the early phase of their criminal careers in the late 1960s. Then virtually unknown street punks, they later would seize control of the Mafia's Gambino Family, the most powerful criminal organization in the United States.

Richard Gotti, John's untalented brother, in 1963, following his arrest on still another botched crime.

Angelo Ruggiero, John Gotti's *goombah*, in 1968 after his arrest on hijacking charges. The mug shot shows one of the few occasions when Ruggiero is not talking.

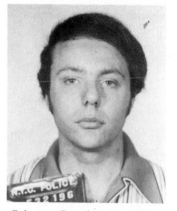

Salvatore Ruggiero, Angelo's brother, in 1971 following an arrest for hijacking. Subsequently, he would become a major heroin trafficker whose accidental death in 1982 set off a critical series of events that directly affected John Gotti's criminal career.

Wilfred (Willie Boy) Johnson, the half-Indian, half-Italian hood who maintained an incredible triple life for nearly twenty years, and initiated the downfall of his closest *goombah*, John Gotti.

The cadaverous-appearing Anthony (Tony Roach) Rampino, another of John Gotti's most trusted *goombata*, captured on a police surveillance videotape in 1979 as he stands in the doorway of a Mafia social club.

Carmine (Charley Wagons) Fatico, the Gambino Family *capo* who was John Gotti's mentor in organized crime. By the time this police mug shot was taken in 1975, Fatico, old and ailing, was in the process of being replaced by his protégé.

Donato (Danny Wags) Fatico, Carmine's brother and partner in crime, following his arrest in 1971 on hijacking charges. Danny Wags, who aided his brother in the running of the Fatico crew, was another mentor and important sponsor of the ambitious street hood named John Gotti.

Alphonse (Funzi) Tarricone, the huge and dimwitted strong-arm hood, shares a laugh with John Gotti, back to camera, in 1979 during a curbside meeting in front of the Bergin Hunt and Fish Club. Tarricone considered, and later rejected, an FBI plan to make him an informant against John Gotti, who had bankrolled his loan shark operation.

Ralph (Ralphie Wigs) Galione, the triggerman in the McBratney killing. Galione, noted for his ill-fitting hairpiece, was himself murdered shortly after the killing.

The Bergin Hunt and Fish Club in Ozone Park, Queens. Founded by Carmine Fatico, it later became the headquarters of John Gotti. The man in the doorway is one of the club's more sinister habitués, Anthony (Tony Roach) Rampino.

FBI Special Agent Patrick Colgan, who miraculously escaped death when one of Carmine Fatico's hoods fired a pistol at him at point-blank range. The attempted murder of Colgan ignited a full-court FBI press against the Fatico crew.

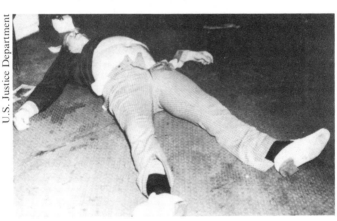

The body of James McBratney lies sprawled on the floor of a Staten Island tavern after he was murdered by John Gotti and two confederates. The 1973 killing of McBratney, who had kidnapped and murdered the son of Mafia godfather Carlo Gambino, provided a major boost to John Gotti's criminal career.

The 1973 championship softball team at the federal penitentiary in Lewisburg, Pennsylvania. Composed almost exclusively of Mafia convicts, the team was noted for its ability to win close calls by umpires. Among its more interesting members were Angelo Ruggiero (14), John Carneglia (13), and Oreste (Ernie Boy) Abbamonte (5), all of whom later went into the heroin business. Other teammates of interest were Salvatore (Sally) DeVita (12), a transvestite hood, and James Cardinali (17), who later became a federal witness against Carneglia and John Gotti.

A trio of mafia convicts poses for a snapshot in 1973 during an outdoor exercise period at Lewisburg. Angelo Ruggiero is at right; at left is Carmine (The Snake) Persico, then boss of the Colombo Family. In the middle is *Mafioso* Louis (Gigi) Inglese. The three men were prominent members of the prison's "Mafia Manor" section.

Angelo Ruggiero talks with Gene Gotti, out of range of the camera at left, in front of the Ravenite Social Club in Manhattan. Their 1979 conversation was captured by a police surveillance team, which took the picture through a partially opened curtain of an apartment window just across the street.

Paul Castellano, trailed by members of his family, leaves a Brooklyn funeral home in 1976 following services for Carlo Gambino. Castellano succeeded Gambino as head of the powerful Mafia organization that bore the departed godfather's name, but was murdered during a power grab by John Gotti nine years later.

FBI Special Agent Martin Boland, who converted Willie Boy Johnson into a valuable FBI informant. Later, to Boland's dismay, a federal prosecutor revealed Johnson's secret life in an attempt to force him to become a prosecution witness against John Gotti.

FBI Special Agents James Abbott, left, and Bernard Welsh, who played key roles in the FBI assault against John Gotti and his crew. Abbott served as control agent for Willie Boy Johnson, while Welsh was a special nemesis of Gotti.

FBI Supervisor James Kossler, the self-described *"capo di tutti frutti,"* testifies before a Senate Judiciary Committee hearing on organized crime in 1980. One of the FBI's most noted organized crime experts, Kossler is credited with formulating the scheme for a renewed federal attack on organized crime that virtually destroyed the New York Mafia.

New York City Police Department detectives Michael (The Falcon) Falciano, left, and Robert Hernandez in 1981 during their assignment to the Queens District Attorney's Squad. Among the more renowned detectives in the entire department, both men later quit the squad over what they perceived as incompetence by its commander during an operation directed against John Gotti and his crew.

The Ravenite Social Club on Mulberry Street in the Little Italy section of lower Manhattan, as it appeared in 1979, when it was the subject of an extensive surveillance operation by the Manhattan District Attorney's Office. After he became head of the Gambino Family in 1985, John Gotti transferred his headquarters there from the Bergin Hunt and Fish Club in Queens. By that time, in an effort to balk any further police and FBI surveillance, the windows had been bricked over on Gotti's orders.

New York City Police Department Detective John Gurnee, with one of the surveillance devices of his own design, a parabolic microphone, at the window of the police surveillance post overlooking the Ravenite Social Club in the summer of 1979. It was through that microphone that Gurnee and his team of surveillance experts recorded a number of incriminating conversations by unsuspecting *Mafiosi.*

Duke, the remarkable guard dog at the Ravenite Social Club, who became a devotee of Mrs. John Gurnee's finest meatballs and resisted the best efforts of modern medicine to put him to sleep.

The certain sign that Mafia business is being transacted at the Ravenite: Cadillacs and Lincolns of *Mafiosi* parked wherever their owners feel like parking.

Gambino Family underboss Aniello Dellacroce, in a foul mood, contemplates the street outside the Ravenite in the summer of 1979 after discovering that police had planted a bug inside the club.

John Gotti gestures during an animated conversation with Dellacroce in front of the Ravenite during Detective John Gurnee's surveillance operation in 1979. Discovery of the bug planted inside the club drove Gotti and other *Mafiosi* in the club out into the street to discuss business —and right into range of Gurnee's cameras and microphones.

Another photo from the 1979 surveillance operation, showing John Gotti, left, and Angelo Ruggiero, right, in conversation with an unidentified *Mafioso*.

Angelo Ruggiero and Dellacroce discuss business while strolling along the street outside the Ravenite in 1979. Police suspected these conversations mostly concerned Ruggiero's growing narcotics operation.

Police surveillance cameras
record a time-honored tradition: Gene Gotti kisses a fellow *Mafioso* in greeting while
Mark Reiter, Gotti's partner
in the heroin business, looks
on at left.

FBI Special Agent William
Noon, whose dogged pursuit
of Angelo Ruggiero and his
fellow narcotics dealers led an
FBI effort to eliminate the
Gotti crew's chief source of
income.

One of the occurrences filmed
during Operation Acorn that
most intrigued police and federal agents: Dellacroce, right,
and notorious narcotics trafficker Richard (Red Bird)
Gomes talk with Gene Gotti,
partially hidden at left. This
photo, in conjunction with
other evidence, convinced
police that Dellacroce was
aware of a large-scale narcotics
operation overseen by John
Gotti and his brother Gene.

One of the last happy moments
in the lives of two *Mafiosi*,
Armond Dellacroce, left, son
of underboss, Aniello
Dellacroce, and Angelo
Ruggiero, during some
affectionate horseplay outside
the Ravenite in the summer
of 1979. Only a few years
later, Dellacroce would be
dead of a cocaine overdose;
Ruggiero, facing charges of
heroin trafficking, would die
in 1989 of cancer.

U.S. Justice Department

Peter (Little Pete) Tambone, infamous heroin trafficker, caught in a police surveillance photo as he strolled along a street in Little Italy in 1979. Gambino Family boss Paul Castellano's plan to murder Tambone ignited a series of events that resulted in Castellano's own death.

Michael Hochman

Federal prosecutor John Gleeson, whose successful prosecution of a close friend of John Gotti on heroin trafficking charges played an important role in the eventual destruction of the entire Gotti-Ruggiero narcotics operation.

U.S. Justice Department

The Staten Island home of Aniello Dellacroce, whose tight security screen was penetrated by a team of FBI electronics experts. A cunningly concealed bug recorded highly incriminating conversations among Dellacroce, John Gotti, and Angelo Ruggiero.

Defense attorney Jeffrey Hoffman, whose surgical dismemberment of key government witnesses helped destroy the federal racketeering case against John Gotti and his codefendants.

Willie Boy Johnson's defense lawyer, Richard Rehbock, who balked government efforts to force Johnson into becoming a witness against John Gotti, then demolished the case confronting his client.

Former teenage gang leader turned bank robber Matthew Traynor. Slated to be an important prosecution witness against John Gotti, Traynor later changed his mind and became a witness on Gotti's behalf—testimony which earned him a five-year sentence for perjury.

Frank DeCicco, the mobster close to Paul Castellano, whom he betrayed to John Gotti. DeCicco, seen here in a 1967 police mug shot, sought to hitch his future to Gotti's rising star, but never got to enjoy the fruits of his treachery: he was blown up by a car bomb in 1986.

Joseph (Joe Piney) Armone, veteran heroin trafficker from the infamous "French Connection," in conversation with a fellow mobster near the Ravenite Social Club in 1979. As an important signal of his support for narcotics trafficking by the Gambino family, John Gotti named Armone to a top leadership position in 1986.

In a significant moment captured by police surveillance cameras, John Gotti, right, and Frank DeCicco confer during a stroll in Little Italy on Christmas Eve, 1985, a few weeks after the assassination of Paul Castellano. Both men were recorded discussing a realignment of the family, including a big promotion for DeCicco.

represented one of the few half truths Johnson told the FBI, for in fact there were *three* killers of Plate, not two; Johnson was the third.) The two revelations concerning John Gotti were unusual, for Willie Boy customarily was careful in discussing him. As the FBI began to realize, Johnson had a curious relationship with Gotti, at one point remarking to Boland, "Sometimes I love him, and sometimes I hate him." He did not provide much elaboration, except for occasional hints, among them complaints about Gotti's gambling habit, which often involved, he said, bets of up to one hundred thousand dollars a week. Some of that action, Johnson complained, would be laid off at his own modest wire room, but Gotti occasionally would not honor the debt, forcing Johnson to absorb the loss. On other occasions, Johnson would say bitterly of Gotti, "You know, he wears these expensive suits now, but he's still a lot of bullshit; he's still a mutt. Don't be fooled by that smooth exterior."

Underlying Johnson's bitterness was apparent resentment over his continuing lowly status in the Fatico crew, a seemingly permanent state of inferiority, despite all his loyal service. He resented how Fatico and Gotti always treated him like a peon: "They still see me as a gofer and make me handle swag."

Johnson usually would precede such remarks by saying, "If this gets out, I'm dead." That simple statement of fact was unnecessary, for the FBI was perfectly aware of the danger its star informant was in, and it took elaborate pains to keep Johnson's existence secret. The tight security—only a handful of FBI officials were aware of the specific identity of BQ-5558-TE—was part of a larger, more delicate arrangement by the Bureau to keep its great source active and productive for as long as possible.

The Johnson-FBI arrangement had several important components, the chief of which was Johnson's insistence that he absolutely, positively would never testify against any *Mafioso* before any grand jury or in court. The FBI solemnly promised Johnson that he would never be compelled to testify. At the same time, it was agreed that the FBI would exert maximum effort to keep Johnson a secret; if action on any Johnson revelation might disclose his identity, then that action would not be taken. And most interesting of all, whatever Johnson told the FBI, he would not be paid for it.

For reasons that Johnson refused to discuss, he did not want to be thought of as an informant; apparently, he believed that if he did not accept any money from the FBI for his services, then he was not really an informant. Since a conventional informant can receive up to seven thousand dollars a month, depending on quality of information provided, the FBI happily assented to this condition. Except for one hundred dollars Johnson once borrowed from Boland as an "emergency personal loan"—which was promptly paid back, Boland declining an offer of "vig" on it—Willie Boy did not receive a dime from the Bureau. (Although he did make some profit: his information solved a number of major hijackings for the FBI, and in cases where insurance companies offered large rewards for recovery of stolen goods, the Bureau provided confidential affidavits attesting that Johnson was directly responsible for recovery of hijacked goods. Johnson collected the rewards, in one case thirty thousand dollars for recovery of a large shipment.)

But the real sticky part of the Johnson-FBI relationship was how Willie Boy earned the rest of his income. Simply put, Willie Boy was a crook. That fact created a delicate situation, for by law, the FBI could not "sanction" his criminal activities. On the other hand, it would have been idiotic to tell Johnson he henceforth was to commit no crimes of any dimension. The man had been a criminal since the age of nine, and crime was clearly the way he earned his money. More to the point, if he suddenly became an upstanding citizen, he would lose the cover that enabled him to operate in the Mafia—and his value as an informant.

An elaborate compromise was worked out: in effect, the FBI would look the other way when Johnson participated in what he claimed to be his major source of income, illegal gambling—a crime, to be sure, but one the FBI was willing to overlook for the pragmatic purpose of keeping a prime informant active. But the FBI made it clear that more serious crimes would not be tolerated, particularly anything to do with narcotics. As Boland repeatedly warned Johnson, "Get this straight, Willie. If we catch you involved in something like drugs, I will lock you up myself.''

From all appearances, Johnson seemed to keep his end of the bargain, although the FBI had reasons to suspect that its star informant occasionally forgot to mention his own involvement in more serious crimes, such as his participation in the murder of Anthony Plate. And he also forgot to mention his involvement in a robbery in 1974, for which the State of New York convicted him and sentenced him to three years in prison. But to his credit, Johnson did not seek, as many other informants in the same situation routinely did, intervention by the FBI to get the charges reduced or dropped.

Johnson's release from prison in 1977 coincided with a personnel crisis in the FBI–Willie Boy arrangement. Boland, scheduled to be transferred to the FBI's Tampa, Florida, field office, was to turn over his function as control agent to someone else. Who that new man might be involved a critical choice, for informant-agent relationships tend to be very personal; the informant, after all, is entrusting his very life to the control agent. Only rarely would an informant willingly accept a new control agent, a man he did not know—or trust.

The FBI's first choice as Boland's replacement, his longtime partner, Bernard Welsh, was finally vetoed: involved in several major organized crime cases, he was too well known to the Mafia. Someone might spot Willie Boy with Welsh, put two and two together, and that would be the end of the informant.

The eventual choice was a shrewd one: James Abbott, a former New York City cop who had joined the FBI because he thought it would provide him with a more challenging law enforcement career. His first FBI assignment was in Atlanta, a city that the native New Yorker found unbelievably boring; homesick for the city for which, like most New Yorkers, he had a love-hate relationship, Abbott applied to return to New York City. A product of the streets, the stocky Abbott could give a convincing impression of a Mafia street hood, a persona that led him into FBI undercover operations against organized crime.

It made him just about ideal to become Willie Boy John-

son's new control agent, for the informant clearly did not
trust any agent who did not strike him as street wise. But
would Willie Boy accept Abbott? Boland arranged a meeting
with Abbott, Willie Boy, and himself at a Queens diner, a
meeting that Boland opened by telling Johnson that there
would be a switch in control agents because of his pending
transfer. Johnson was clearly unhappy about being handed
over to someone else.

"If you're leaving, that's it, right?" Johnson asked
Boland.

"No," Boland said, "that's *not* right, Willie. You're
going to deal with Jim; he's okay, Willie, you'll see."

In the beginning, Johnson's relationship with Abbott was
a rocky one, and Boland was flown up from his new post in
Tampa on several occasions to calm Willie Boy down and
reassure him that he could trust his life to Abbott, just as he
had with Boland. Gradually, Abbott and Johnson established
a close bond, and when Willie Boy finally warmed to his
new control agent sufficiently, he provided several stunning
pieces of intelligence.

Among them was the interesting news that John Gotti,
esteemed by Dellacroce and gradually supplanting Carmine
Fatico as *capo* of the Bergin crew, was dealing directly with
the Gambino Family underboss in business matters. At first,
Johnson revealed, these discussions took place at Dellacroce's headquarters, the Ravenite, when Gotti and chief
goombata—Johnson, Angelo Ruggiero, Gene Gotti, Tony
Roach Rampino—arrived every Tuesday for a business dinner
at the club. Later, however, as Dellacroce's medical condition steadily worsened, Gotti and Ruggiero spent more and
more time at Dellacroce's home on Staten Island. Johnson,
who had been there with Gotti, had plenty of useful details
to relate, such as the fact that when Gotti and Dellacroce had
something especially sensitive to discuss, the *capo* would
arrive late at night; Dellacroce would turn out all the lights
in the house, hoping that would convince any police or FBI
surveillance teams he had retired for the night. More significantly, Johnson could pinpoint precisely which areas of the
house were used for discussions of Mafia matters, the perfect
basis for a wiretap warrant, which allowed the FBI to plant

an electronic bug right beside Dellacroce's sickbed, his chief business office during his last years.

That was damaging enough, but Johnson was to cause a small earthquake with his next revelation, which began quietly enough. "Angelo's doin' drugs with John Carneglia—real big," Willie Boy mentioned to Abbott one night in 1981. Abbott came fully alert: for some time, the DEA and the FBI had been aware of the drug ring operating out of the Bergin, but proof was always just out of reach. What the FBI needed was some kind of attack point—and now Johnson was giving it to them.

"Tell me more," Abbott pressed and Johnson fleshed out details of what the FBI already knew or suspected: Gene Gotti, Angelo Ruggiero, John Carneglia were the main characters in a large-scale narcotics operation that involved another dozen people. Their main product was high-grade heroin, which was sold to contacts as far away as Detroit. The ring's main business office, oddly enough, was Angelo Ruggiero's house, where the voluble Quack-Quack presided over a sort of local hospitality inn for the traffickers, who would drop by to discuss various aspects of the business.

Johnson's motive for this startling revelation, Abbott perceived, was personal animosity: for reasons which were not entirely clear, he hated Ruggiero, and of all the Bergin crew members, Willie Boy seemed most intent on hurting the man he called "that fat fuck" in some way. However, Johnson pointedly did not include John Gotti in his discussion of the Bergin narcotics operation, insisting to Abbott that he didn't know much about that subject. Abbott suspected that was a lie, but Johnson nevertheless had provided the FBI with a stunning gift, including precise sketches of the interior of the Ruggiero home on Long Island, accompanied by recommendations on the best places to plant a bug.

Again, Johnson's revelations formed the essential legal foundation for another court order, this one for bugging Ruggiero's house. Johnson had noted that Ruggiero was incapable of keeping his mouth shut for more than ten seconds at a time, and therefore the FBI could anticipate extensive conversations. In fact, what the FBI got, almost immediately after it succeeded in planting the bugs early in 1982, was an ocean of highly incriminating conversations—most of it from the man who just could not shut up. And thanks to that stream of Ruggiero chatter, the FBI was provided with one of the most remarkable oral histories ever recorded on the progress of a major criminal conspiracy.

When the FBI bugs were switched on, the narcotics operation was at a midpoint. Sal Ruggiero had fled indictment in 1975, and since then, under another name, had been in secret contact with his brother. The Ruggieros, with John Carneglia and Gene Gotti, managed an operation that distributed narcotics (heroin, mostly) via selected middlemen to customers over a huge area, from Michigan to Canada. The four men tried to keep as much distance as possible between themselves and the actual distribution as a legal precaution.

Any connection between John Gotti and the ring was never discussed openly, although FBI monitors on the Ruggiero bug one day heard an intriguing conversation between Gene Gotti and Angelo Ruggiero, during which Ruggiero recounted, bitterly, how John Gotti had upbraided him severely for referring openly in front of him to a package of "stuff" in the trunk of a car. Alarmed, Gotti told him never to mention such things in front of him again. "Who are you kidding?" Ruggiero snapped back at him, and accused him of being a hypocrite.

Aside from such minor flare-ups, the Ruggiero-Gotti drug operation was running along smoothly (in one four-month period, the main participants split over two million dollars in profits), but then the one event they could not have anticipated occurred: in May 1982, Sal Ruggiero was killed in a plane crash. His death set off a mad scramble, for Angelo now faced two major problems: first, he had to make sure there was no evidence lying around that would connect him to his brother during the period when Sal was a federal fugitive—and thus expose Angelo to the stiff charge of harboring a fugitive from justice. Second, he had to undergo the considerable legal risk of taking charge of his brother's end of the narcotics operation, an action that would bring him, dangerously enough, into much closer contact with the nuts and bolts end of the business.

And that, as things turned out, is where it began to go seriously wrong. The problem was Angelo Ruggiero, the man whom the FBI began referring to as "the Perle Mesta of the mob." Ruggiero not only threw himself into the considerable task of reorganizing his dead brother's drug operation, he could not stop talking about it.

"Dial any seven numbers, and there's a fifty-fifty chance that Angelo will answer the phone," John Carneglia often complained about his chattering business partner. It was an accurate evaluation, for although the FBI hounds clearly were on the trail—aroused by the discovery that the man killed in the plane crash was in fact Sal Ruggiero, they were sniffing everywhere—Angelo went on chattering, as though nothing had changed. Hour after hour, day after day, Ruggiero sat in the eat-in kitchen of his home, discussing with a long list of visitors the vagaries of the narcotics business. Ways of erasing any possible trace of a connection between his dead brother and himself were worked out. Claims by business associates of the late Sal Ruggiero that they were owed money were disposed of (Ruggiero threatened to put two of the men in his swimming pool with a man-eating shark). Further narcotics deals were hammered out (to Eddie Lino, a Bonanno Family associate and heroin trafficker: "Do you have anyone who can handle H [heroin]?").

Ruggiero's electronic web hummed almost around the clock as he tried to become a drug czar, all the while convinced that he could keep word of this ever more sprawling operation from Paul Castellano. But Ruggiero talked too much, and it was only a matter of time before Castellano, already suspicious, would have some proof.

The moment that Ruggiero dreaded arrived when Castellano suddenly called John Gotti and Dellacroce to an urgent meeting and announced that "two friends of ours" had told him that Peter (Little Pete) Tambone was selling narcotics. Angry, Castellano said he was going to the Commission for sanction to murder Tambone as an encouragement to others in the family to obey the edict barring dealing in dope. Staring straight at Gotti, Castellano said, "Johnny, we got a problem with Little Pete. You know that anybody that gets straightened out that moves *babania* gets killed." (In other words, anyone formally inducted into the Mafia caught dealing in narcotics was to be murdered immediately, with no appeal.)

All of which meant that the Gotti-Ruggiero drug operation now had a dangerous political complication to worry about. Clearly, Castellano was still suspicious that John Gotti and Dellacroce were mixed up in drugs. News of the narcotics involvement of Tambone—known to be close to Gotti—heightened that suspicion. As part of his attempt to dampen Gotti's ambitions, Castellano had seized on the Tambone matter. The situation was delicate: if Gotti defended Tambone too actively, that would provide Castellano with evidence that Gotti himself was involved. On the other hand, both Gotti and Ruggiero were not about to let their friend Little Pete Tambone get slaughtered—or themselves, for that matter.

Following some intricate Mafia politics, it was finally decided that Tambone would be "chased" (banished forever) from the Mafia. But it had been a very close call for Gotti, and in the process, a drastic solution to the ongoing problem of Paul Castellano began to germinate. As Ruggiero summarized it, "Maybe it's time to turn the tide."

Although no one knew it at the time, this whole chain of events would result in serious consequences to all concerned, most prominently Paul Castellano, who would wind up sprawled on a Manhattan street, six bullet holes in his body. John Gotti, Angelo Ruggiero, John Carneglia, Gene Gotti, and a dozen other men would find themselves in courtrooms, fighting for their lives against an implacable electronic enemy: the FBI's chattering bugs for which Willie Boy Johnson was directly responsible.

As for Willie Boy himself, death would come to the supposedly dull-witted Mafia hood who nevertheless managed to pull off an incredible high wire act for nearly sixteen years, living in one world while at the same time trying to destroy it in another. He would finally be consumed in the very same firestorm he had created, but before that happened, he would provide the FBI with further insights into some more dark doings of the Gambino Family. And one of the darkest went under a diminutive nickname that made it sound like a collection of small, cuddly dogs: the Westies.

*   *   *

How to describe the Westies? The standard police blotter summation: a band of violent Irish-American organized criminals who operated in the "Hell's Kitchen" neighborhood of Manhattan's West Side along the Hudson River (the original setting for *West Side Story*). Descendants of the original Irish gangs that once dominated organized crime in New York City until the Jews and Italians took it over, the Westies had a hard core of about two dozen members who, during a fifteen-year period beginning in 1972, carried out over thirty murders, and were involved in narcotics, labor racketeering, kidnapping, loansharking, and extortion.

But the real flavor of the Westies can be summarized in the case of one Westie, Patrick (Paddy) Dugan. In 1981, despite warnings from Westies leader James Coonan, Dugan continued his nonsanctioned shakedowns of loan sharks, and to underscore his defiance of Coonan, murdered one of Coonan's friends. Angered, Coonan murdered Dugan, as was his custom cutting Dugan's body into small pieces with a machete. The severed fingers were added to a bag full of the fingers of other murder victims that Coonan carried around to frighten various people into being more cooperative.

On reflection, Coonan decided that Dugan was not such a bad sort after all, and took Dugan's severed head to a local tavern. There, he propped it up on a bar, and for the next several hours, Coonan, members of the Westies gang, and mourning friends of Dugan toasted his memory, at one point touchingly lighting one of Dugan's favorite brand of cigarettes and putting it into the dead head's lips.

Like some terrible ghosts from the past, these savages stalked Hell's Kitchen, murdering even Mafia hoods who had the temerity to invade their turf. And that, Willie Boy Johnson noted to the FBI one day, represented a serious political problem. Paul Castellano, especially, was increasingly agitated over the continued assaults against his men, some of whom had been thrown into the Hudson River.

As Johnson recounted, Castellano, a Mafia diplomat in the Gambino tradition, in 1977 held a big sitdown with Coonan and the Westies and reached an accommodation: the Hell's Kitchen gang and the Gambino Family would enter into a partnership. The Westies, who seemed to enjoy killing, would carry out contract murders for the Gambino organization, in return for which the gang would be given a percentage of profits from loansharking and other activities.

Castellano ordered Dellacroce, the family's lord high executioner, to set up some sort of liaison arrangement. Dellacroce immediately thought of John Gotti for the job. A subsequent meeting between Coonan and Gotti resulted in a remarkable affinity between the two men; as Coonan was to say admiringly to his men later, "I just met a greaseball tougher than we are."

Gotti's working arrangement with the crazies of Hell's Kitchen caused a sigh of relief throughout the Gambino organization, the theory being that the kidnappings and murders of Gambino associates would now end, and with Gotti as the Mafia's representative, his reputation would keep the wilder impulses of the Westies in check. He was only partly successful, because the Westies were still killing people and then carving them up, and the gang members were still spending their nights in West Side bars, playing Russian roulette for a thousand dollars per turn of a loaded pistol chamber.

But at least they weren't killing any more Mafia people. Besides, there were some immediate business benefits: the Westies and the Mafia cooperated in infiltrating the unions that represented personnel working aboard the U.S.S. *Intrepid,* the floating aircraft carrier museum anchored in the Hudson River. The carrier had survived kamikaze attacks in World War II, but was nearly sunk by a sophisticated skimming scheme that siphoned off ticket receipts and nearly drove the museum into bankruptcy. Additionally, the Westies had their hooks into some of the backstage unions at Broadway theaters (one of the reasons why Broadway ticket prices are so high).

The intelligence about the Westies-Gotti link, like many other things Johnson told the FBI, provided the Bureau with the kind of detail essential to filling out its portraits of certain mobsters, John Gotti among them. The FBI would have loved Johnson to fill in the details on another incident involving Gotti, but in this case, Johnson was notably reticent. His reticence was not particularly surprising, because the FBI

suspected he had played a criminal role in the event, which
was nothing less than the complete unhinging of John Gotti.

It began on the early evening of March 18, 1980, when
one of Gotti's Howard Beach neighbors, John Favara, driving
home in the face of a brilliant setting sun, did not see the
twelve-year-old boy on a minibike suddenly dart out from
behind a garbage dumpster parked on the street where Favara
lived. The car slammed into the bike, and the boy was
instantly killed.

Favara was distraught, an anguish that deepened when he
learned the victim was Frank Gotti, the younger of Gotti's
two sons. Favara knew his neighbors the Gottis slightly, but
quickly got the idea that they were not about to forgive him
for a tragic accident even though it clearly was not his fault:
when he tried to approach Victoria Gotti to offer his deepest
sympathies, she smashed him in the head with a baseball bat.

From that point, Favara's life became a living hell. His
car was stolen; it was found later with the word *murderer*
scrawled in the dust on the hood. He opened his mailbox one
day and found a funeral card and a picture of Frank Gotti
inside. Amid whispers in the neighborhood that he was about
to be killed, Favara asked some neighbors who also knew
the Gottis what he should do. One neighbor said, "Look,
you've got two choices. One, move. Two, get a gun and kill
John Gotti." Local police, also convinced that Favara was
about to be murdered, had similar, amended advice: to avoid
trouble, he should sell his house and move elsewhere.

Favara took steps to do just that, but it was too late. Two
months later, on the very day he was scheduled to close on
his new house, he had just finished work at a Long Island
convertible sofa firm when three men pulled up in a van.
They jumped out and headed for Favara, who had begun
packing a .22-caliber pistol. He managed to get the gun out,
but one of the three men smashed him in the head with a
two-by-four as he fired a shot; the shot went wild, and the
limp body of Favara was thrown into the van and driven off.
John Favara was never seen again.

No great feat of police science was required to deduce that
Favara had been murdered by men sent by an unforgiving
John Gotti. But detectives investigating the abduction and

probable murder were puzzled why Gotti, an exceedingly shrewd hood, would take the risk of ordering a murder in which he would be the obvious chief suspect. They did not realize the place that Frank Gotti occupied in his father's psyche.

Like many other *Mafiosi* of attainment, John Gotti had a strange schizophrenia about his chosen profession. On one hand, he was perfectly willing to admit—privately—that he was a crook and a mobster. On the other hand, it was not a life he wanted for his children. Many Mafia leaders suffered from the same syndrome. They would spend part of their considerable fortunes to send their sons to the finest private schools and provide every possible advantage to turn them from a life of crime. Yet, those very same sons grew up in households where "them"—FBI agents, police detectives, judges, prosecutors—were always discussed as the enemy. In the tight world their fathers inhabited, the sons encountered other men just like their fathers: products of the streets whose descriptions of themselves as ordinary "businessmen" were belied by the lurking bodyguards and lifestyles that clearly had nothing to do with business.

A few Mafia bosses had managed to achieve their dream of successful sons. The godfather of the Mafia family named in his honor, Gaetano (Three Fingers Brown) Lucchese, everlastingly boasted about his oldest son, who went to West Point, beginning a successful military career and life that studiously avoided any connection whatsoever with his father's business. But most Mafia bosses failed to keep their sons away from organized crime, and usually produced images of themselves, junior mobsters who spent their early criminal careers in precise imitations of their fathers.

John Gotti desperately wanted his two sons, John Jr. and Frank, to be successful men in any endeavor other than crime. He failed with John Jr., who despite years spent in military school, soon drifted into the fringes of organized crime. Known as "baby mobster" among the Bergin crew, he was a stocky, barrel-chested young man who demonstrated little mental agility, but strong ambition to become his father's successor, in image as well as deed. But Frank was an entirely different matter. From an early age, the boy showed exceptional brightness, and the teachers of the expensive private school where Gotti enrolled him raved about his academic abilities.

The proud father periodically besieged members of the Bergin crew with the boy's report card. "Look at that, four fucking A's!" a beaming Gotti would say, thrusting the card at street hoods who could barely read the words. "Did you ever hear of a kid who was so smart in school, huh?"

The hoods would also be encouraged to read the enthusiastic comments the teachers wrote on the back of the report card. "Lookit what this teacher says about him!" Gotti would command. The hoods would read and make respectful sounds; it was considered politic to note how the boy's academic achievements certainly demonstrated a strong genetic similarity to his father.

Gotti often mentioned Frank's quick mind and probable future at a prestigious Ivy League university, followed by glittering success in some unspecified field. As his *goombata* came to realize, Frank was the future that John Gotti never achieved; in the boy now reposed all the hopes and dreams that his father perhaps once held, visions suffocated by the tenements and mean streets that destroyed many such dreams.

That is why Frank's death had such a strong impact on his father. In fact, as people who knew John Gotti quickly discerned, he was completely devastated, and Bergin crew members had never seen their boss so completely out of control. At the boy's funeral, Gotti could not be torn away from the casket; hours before services began, he was constantly fussing over Frank's formally dressed body, and screaming at Bergin crew members.

"Lookit those fucking shoes!" he shrieked at one crew member assigned the job of polishing the new shoes on the body. "You were supposed to shine the shoes! I'll fucking kill you if you don't get those shoes shined right!" For at least the tenth time, the hood dutifully began repolishing the shoes.

"Jesus Christ, who the fuck was supposed to do the hair!" Gotti screamed, as another hood recombed the boy's hair for what seemed to be the hundredth time. "You fucked up the hair! I'll kill you, you stupid motherfucker!" Gotti snatched the comb from the man's hand, and, sobbing, recombed Frank's hair yet again. Then he fussed over the rest of the body, occasionally stroking the dead face, whispering words that no one could hear. The Bergin crew heaved a collective sigh of relief when the ordeal was finally over.

But it was not over for John Gotti. He did not want to take the legally dangerous step of murdering John Favara in revenge, but Victoria Gotti—equally devastated by the loss of their son Frank—was nearly beside herself in grief-stricken rage. What, she demanded to know of her husband, did he propose to do about John Favara, "that no-good sonofabitch"? How could she possibly function knowing that the killer of her son was walking around loose, *right in the same neighborhood?* Did John Gotti think she was supposed to forgive and forget?

John Favara's fate was sealed. While Victoria Gotti constructed a small shrine in her living room, complete with votive candles, Frank's portrait, and black curtains, her husband achieved some peace at home by ordering the dispatch of Favara. Of course, only his closest *goombata* could be given this most personal of all murder assignments, *goombata* who would not question, and who would understand why, in the balance of things, it had to be done; *goombata* would do it uncomplainingly and loyally.

And so, as John Gotti and his family went to Fort Lauderdale for a vacation (and an alibi), Willie Boy Johnson, Funzi Tarricone, and Tony Roach Rampino jointly removed John Favara from the face of the earth. The specifics of Favara's actual death remain a mystery: some days after his disappearance, police received an anonymous phone call from someone who seemed to have a very well-informed knowledge of the entire matter. According to the caller, Favara had been held captive until Gotti returned from Florida. Then, in a blood lust to purge himself of the pain of the death of his son and all that represented, John Gotti ignored his neighbor's pleas for mercy and dismembered him with a chain saw.

Police investigating Favara's disappearance had no proof of Gotti's personal involvement, but they were quite convinced from the first moment that at the very least, he had given the order for Favara's disposal. Investigating detectives had one promising lead: the owner of a diner across the street from where Favara had been abducted saw the actual encounter between Favara and the three men in a van. Shown a picture of Willie Boy Johnson, the diner owner could not be certain, given the distance from which he had seen the encounter, but the picture certainly bore a strong resemblance to the man who hit Favara with some kind of club.

This promising lead disappeared two days after his conversation with police when three men, including Willie Boy Johnson, entered his diner. They took seats at the counter, ordered three cups of coffee, and for the next two hours just sat there, staring fixedly at the diner owner. And while they stared, they slowly stirred their spoons in the cups of coffee. As the diner owner felt sweat running down the back of his neck, the three men quietly sat, slowly stirring, never taking a sip. Finally, they left.

The diner owner got the message. He sold the diner, and without bothering to leave a forwarding address, moved to another state. He was never seen again.

Distressed by this turn of events, detectives decided to talk to Gotti. They went to the Gotti home, where they found Victoria Gotti dressed all in black. Her husband was at the Bergin. Clearly shattered, she admitted having struck Favara in the head with a baseball bat; told that police suspected he had been murdered, she said simply, ''I'm not sorry.''

She claimed to know nothing about Favara's disappearance or probable death, and as she spoke, the fascinated detectives stared at the shrine to Frank Gotti in the living room. Judging by the overall atmosphere of gloom in the house, they began to get the impression they were in a funeral chapel.

One detective, unable to resist the opportunity, asked her, ''Mrs. Gotti, do you know what your husband does for a living?''

Victoria Gotti was ready with a timeless answer, one that detectives involved with organized crime had heard for many years in many different ways. ''I'm an old-fashioned woman,'' Victoria Gotti said, lifting her head in a gesture of proud defiance. ''I don't ask him what he does. He provides.''

The detectives then sought Gotti at the Bergin club.

Dressed entirely in black (with monograms on his shirt and socks), he sat behind his desk confidently, puffing on a large cigar as the detectives asked leading questions about his suspected role in Favara's death.

"You should be more *circumspect* in here," he said, drawing out the three syllables of the word, as if the cops might not understand it. "This place is bugged." Addressing the specific issue of Favara's death, Gotti smiled, pointed out that he was in Fort Lauderdale at the time, and added, "You know, I wouldn't be that stupid." With that comment, Gotti closed the discussion.

Sitting back in his chair, puffing on his cigar, he stared at the representatives of his greatest enemy, the New York law-enforcement establishment. They had nothing solid on him, and John Gotti knew it. Like many other cops and FBI agents he had encountered as his criminal notoriety grew, Gotti could see the frustration in their faces, that tightening around the lips as they tried to mask the fury inside them with a detached professional exterior. He relished the sight of these men who tried to ignore Gotti's patronizing smile and the smirks of the Bergin hoods as they asked the questions Gotti brushed easily away, like a man batting away some pesky flies.

In the end, the detectives, who were convinced John Gotti had arranged for the death of his neighbor, walked away in frustration. They left with the same frustration felt by his other enemies: the FBI and DEA agents who were persistently trying to prove he was a drug pusher, and the cops who were always sniffing around the Bergin looking for evidence that he was a Mafia *capo*, and detectives like John Gurnee who spied on him from a window on Mulberry Street, and the grand jury that couldn't even get his name right.

They would all walk away in frustration, Gotti was convinced; his *goombata* were solid, unquestioning, loyal. He was too clever to be brought to justice.

In that air of confidence, the thought could not have crossed his mind that his half-Indian *goombah* was betraying him, and that the betrayal ultimately would lead to his destruction.

7

The Preacher and
The Falcon

The whistle blows, and Big Joe wants us.
— MICHAEL (THE FALCON) FALCIANO

DRIVEN by a howling wind, the sleet began falling just after midnight during one cold night in the winter of 1980; by 3 A.M., with the storm in full force, it seemed as though the very heavens were concentrating their entire furies on the nondescript car parked on a Queens street. A distinct possibility, for Higher Authority could not have been pleased with some of the conversations taking place inside that car.

"It just shows you," Detective Michael Falciano complained, "how it's all bullshit! A Polish Pope! A fucking Polish Pope! Are they crazy? Everybody knows the Pope has to be Italian! How can you run the Roman Catholic Church without an Italian Pope? Well, thank God at least Jesus Christ was Italian."

"Don't be ridiculous; Jesus was a Jew," Detective Robert Hernandez said. Occasionally switching on the wipers to keep his field of vision down the street clear, he was simultaneously trying to concentrate on the words coming out of a tape recorder.

"No, he was Italian; he was a Roman," Falciano insisted.

"Mike," Hernandez began wearily, "we've been through this a thousand times. I'm telling you, Jesus Christ was a Jew. That's a fact. End of story."

"So you say," Falciano said. He glared at the tape

recorder between them on the front seat, listening for a
moment as the Catholic theological lecture and its accompanying organ music droned on. "Of course, if you believe
what *they* tell you . . ."

Hernandez did not reply, and the soothing sounds of organ
music and Catholic homilies flowed around the inside of the
unmarked police car. Falciano listened for another minute,
occasionally muttering, "What a load of bullshit," then
reached the end of his patience.

"I can't stand this shit no more, Bobby, I'm telling you!"
Falciano said, opening the door. "I'm gonna get some
coffee."

"For God's sake, don't go out, Mike," Hernandez
pleaded. "You'll freeze to death out there."

"I don't give a shit if I get pneumonia!" Falciano shouted.
"I'd rather die than listen to this goddamn, mind-bending
Vatican propaganda!" He left the car, slammed the door shut,
and headed out into the storm. A few minutes later, looking
like a drowned rat, he returned with a container of coffee
from the corner coffee shop.

Newly energized, Falciano recommenced the ongoing theological debate that seemed to preoccupy both men. There was
no resolution of this wide-ranging struggle across the entire
spectrum of everything from the basic (does God really
exist?) to the arcane (is the doctrine of prodigalism of any
worth?), and there never would be. It had been touched off
when Hernandez, a devoutly religious man, began passing
the long, empty hours of stakeout or surveillance duty by
listening to tapes of sermons and lectures on the intricacies
of Roman Catholic theology, often nodding in agreement. Falciano, a self-described "ex-Catholic, total goddamn atheist"
(Hernandez preferred the term *lapsed*), was alarmed at this
development, and sought to convince his friend and police
working partner that a strange and evil force emanating from
somewhere inside St. Peter's Basilica had seized control of
his mind. For his part, Hernandez sought to persuade Falciano that a modification of some of his theological positions—
such as his conviction that the Catholic Church wasn't worth
a damn "since the Italians lost control of it"—might lead him
back into the welcoming fold of the church of his childhood.

Nevertheless, the debates helped pass the hours during that winter of 1980 in the most humdrum of all police investigative procedures, the surveillance. From late evening until dawn, Hernandez and Falciano sat in an unmarked car just down the street from the Bergin Hunt and Fish Club in Ozone Park, Queens. They were to note on a surveillance log all those who entered and left the club, and the license plates on their cars. For weeks, the two detectives sat there, occasionally peering through binoculars, filling up pages of log sheets with what appeared to be the trivia of comings and goings at the plain storefront with the red door.

But those log sheets were the essential foundation for an assault just then under way against the Bergin and its members. The assault was being mounted by the Queens District Attorney's Squad, to which both Falciano and Hernandez were assigned. The objective, as stated to both detectives, was to destroy the Bergin crew and its new *capo*, John Gotti.

Veteran detectives who had been assigned from other squads as reinforcements for the Queens D.A. Squad, Hernandez and Falciano owned vaunting reputations as among the best detectives in the entire department. Of the two, Falciano was the more noted, and there was not a squad room in the city that did not have its share of stories about the man known as "The Falcon."

Falciano acquired that nickname during a thirty-year police career when, as a young plainclothes detective, he was assigned the job of breaking up an extensive Mafia gambling ring that used racing pigeons to transmit betting slips. The ring remained impervious to police raids, because every time the cops moved in, the *Mafiosi* simply released all the pigeons from their cages; without the pigeons—and the evidence of the bets written on tiny pieces of rice paper—there was no case. Falciano studied the problem awhile, and came up with a solution: he bought a falcon. On the next raid, he released his falcon to bring the pigeons to earth. Unfortunately, his first choice was an extremely hungry falcon, who ripped the pigeons (and the evidence) to shreds. Falciano kept experimenting, finally finding a less-savage falcon who delivered the evidence—a result of small comfort to Falciano's superiors, compelled to justify to unamused higher-ups those vouchers for purchases of falcons.

Squat and stocky, with curly, graying hair and glasses, Falciano looked and spoke like a Mafia godfather; on occasion, another detective would be compelled to verify to a disbelieving suspect that this Runyonesque character actually was a cop. Falciano took it all in stride, for his success as a detective was attributable largely to the fact that most people could not believe he was one. Among the stories told in squad rooms about The Falcon was the time when the wife of a drug trafficker stood in a court hallway, enduring the fury of her defense attorney. *"You let him into the fucking house?"* he screamed at her, unable to believe she had actually admitted a police detective with no warrant into her home. And he could not believe she had sat there in her living room—*"serving him coffee, for Christ's sake!"*—with this detective, this nice Italian man, she said, who claimed he only wanted to come inside and sit down, and who talked to her so gently about life. And before she knew it, this nice man with the gravelly voice who sounded like Marlon Brando in *The Godfather* spotted the seventeen kilos of cocaine in the open suitcase.

Other detectives were astounded by Falciano's ability to talk himself into just about anyplace. They also marveled at his volubleness, for he was a man who never seemed to stop talking—a running stream of consciousness on his personal life, current political events, developments within the police department, the superiority of Italian cuisine, the personality of his long-suffering Irish wife, the assumed sexual peccadillos of his superiors, and whatever else came into his mind. It was a constant blizzard of words, all delivered in a rich New York City inflection. A tactile man who stroked, squeezed, and caressed every human being he encountered (he disconcerted some detectives by his Old World Italian habit of kissing men he admired), Falciano was not so much a police detective as he was a force field.

Hernandez, by contrast, was quiet, studious, and extremely serious. A street cop who had won promotion to detective by virtue of his amazing record of felony arrests, Hernandez was a husky, swarthy man totally devoted to his job. He had a number of short fuses, among them any reference to himself as Puerto Rican or Mexican (he was in fact born of Cuban parents). There was also the sensitive matter of his religious devotion; he was perceived by other detectives as tenaciously brilliant, but pious, a combination that instantly suggested his nickname: "The Preacher."

The pairing of The Preacher and The Falcon as working partners in the Queens squad seemed almost perverse, given their wildly contrasting personalities. "My God, I'm being paired up with the Swiss Guard," said Falciano, the relentless agnostic. Hernandez, on the other hand, did not know quite what to make of The Falcon and his nonstop chatter, but after some adjustments, a deep respect and fondness grew between them, and they were to become a highly effective police team. Among the essential adjustments was the matter of official paperwork: early on, Falciano handed Hernandez a report he had just completed.

"What the hell is this?" Hernandez said as he read several pages.

"It's a police department report; what do you think it is?" Falciano replied.

"Falcon, this is not a police report," Hernandez said, citing long passages on the probable psychological motivations of the criminal suspect, weather as a possible factor in the crime, and random thoughts about the crime under discussion. Hernandez was right: it was a Tolstoyan novel, not a police report. After some argument, it was agreed that Hernandez thereafter would do all the report-writing, in prevailing police officialese.

That settled, the new team embarked upon the mission for which their unique talents had been enlisted: war against the Mafia in Queens. Hernandez had served several years in the police department's Safe, Loft and Truck Squad, where a small elite unit, including Hernandez, was known as the terror of Mafia hijacking crews. In the process, Hernandez became something of a walking encyclopedia on *Mafiosi* who liked to steal trucks, including a young punk named John Gotti.

Falciano's knowledge of the Mafia was much more personal. He grew up in East Harlem on the same streets that produced Lucky Luciano and a number of other boys who later became famous Mafia bosses, a circumstance that worried his father, who feared the boy would join a *borgata* and "become a bum like Luciano." As young boys, Falciano and his friends watched in horror one day when a handsome local hood, who had made the error of conducting an affair with the wife of a Mafia boss, was seized by six men in broad daylight outside a vegetable store. They beat him up, then stripped him naked and sodomized him in turn. In a final act of contempt, they shoved a banana into his anus and left him lying there. The following morning, Falciano, on his way to school, saw the humiliated hood sitting on the parapet of a six-story building. As Falciano watched, the hood leaped from his perch, his body smashing into the pavement near the boy's feet.

Little wonder, then, that Falciano's father decided on a drastic solution to get his son out of the neighborhood: at the age of seventeen, he was ordered to join the Marine Corps. During his military service, Falciano was detailed to the Office of Naval Intelligence for a strange assignment: he was to play the part of a young Marine on liberty in Naples, where he was to strike up an acquaintance with the newly exiled Lucky Luciano and report anything he saw or observed. The old neighborhood connection quickly won Luciano's confidence, and Charley Lucky began treating Falciano like a son. At one point, Luciano, who pumped Falciano endlessly for news about the people he remembered from East Harlem, asked him about a small Italian bakery. As Falciano rapturously described the delicacies the bakery still produced, the homesick Luciano suddenly burst into tears. "Oh my God, Mike," he sobbed, "what I would give for one hour back there, *one hour!*"

After his discharge, Falciano joined the police department. But among the people he sometimes called *gintaloons* (an untranslatable Sicilian slang term roughly meaning "lumbering hood"), Falciano was not regarded as a policeman. To them, he was a man of the old ways from the old neighborhood, the man who would hug and kiss them and exchange gossip in Sicilian. Even when he arrested them, they seemed to regard him as some kind of kindred soul.

Because Falciano had never operated in Queens before

being assigned to the D.A.'s squad in that borough, he was not known to John Gotti and the Bergin crew. They did know Hernandez from the days when he operated against hijackers. His reputation was "straight" (meaning a police detective who does not shade testimony to cover lack of critical evidence). "Bobby," as he was invariably called by the Bergin crew members, had locked up a number of them for hijacking, but none seemed to take it personally—including John Gotti. Indeed, one especially cold and bitter winter night in 1980, Gotti noticed Hernandez and another detective he did not recognize parked on surveillance duty near the Bergin. As the hours passed and the two cops did not move from their unmarked car, Gotti shook his head.

"This guy Hernandez ain't human," he said, ordering one hood to take a pot of hot coffee to the detectives' car.

"Johnny says to give you this," the hood said, handing the pot of coffee to Hernandez.

"What does The Falcon get?" demanded Falciano, the other detective in the car.

"Huh?" the puzzled hood replied.

"I said, damn it, what does The Falcon get? *Where is the Big Elephant?*"

The hood stared, uncomprehending, as Hernandez began to laugh hysterically, aware that this was Falciano's standard metaphysical demand in all situations in which he felt he was not receiving his proper share of respect. He was most apt to spring it on befuddled Mafia hoods who would try to figure out what Falciano meant. Actually, it didn't mean anything in particular, and was primarily a means used by Falciano to gain the initiative in encounters with assorted *Mafiosi*. (Many police detectives used the same trick, since it tended to rattle suspects.)

Falciano's metaphysics, repeated to Gotti, caused him to shake his head again: the cops in Queens were definitely getting weirder. But he was also smiling, for in a way, he relished such developments; they made things more interesting, at least. Gotti long ago had accepted the inevitability of surveillance by the police and FBI, especially around the Bergin, along with the certainty that his law enforcement adversaries would attempt to make his daily life difficult. It amounted to a form of hand-to-hand combat, and attempts to enliven the grim game with a few occasional twists were to be welcomed.

Gotti managed to find delight in such games, even when they caused him some inconvenience. For example, there was his running war with FBI Special Agent Bernard Welsh, who had become a special nemesis. Welsh, a man of impish humor who was fond of practical jokes and liked to make Gotti's life complicated, one day discovered that the *capo* habitually visited the racetracks (where he would lose huge sums to a gambling habit in which he was the eternal loser). New York State law strictly prohibits convicted felons from even walking through the gates of a racetrack, so Welsh informed security at Gotti's favorite racetrack that a convicted felon named John Gotti—usually accompanied by some of his friends, also convicted felons—was a habitué of the track. The next time Gotti arrived at the track, with Angelo Ruggiero in tow, he was met by a security detail that informed him sternly he was prohibited from entering the place. Watching from a distance, Welsh could see Gotti's face turn bright red as his temper reached critical mass. But Gotti checked himself just in time, and he stalked out, muttering, "This is Welsh's doing, I just know it."

A few days later, while Gotti and Ruggiero were driving along a highway, Welsh, following behind, pulled up alongside their car, rolled down the window, and shouted at Gotti, "Hey, John, I haven't seen you at the track lately; have you been away?"

"Nah," Gotti replied, laughing. "Listen, Bernie, I just figured out you did me one hell of a favor. You don't know how much money you saved me!"

Both Welsh and Gotti laughed, but Ruggiero was not amused. "Fucking FBI wiseasses think they're funny," he groused to Gotti as Welsh sped away. "If it was up to me, I'd put a bullet in his fucking head."

Ruggiero was even less amused when two FBI agents one day strolled into the Bergin and solemnly informed Gotti they wanted to apply for membership in the Bergin Hunt and Fish Club. Gotti instantly joined in the fun, just as solemnly replying that the two men would have to fill out applications, be "adjudged of good character," obtain valid state fishing licenses, and then pay an initiation fee—which, in their case, he estimated would come to somewhere around a half-million dollars.

"Fucking pains in the ass," Ruggiero complained as the agents departed. "Jesus, John, why do you play fuck around with these people?"

"Ah, you gotta have some fun in this business, Ange," Gotti replied.

Not too long afterward, Gotti demonstrated what he meant. It was Wednesday night at the Bergin, time for the regular dinner. The atmosphere was somewhat tense, since some of the Bergin crew members were grumbling about the FBI surveillance van parked right near the front door; two agents inside were noting everyone who came in or out. Some of the hotheads were talking about upending the van while the agents were still inside it.

"No, no," Gotti commanded. "Here's what we do: we have some fun." As the dinner hour approached, and the heaping bowls and plates of rich Italian food were carried into the Bergin, Gotti ordered the club's windows and front door opened wide. Outside, the two FBI agents began munching their standard surveillance duty fare of tuna fish sandwiches. Gotti and the Bergin crew watched as the agents' stoic expressions slowly melted while the aromas of pasta, sausages, and tomato sauce wafted into the van's open windows. For the next several hours, the agents appeared to be almost in agony as the aromas continued to pour out of the club and into the van.

Although such moments provided a light note in the never-ending war between Gotti and his law enforcement adversaries, he was aware that the war had potentially serious consequences. In the case of the Bergin, he assumed that some kind of direct attack by the Queens D.A.'s Squad was inevitable. "Don't ever say anything on these phones you don't want played back to you," he often warned crew members who used the three pay phones in the annex next to the club. But, as Gotti and everyone else at the club knew, the phones were in use almost around the clock for illegal gambling operations. Thus, it was only a matter of time before the police would focus on them. Nevertheless, the prospect did not especially worry Gotti; even if the cops could prove illegal gambling, so what? Judges were notoriously lenient in gambling cases, and those so accused usually walked out of court with the wrist slap of a fine; the courts traditionally did not take gambling, a classic so-called victimless crime, very seriously.

To the discomfort of both Hernandez and Falciano, the Queens D.A.'s assault on the Bergin concentrated on gambling. They were not impressed with the expenditure of manpower and time to prove that illegal gambling operations were run from the Bergin, and that not too far away, in a local apartment, the crew had a wire room. As both detectives were aware, illegal gambling is among the easiest crimes to prove, since it requires an extensive, highly visible operation. Even a police academy rookie could find a wire room: he merely listened at the doors of suspected apartments. When he heard someone answering "hello" with no accompanying sound of a phone ring, that was a wire room: illegal gamblers substitute lights for phone rings, so that the constant jangling of the telephones does not annoy neighbors, who might call police to complain.

In the view of the unenthusiastic Hernandez and Falciano, gambling was the least of what went on at the Bergin; with a crew involved in loansharking, murders, hijackings, and narcotics, those were the kind of things the squad should be pursuing. And instead of having a platoon of detectives carrying out surveillance and wiretaps to prove what everybody knew—that *Mafiosi* do a lot of illegal gambling—such resources were more productively targeted against individual members of the Bergin crew known to be involved with really serious crimes. As Hernandez impolitically pointed out to Lieutenant Remo Franceschini, commander of the Queens D.A. Squad, such "targeting," standard procedure in the specialized police squads, had proven valuable.

That kind of talk displeased Franceschini, a small man usually dressed in fine-tailored suits. Something of a martinet, Franceschini was a figure of considerable controversy within the police department; some detectives pronounced him an insufferable egotist, and repeated gossip about him, such as the day he was seen walking *backwards* on a windy day so that the prevailing wind would not disturb a hairpiece he wore to conceal a bald spot toward the front of his head. However, Franceschini's defenders pointed out that, like all D.A. squad commanders, he worked directly for the district attorney—in Franceschini's case, Queens District Attorney John Santucci, a notorious publicity hound. A common malady among district attorneys who have to run for reelection every four years, it mandated that Franceschini wanted as many arrests as possible, especially in Mafia cases. No matter that the charges were trivial and resulted in very little jail time; the publicity would convey to voters the impression that the district attorney was alert and active in dealing with the menace of organized crime.

And that is precisely why Franceschini had his men concentrate on gambling in what he called Operation Wedge, the supposedly grand assault on the Bergin; the D.A. at some point could round up a bunch of the Bergin mobsters, arrest them on gambling charges, then drag them before newspaper photographers to arraignment. That would get a lot of space in the newspapers and television news, which would seldom bother to report the final outcome several weeks later: average $250 fines, and little or no jail time. It was a joke: the mobsters would be back operating out of the Bergin before the ink was dry on their arraignment papers.

Hernandez and Falciano much preferred the "targeting" method: picking out one especially active member of the Bergin crew known to be deeply involved in major crimes, subjecting him to detailed surveillance, and slowly building a case that might ensnare other crew members. To demonstrate how that technique might work, they selected one of the more interesting Bergin crew members, an active hood known to be close to John Gotti.

His name was Willie Boy Johnson, and in selecting him, The Preacher and The Falcon were playing with an extra ace: they knew Willie Boy's great secret.

Hernandez had discovered the secret two years before, in 1978, when he began a tail on Johnson as he left his home. But instead of heading toward the Bergin, Willie Boy drove to a quiet residential neighborhood. There, he parked his car, walked several blocks, then entered a parked car with a man in a business suit behind the wheel.

Hernandez reached into the back of the unmarked police car for a toolbox he kept for just such purposes. Dressed casually and carrying the box of tools, Hernandez left the car and walked past the car containing Willie Boy and the man in the suit. Engaged in conversation, they hardly paid attention as the repairman strolled by and entered a nearby apartment building. Hernandez hung around the apartment building lobby for a while, then left, walking back past the car with Willie Boy inside. Hernandez noticed the man behind the wheel writing something down on a legal pad.

Hernandez later checked out the plate number of the car in which he had seen Johnson, and instantly got confirmation of his initial suspicion: the car was registered to some vague-sounding upstate security firm—a favorite ploy adopted by the FBI in registering its unmarked cars used in undercover organized crime investigations. Obviously, Johnson was an FBI informant.

Hernandez kept this interesting piece of intelligence to himself, hoping it might come in handy someday. That opportunity did not arise until two years later when, assigned to the Queens squad, Hernandez again targeted Johnson. One night, Hernandez, trailing Johnson, spotted him furtively slipping a satchel into the trunk of his car. "Mind if we look?" Hernandez said as he pounced. Willie Boy shrugged. "Go ahead."

Inside the satchel, Hernandez found fifty thousand dollars in small bills. Johnson then committed a mistake. "You take what you want," he told Hernandez, who immediately answered, "You're under arrest for attempted bribery, Willie."

Back in the Queens squad room, Hernandez began to play out an intricate game whose moves he already had preplanned. First, he recommended to Franceschini, Johnson should be handled in the grand jury by a sealed indictment (voted, but not formally handed up) as a form of control: he would be induced to cooperate, with the threat of unsealing the indictment at any point he became uncooperative. Second, Johnson would be told that Hernandez was aware he was an

FBI informant, and that henceforth, he was also to provide information to the Queens D.A. Squad.

Franceschini made a face, and following a conference with District Attorney Santucci, told Hernandez that Johnson would be jailed on a bribery charge. The district attorney apparently believed this would produce good publicity, indicating incorruptible officers in the squad.

Hernandez shook his head. "You don't agree with that?" Franceschini asked.

"No," Hernandez snapped. "I think you're blowing the biggest chance this office ever had."

Franceschini exploded. "Look, you're nothing but a fucking detective, and you do what the fuck I tell you!"

By this point, it was 2:30 A.M., and tempers were very short. Hernandez threw a chair at Franceschini, yelling at him, "Don't you ever talk to me like that again!" Falciano grabbed Hernandez and dragged him away, just as he was about to take a punch at his superior.

Later, Franceschini relented, and it was decided that they would handle the Johnson matter Hernandez's way. Still, Franceschini insisted, the police would confiscate Willie Boy's fifty thousand dollars on the grounds that it was drug money.

Falciano snorted. "Remo, no way that's drug money. In the first place, it's all in small bills, a lot of them one-dollar bills. Drug dealers don't sell drugs for a dollar. Second, look at some of these bills: they've got numbers written on them. Obviously, it's gambling money, probably numbers."

But Franceschini refused to budge, and an already rocky relationship with the two detectives imported into Queens deteriorated further. By this point, Falciano had begun referring to Franceschini privately as "The Prince of Darkness." Back on the streets, working with Hernandez, he bemoaned their fate. "Oh, why did we ever come to this hell on earth?" Falciano wailed. "Bobby, we are in the hands of a maniac, the Captain Queeg of the New York City Police Department. The man is crazy, and he will make us crazy, too."

"Well, he's not going to make *me* crazy," Hernandez said. "Look, right now, we have potentially the greatest informant on the Bergin crew that this office has ever seen.

We've got a pipeline right into the place. Let's develop Willie Boy as an intelligence source; this is the guy who can tell us what's going on inside that place.''

But to the fury of both Hernandez and Falciano, Franceschini had different ideas. He wanted Johnson to provide information on specific crimes about to be committed—a load of bootlegged cigarettes to arrive at a particular place, a truck targeted to be hijacked—so that his squad could swoop in and make arrests, as many as possible, all with maximum publicity. Further, Franceschini said, Johnson would be told to encourage Bergin crew members to commit crimes only in Queens.

This plan led to another Hernandez-Franceschini confrontation, with Falciano unsuccessfully playing a role as a mediator. Franceschini ignored the urgent pleas of the two detectives: he was not interested in organized crime intelligence from Willie Boy Johnson; he wanted lots of cases to build up the squad's statistics. Johnson himself was unhappy with the plan, arguing that providing such information inevitably would point to him as a snitch. In meetings at Franceschini's office, Johnson begged not to be put in that position. ''You're gonna get me killed,'' Johnson said, as he sat at a table across from Franceschini, who treated him with contempt. Falciano noted that Franceschini had concealed a tape recorder under the table to record Willie Boy's comments surreptitiously—but Willie Boy, aware of the hidden machine, sometimes would arrive with an electromagnet concealed in one hand to erase the tapes.

In meetings with Willie Boy throughout Queens, Falciano and Hernandez worked out their own special arrangement: he would occasionally give Franceschini assorted minor crimes, while he would demonstrate his real value by providing intelligence to the two detectives. They agreed he would never be compelled to testify, but if they caught him selling dope, as Falciano put it, ''You don't even want to think what we will do to you.'' Representing still another intricacy in Willie Boy's complicated life, the arrangement began to come unglued almost at once.

Johnson had thrown Franceschini a small bone: John Gotti, Gene Gotti, and Angelo Ruggiero were running an illegal casino in Little Italy. In the course of passing on this tidbit, Johnson made the mistake of mentioning that Paul Castellano was known as "The Pope" around the Bergin. Franceschini led a highly publicized raid on the place, and at one point, jumped atop a craps table and shouted, "How's The Pope gonna like this?" It was an appalling blunder, and John Gotti within minutes got a phone call from a friend in Little Italy: "Johnny Boy, you got a rat, a fuckin' rat!"

Johnson was almost beside himself with rage the next time he met Hernandez and Falciano. "Does your boss have shit for brains?" he demanded. "Jesus Christ, he might as well point a gun to my head; don't you think Johnny started looking around the Bergin, trying to figure out which of us told that moron Franceschini about Castellano?"

Hernandez and Falciano got Johnson calmed down, a feat they managed only because Willie Boy had grown very fond of them—especially Falciano. To Hernandez's amazement, Johnson treated Falciano like a brother, confiding in him the most intimate details of his personal life, opening up to him as he never had for any other man. The relationship deepened despite several Falciano habits that annoyed Johnson, especially the detective's practice of rummaging through the informant's pockets and the glove compartment of his car for the packs of mints Willie Boy invariably stocked. Then Falciano would eat all the mints.

"You know, Falcon," Johnson said at one point, "if you like my mints so much, why don't you buy your own?"

"Because," Falciano replied, "you should offer me your mints as a sign of your respect."

"Oh, right, sure," Johnson replied, struck by Falciano's sudden descent into Mafia logic.

For their part, Falciano and Hernandez were disturbed by Johnson's occasional lack of concern for his own security. Hernandez endlessly lectured Willie Boy on such elemental precautions as checking the rearview mirror of his car for any possible tails (perhaps by fellow *Mafiosi* trailing him to discover the identity of the informant Gotti was convinced existed somewhere in the Bergin). Falciano had the unsettling experience one day, as he was making a phone call from an outdoor booth not too far from the Bergin, of seeing Johnson approach him and call out loudly in the traditional Brooklyn greeting, "Hey, Falcon, howya doin'?"

"For Christ's sake, Willie," Falciano hissed at him, "get the hell away from me. What if somebody sees us together?"

"Hey, what'd I do wrong?" Johnson asked, befuddled that Falciano was upset. Falciano then patiently tried to explain to him why it was not an especially bright idea for a police informant to be seen talking with a police detective in broad daylight. (A similarly patient explanation was required to make Johnson understand why neither Falciano nor Hernandez could accept his invitation to go fishing with him; the risk was too great that the three men might be spotted together.)

As the Falciano-Johnson relationship grew warmer, Falciano's boss, Remo Franceschini, become more displeased. He began to wonder aloud why the detective seemed to enjoy the company of the man Franceschini called "the dirtbag." Falciano bristled: "Listen, Remo, I'd rather have Willie Boy over my house than you."

Meanwhile, Johnson developed a deep animus for Franceschini. "You know what I wonder about?" Johnson asked Falciano one night. "How come [District Attorney John] Santucci doesn't get rid of Remo?"

"Yes, well, Hitler was told to get rid of Himmler many times," Falciano replied. "And he never did."

Johnson's trust in Hernandez and Falciano was total, and it would be tested in full measure when still another serious incident involving Franceschini arose.

Hernandez's home telephone rang late one night; a clearly agitated Willie Boy Johnson was almost consumed by rage. "Is this man crazy?" he said, without any preliminaries.

"Who?" Hernandez asked, although he knew the answer.

"Your idiot of a boss, that's who. You won't believe this: he calls me at home and he says to me, 'I'm gonna be on Channel 7 news; they're interviewing me. I want you to go to the club [Bergin], turn on the TV to Channel 7 at five or six o'clock. Afterwards, ask the guys what they think of me.' "

Hernandez sighed. "Forget it," he said. "Let's meet, and we'll talk."

The resulting meeting was especially tense, for Willie Boy

clearly was no longer interested in being an informant for the Queens D.A. Squad. Let Queens do its worst; jail was preferable to the growing certainty that he was going to get killed. Hernandez and Falciano used every ounce of their considerable persuasive powers to convince Willie Boy to stay on; somehow, they vowed, they would get the Franceschini problem resolved.

Johnson slowly calmed down, and Hernandez decided it was time to play for the big hand; inevitably, Willie Boy would sever his relationship with Queens, so now was the moment to tap into his vast reservoir of knowledge. Up to this point, he had passed on some interesting intelligence about the Bergin crew, but, distressed over his treatment by the Queens D.A., he obviously was holding back.

"Look, Willie," Hernandez said, "we've treated you pretty good." (He meant himself and Falciano.)

"Yeah, right."

"We could've put the word on the street that you were an FBI informant," Hernandez said, pressing on. "We don't treat you like a dirtbag; you chose your life, we chose ours."

"Right, and I appreciate that."

"Okay, so now I really want something—something big. Tell me about John Gotti and narcotics."

Johnson's face tightened. "Jesus, Bobby, don't ask me to talk about Johnny; I can't, I can't."

"All right," Hernandez said, noting the fear in Willie Boy's face. "Tell me about Angelo Ruggiero, then."

Johnson was silent for some time. "Angelo thinks he's a big fuck," he said, finally. He was silent again for a while, then said, "John Carneglia and Angelo are doing big drugs." He went on to explain something Hernandez and Falciano already suspected: Carneglia and Angelo Ruggiero, in concert with Gene Gotti, were running a multimillion-dollar narcotics operation with Sal Ruggiero, the fugitive living under another name. Carneglia was renting an apartment under an assumed name, using it to work out major drug deals, mostly on Sundays. Johnson carefully avoided discussing an obvious implication: neither Carneglia nor Angelo Ruggiero, a close *goombah* of John Gotti, would dare to take such a significant step as narcotics dealing without getting the approval of their *capo*.

But what Johnson had revealed was astonishing enough. Hernandez and Falciano immediately ran to Franceschini, recommending that the squad get a wiretap working on the Carneglia apartment; a priceless opportunity now existed, they argued, to get inside what was clearly a major narcotics operation, almost certainly extending as far as John Gotti himself. But Franceschini said no, and accused Hernandez of making the proposal only to get overtime by working on Sundays.

And with that, Willie Boy Johnson snapped. Infuriated over his treatment at the hands of the Queens D.A. Squad, and even angrier about Franceschini, he summoned Falciano to a late-night rendezvous.

"I'm gonna kill him," Johnson announced.

"Who?" Falciano asked, although he had a faint idea.

"That asshole Franceschini, that's who. I'm gonna fucking blow him away, that cocksucker."

Alarmed, Falciano sought to head him off. "Now look, Willie, you're not gonna shoot *anybody*, least of all a lieutenant in the New York City Police Department. What, are you crazy? I'm telling you right now, you can't shoot cops; you want to shoot a cop, believe me, you're gonna have to do it over my dead body."

Summoning all his rhetorical gifts, Falciano worked hard to cool Johnson's white-hot fury. But nothing he tried seemed to work. Finally, Falciano realized he was talking to Johnson on the wrong level; a man like Willie Boy was undeterred by conventional arguments, even when Falciano made it clear that he was prepared to shoot Johnson on the spot if he so much as lifted a finger against a cop. Falciano then decided on a wholly different tack, one more attuned to Johnson's own world.

"Listen to me carefully," Falciano said, and went on quietly to note that a prominent *Mafioso* whom Johnson respected (and greatly feared) was in fact Falciano's cousin. "If you shoot Franceschini, he won't like it. You catch my drift, Willie?"

Johnson looked stunned. "Gee, Falcon, you should've told me that he's your cousin," he said. "That changes things."

To Falciano's relief, Johnson then visibly relaxed. Within minutes, his temper finally cooled, Johnson seemed to have forgotten all about his intent to murder the detective lieutenant who was causing him so much grief.

But from that moment, Johnson refused to have anything further to do with the Queens D.A. Squad. No amount of coaxing from Hernandez and Falciano would change his mind. In truth, there was not much conviction behind the effort of the two detectives; they had reached the end of the line, and saw no further point to working in the squad—where, they were convinced, by incompetency or design, there was no real interest in bringing to justice John Gotti and his crew (or the Mafia in general, for that matter).

Falciano had the sense that things were becoming seriously unhinged in Queens. Having talked Willie Boy Johnson out of murdering the Queens D.A. Squad commander, Falciano was suddenly confronted with another crisis: one of the squad detectives, who as a boy had seen his father gunned down by Mafia hoods, was steadily losing his grip. One night, he went over the edge.

Falciano encountered him wandering in a near-incoherent state, loudly proclaiming his intention to murder Tony Roach Rampino, one of John Gotti's closest *goombata*. "I'm gonna do it, Falcon," he vowed, waving his gun. "I'm gonna shoot that cocksucker hood. I don't give a shit what happens, but he's dead!"

This time, Falciano did not try persuasion. "I'll shoot you right now if you don't put that gun away," he threatened. The shock treatment worked: startled by the sudden hard edge to the man he had known as the jovial raconteur, the detective slowly returned to normal. "You wouldn't really shoot me, would you, Falcon?" he asked, smiling.

"Damn right I would," Falciano replied, evenly.

To Falciano, the incident was the last straw; it was time to leave the Queens D.A. Squad. Hernandez reached the same conclusion. In a red-hot anger, he confronted Franceschini, demanding to know why the squad bothered with only relatively trivial pursuits involving the *Mafiosi* of the Bergin; why the investigation of gambling, when narcotics, hijackings, and every other felony flourished in Queens? Why the obsession with small-time bookies when, as everybody in Queens knew, the local judiciary and political systems were totally corrupt? Why wasn't the squad doing anything about it?

Hernandez did not get a satisfactory answer, and quit the police department. Falciano tried to talk him out of it, but when that failed, The Falcon decided he, too, no longer wanted any further part of the Queens D.A. Squad. Thirty years in the department had provided him with a network of high-level friends; Falciano called one of them the day Hernandez quit and said, "Get me out of this cesspool; not tomorrow, not next week, not next month, *today!*" Within hours, Falciano was transferred to an elite task force of detectives.

Coincidental with the departure of Falciano and Hernandez and the end of Willie Boy Johnson as a Queens informant, there were unmistakable signs that the FBI—now the exclusive recipient of Willie Boy's information—was beginning to target its considerable resources against the Bergin crew and its *capo,* John Gotti.

One clue was the unusually large group of detectives from the police department's Public Morals Division that raided the Bergin in June of 1981 and confiscated an extensive store of fireworks. The fireworks were to be used in what had become a tradition on 101st Avenue, a large July 4 block party and fireworks show—the fireworks part, since it was unlicensed, was illegal in New York. While Gotti and the Bergin crew were angry over this raid, they failed to notice that some of the detectives were in fact FBI agents. Those agents were scouting the Bergin for purposes of installing bugs, having already been informed by Willie Boy Johnson of the best spots for their installation.

As the raid concluded, an FBI agent picked up one of the Bergin pay phones, and in a cryptic message to Bruce Mouw, supervisor of the Bureau's Gambino squad, reported that the raid had gone off as planned. Almost immediately, Mouw received another call, this one from Remo Franceschini, congratulating the FBI on the raid.

Why Franceschini chose to make this curious call remains unknown, but Mouw was alarmed: obviously, the Queens D.A.

Squad had a tap on the Bergin phones, which would complicate the FBI's plan to draw up an electronic web around the club. Mouw went to Queens District Attorney Santucci to discuss what he carefully called "a possible conflict of interest" between the two jurisdictions.

Mouw was dismayed to find that Santucci was not about to cooperate. He told Mouw that the Queens D.A. Squad had tapped two of three phones in the Bergin annex, and installed a bug in the rear of the club, where Gotti had his office. (Santucci did not know that the bug failed to pick up any incriminating conversations because Gotti was aware of it, having been informed of its existence by a corrupt assistant district attorney in Santucci's own office.)

Santucci called the Bergin wiretaps "valuable" because they had resulted in nearly two dozen arrests for illegal gambling. Mouw was clearly unimpressed: considering what Gotti and his Bergin crew were involved in, those gambling arrests were not much to show for wiretaps. He tried to convince Santucci to leave the Bergin alone, so that the FBI electronics experts could do a real job on the club, along with its satellite, the Our Friends Social Club, just down the block. It sounded very much as if the FBI planned to wire up the entire street.

To Mouw's annoyance, Santucci gave the impression that his squad of detectives was a competitor to the FBI, and that it would continue Operation Wedge in the hope of making more gambling arrests. He did offer a compromise of sorts: the FBI would be "permitted" to attack the Our Friends Social Club, while Queens would concentrate on the Bergin. (Operation Wedge finally failed because still another corrupt official in Santucci's office sold information about the bugs to Gotti; he and his crew simply transferred sensitive conversations to untapped phones.)

Mouw gave up any further attempt to get cooperation from Queens, but in one sense, it hardly mattered. The fact was that at that moment, the FBI was in the grip of a breathtaking vision: it planned nothing less than the destruction of the entire New York Mafia in a series of massive, coordinated blows. All the *Mafiosi* of consequence were targeted to be swept up in this whirlwind; from soldiers to godfathers, all were to be put in prison. "Untouchables" like Aniello Della-croce and Paul Castellano, along with the godfathers of the ruling Commission, were prime targets. And so were men like John Gotti, at that time a relative unknown outside the Mafia world, simply one of a number of active *capi* targeted for destruction. Ironically, however, it was this new crusade that was to make Gotti a figure of national infamy.

The moment when the FBI crusade began can be set with precision. On a sunny day in June 1980, FBI Special Agents James Kossler and Julius Bonavolonta, veteran agents in organized crime work, were attending a legal seminar at Cornell University in upstate New York on organized crime.

Among the speakers was a Notre Dame University Law School professor, Robert Blakey, author of the Racketeer Influenced and Corrupt Organizations Act, popularly known as RICO. Originally designed to provide prosecutors with a weapon against organized crime infiltration of labor unions and businesses, the law could be used more effectively to combat the entire structure of organized crime, Blakey believed. He was upset that federal prosecutors and the FBI had not understood RICO's potential as a prosecutorial weapon.

To the discomfort of other seminar participants aware of the FBI agents' presence, Blakey proceeded to criticize the FBI severely, arguing that the Bureau spent too much time making cases against individual criminals instead of the structure of organized crime that enabled them to flourish. In effect, Blakey demolished the entire FBI war on organized crime to that point as a virtual waste of the taxpayers' money. When Blakey was finished, some of the seminar participants expected the two agents to shoot him. Instead, Kossler turned to Bonavolonta and said, "You know, he's absolutely right."

In that moment, like a huge aircraft carrier suddenly switching course, the FBI began to overhaul its war against the Mafia in New York. Less than a year after that Cornell seminar, Kossler was given the formal title of Coordinating Supervisor of Organized Crime Squads; asked to describe the job, the self-effacing Kossler liked to say, "I am supervisor of supervisors; that is to say, *capo di tutti frutti*."

Kossler was considered an organizational genius within the Bureau and, given a free hand, he designed a completely reorganized FBI structure targeted against the Mafia. Instead of individual squads oriented to combat specific crimes, such as hijacking or gambling, Kossler recommended the creation of nine elite squads, five of them targeted against the five Mafia families, two against labor racketeering (at that point considered the most serious Mafia threat), one against organized crime on Long Island and its two suburban counties to the east, and one against organized crime in Westchester County, the suburban county bordering New York City on the north.

There were several significant changes in the way these squads would operate. Most important, they would operate primarily against the structures of the individual Mafia groups, rather than individual members. Cases would be developed against the structure as a "continuing racketeering enterprise," as Blakey recommended. Another significant change: the FBI's organized crime effort would be a joint one, operating with detectives of the New York City Police Department's elite Organized Crime Control Bureau (whose personnel would make up about a third of the two hundred forty people assigned to the new effort against the Mafia).

These changes were nothing less than remarkable for the FBI, in a number of ways a curious organization with a mixture of traditionalist policies and modern technology. For many years regarded as the most hidebound of all law-enforcement establishments, it was overhauled and reoverhauled relentlessly after J. Edgar Hoover's death in 1972; by 1980, Hoover would not have recognized the place. Few agents remembered that in 1959 the Bureau's biggest and most active branch, the New York field office, had a grand total of four agents investigating organized crime, at a time when the Mafia was enjoying phenomenal growth. That very same year, over four hundred agents in New York were assigned the job of probing the "Communist conspiracy," spurred by a stream of directives from the autocratic Hoover to investigate such earthshaking matters as whether the head of the American Communist Party drove a limousine or took the subway to party headquarters.

The reorientation of the FBI attack against organized crime was to be enhanced by two other developments. One was the appointment of Thomas Sheer as head of the FBI's New York office. A former street agent who had worked against the Mafia in New York, Sheer was an enthusiastic proponent of Kossler's reorganization scheme. Second was the arrival of a Justice Department official named Rudolph Giuliani as U.S. Attorney for the Southern District of New York, the most active (and publicized) such post in the country. The energetic Giuliani was instantly smitten with the FBI's new approach, having just read Joseph Bonanno's autobiography, which openly discussed the existence of the Mafia's ruling Commission—a "continuing criminal enterprise" if ever there was one.

A prime component of the new war was one of the FBI's greatest strengths, its "techies," the teams who specialized in electronic bugging operations. Regarded as magicians of the black arts by the rest of the Bureau, the teams included locksmiths, expert burglars, undercover operatives (including some of the Bureau's best women agents), surveillance experts, and electronics technicians, sometimes called "buggies" or "Dr. Bugs." Justifiably proud of their reputation to perform the impossible, the techies found their most difficult jobs in Mafia bugging operations. Sometimes, it would take them months to penetrate a tight security screen, only to confront such problems as where to conceal the fireplace-log-sized power cells connected with thin wire to a hidden tiny microphone—both of which also had to be concealed. When the installation was completed, special teams "worked" the site where the microphones had been hidden, ensuring that not even a speck of dust was out of place to warn anyone that the techies had been there.

Once in place, the system was a technological wonder, transmitting and simultaneously scrambling intercepted conversations (so they could not be picked up by scanners) to electronic boosters about a quarter-mile away, which in turn sent the signals to monitoring sites (or "plants") up to several miles away. There, the signals were unscrambled and recorded. Monitoring agents working the "plant" had to be alert for the onset of "sweepers," electronic equipment designed to detect hidden bugs; warned of their approach, the agents instantly would turn off the bugs until the "sweepers" had passed.

The techies were to score their greatest success for the Gambino squad, the largest of the new units working against the Mafia. Their first target in 1982 was the home of Angelo Ruggiero, a choice only partially related to Willie Boy Johnson's revelations about narcotics being discussed there. More to the point, the voluble Ruggiero, the FBI believed, would be the man most likely to discuss a wide range of Gambino Family business; each reference could serve as the basis for still more wiretapping warrants on other homes and businesses of family members.

From the first instant the bugs began transmitting inside Ruggiero's home in April 1982, it was clear they were going to be something special. Bruce Mouw, the Gambino squad supervisor, was called to the plant at the FBI's Kennedy Airport office to hear some of the first intercepted conversations. A notoriously reticent man noted for stoicism, Mouw listened a few minutes, then said, uncharacteristically, "Wow!"

The man who called Mouw to listen was an agent regarded by fellow agents as even more humorless than Mouw, William Noon. Movie-star handsome, Noon was sometimes called "baby face" for his remarkably youthful appearance, which made him look only half of his thirty-four years. Originally trained as an accountant, he showed it: as the hours and hours of tapes piled up, Noon demonstrated an amazing facility for keeping all the many strands organized in his head. One imagined a memory divided into the columns of accountants' ledger books. Noon, who was to become the chief agent in the Ruggiero case, was its historian, memory bank, and interpreter; as defense attorneys were to learn later, to their cost, there was no conversation that Noon could not catalog, recall, or set into the context of all other conversations.

There was a great deal to be organized, for the Ruggiero bug was like a gushing fountain. The conversations could range from the basically criminal, such as Alphonse Sciacia, a noted Mafia heroin trafficker, walking into the Ruggiero home and announcing brightly, "I got thirty things of heroin. That's why I'm here." Or they could be chilling, such as Angelo Ruggiero's warning to two of his business partners: "If I find out anybody's lying, a year from now, or six months from now . . . I promise youse this: youse are gonna die the same way my brother died—in pieces!" Or they might be merely ruminatory, such as Ruggiero's evaluation of the FBI ("fucking rotten motherfuckers"), and the strains of conducting a heroin sales business ("Fuck! This fucking narcotics and this other fucking shit!").

But as Noon realized, the really interesting part of the Ruggiero bugs was the tremors they caused in the hierarchy of the Gambino Family. Paul Castellano was furious when an indictment of Ruggiero and others for drug trafficking in early 1983 mentioned the existence of the tapes. Castellano, it turned out, had lent Ruggiero a hundred thousand dollars, a loan that could be interpreted by suspicious minds as bankrolling Ruggiero's heroin operation—in other words, a very nasty federal conspiracy charge.

When the FBI tapes were turned over to Ruggiero's lawyer, Castellano demanded to see them, but Ruggiero stalled. No wonder: among other things the FBI had recorded were discussions of Mafia Commission business by Angelo with one of his heroin partners, a nonmade man named Eddie Lino. This amounted to a capital offense under Mafia rules, which forbade such discussions. Increasing pressure by Castellano brought Dellacroce into a steadily worsening political crisis that also drew in John Gotti.

"I ain't givin' them tapes up," Ruggiero declared flatly to Dellacroce as he and Gotti sat by the underboss's sickbed. He persisted in this view, even though Dellacroce patiently explained he had no choice: if the boss wants the tapes, he gets the tapes. "You don't understand *Cosa Nostra*," Dellacroce said, wearily.

"Angelo, what does *Cosa Nostra* mean?" Gotti interjected, trying to avoid further confrontation.

As usual, Ruggiero was not listening, and to Gotti's dismay, went on to say defiantly he would never let Castellano see the tapes, and accused Dellacroce of reneging on a promise to back him in his refusal.

"You don't know what the fuck you're talkin' about," Gotti snapped at Ruggiero, aware that the last thing he needed at this point was an angry Dellacroce. When Ruggiero plowed on, Gotti put an even sharper edge to his voice: "Why don't you keep quiet and shut the fuck up?"

He might just as well have asked the planet to stop spinning; by the time the conversation had finished, an irked Dellacroce made it clear the tapes were to be given to Castellano, because the only alternative was a war within the family. Gotti and Ruggiero soothed Dellacroce by hinting that the tapes would be turned over, but in fact they had no intention of doing anything of the kind. Dellacroce did not know it, but Gotti and Ruggiero had begun to consider more radical solutions to the problem of Paul Castellano.

The gathering threads of their plan were detected a year earlier in FBI bugs on other Mafia families, one of which recorded Ruggiero, on a diplomatic mission from Gotti, talking with Colombo Family *capi* to divine their feelings about Castellano. He learned they despised Castellano; one of them, Gennaro (Gerry) Langella said, "Your boss [Castellano] is breaking our fucking balls."

Ruggiero discovered that Castellano was an increasingly unpopular figure throughout the rest of the Mafia. Perceived as cheap and money-hungry, he had antagonized other families by seeking a larger slice of the concrete bid-rigging scheme in which all the families were supposed to share equally. In fact, there were rumbles to the effect that Castellano was in the process of creating his own concrete firm that would function as a monopoly controlling all major concrete work in the entire city.

In 1982, Castellano discovered that his own house had been bugged by an FBI team of techies who somehow had managed to penetrate a supposedly impregnable security system at the Staten Island mansion, including closed-circuit television cameras, bodyguards, frequent electronic sweeps to detect bugs, electronic sensors, and two huge attack dogs who freely roamed his property. To further sour his mood, Castellano heard that Dellacroce's house, too, had been bugged. As the family boss correctly assumed later, these blows were the direct result of the bugs inside Angelo Ruggiero's house. Castellano was furious, and threatened to have Ruggiero killed.

Fearing imminent assassination by Castellano, Ruggiero went into hiding, first in a Long Island motel and later in a Manhattan apartment provided by one of his partners in crime, Mark Reiter. All the while, he was unaware he was under surveillance by police and FBI teams. Meanwhile, the FBI began rolling up his narcotics operation. In June 1982, FBI agents trailed two of Ruggiero's business partners, William (Sid) Cestaro and Salvatore Greco, and saw them drive the wrong way up a one-way street, a standard countersurveillance technique of drug dealers. Another team of FBI agents, anticipating just that move, watched as the two men exchanged packages; when the agents pounced, they caught Cestaro with two bags containing $140,000 in cash, and Greco carrying two kilos of heroin.

The following August, the roof caved in. In a citywide sweep, FBI agents arrested Angelo Ruggiero, Gene Gotti, John Carneglia, and Mark Reiter on narcotics trafficking charges, plus another half-dozen men on related charges. Among those arrested were the Bergin crew's lawyer, Michael Coiro, and John Gotti's ostensible employer, Anthony Gurino, on obstruction of justice charges. Four other men connected with the Ruggiero ring fled.

Castellano was now nearly beside himself with rage, a fury not lessened when John Gotti tried to explain it all away by claiming that the FBI sweep was merely a "clearing up" of Sal Ruggiero's old drug operation. "Listen, Johnny," Castellano snapped, "you better prove you weren't involved," and went on to hint that he was prepared to recall Carmine (Charley Wagons) from retirement and replace his protégé. He also hinted that Peter (Little Pete) Tambone, having once escaped a Castellano assassination order, would now be the subject of another.

Castellano was not able to dispose of Tambone immediately, for Little Pete was out of his reach: summoned before a federal grand jury to discuss his role in the Gotti-Ruggiero narcotics operation and why he had been the target of Castellano's wrath, Tambone decided on the expedient of acting as though he was insane. He showed up in court wearing pajamas and mumbling incoherently to himself, an act that did not impress prosecutors. They hauled him before the grand jury, where Tambone refused to say a word. He was promptly clapped in jail for contempt.

Castellano also was unable to do anything about John Gotti for the moment. Still furious about what he considered firm proof that Gotti was the chairman of the board for Ruggiero's narcotics operation, Castellano suddenly found himself under indictment on charges that one of his crews, run by a homicidal *capo* named Roy DeMeo, had operated a huge luxury car theft ring on direct orders of the Gambino Family boss, who had profited from it. Castellano was also alleged to be aware that the DeMeo crew had murdered twenty-two people, including one man they beat to death in a frenzy, hacked his body to pieces, then adjourned to have a pizza. Subsequently, Castellano was hit with an even mightier legal blow, indictment in Rudolph Giuliani's historic "Commission case," in which all reigning godfathers of the five New York Mafia families were charged, essentially, with being godfathers, their "illegal enterprise" under the RICO statute the Mafia itself.

Castellano's vast legal troubles provided respite to John Gotti, who was confronting his own legal troubles. He became aware that the Eastern District Organized Crime Strike Force was putting together its own RICO case in which the central defendants would be Dellacroce and the middle echelon of the Gambino organization, including Gotti. "They're seekin' to knock the nuts off me," Gotti said, although he remained confident that he would beat the case. After all, no one had managed to plant a bug inside his house, and if anyone had bugged the Bergin, he had tried to be careful in the club; aside from gambling talk, nothing terribly incriminating had been said within the range of any electronic device. There seemed to be no evidence linking him directly to the Ruggiero narcotics operation. Besides, his *goombata* were loyal, so there was no avenue of attack there.

But Gotti was quite mistaken. In fact, cooperative efforts by the FBI and the state's Organized Crime Task Force had resulted in several significant, nonelectronic penetrations of Gotti's little empire.

One was William (Willie) Batista, the old holdover from the original Ruggiano crew absorbed into Carmine Fatico's organization when Fatico led his forces from East New York into Ozone Park some years before. Batista, an engaging old-line hood, who relentlessly chased women and demonstrated genuine culinary talent as an accomplished cook, had done a little snitching for the FBI back in the mid-1960s. He broke off with the Bureau, but in 1972, when FBI agents were trying to track down Buzzy Carrone following his attempted murder of Special Agent Patrick Colgan, they recontacted him to see if he might help. He was of limited aid, but suddenly turned to Colgan and said, "You know, I wouldn't mind a call back." When agents asked if he would be willing to become an informant, Batista replied, with characteristic breeziness, "Sure, why not? Shit, I ain't making any money here anyway."

This astonishingly easy recruitment of an informant produced a Bergin crew member whose effectiveness was in inverse proportion to his distance from a crime; arrested eighteen times in twenty-seven years, Batista tended to get vague on any crimes in which he was involved. Nevertheless, the Bureau found him useful as a check on its star informant, Willie Boy Johnson; Batista hated Johnson, and insisted to the FBI that Willie Boy was a heroin dealer. At one point he told Colgan, "You know, Willie Boy is a fucking informant." Trying to keep the concern out of his face, Colgan asked how Batista knew that; he was relieved to hear him reply that it was "just a feeling." Colgan disabused him of the notion.

Another penetration was named Dominick Lofaro, a former upstate Mafia associate who joined the Queens crew of a Gambino *capo*, Ralph Mosca, a specialist in gambling operations and a good friend of Gotti. Arrested on heroin charges, Lofaro was converted by the Organized Crime Task Force into an informant: equipped with a concealed body recorder, Lofaro accompanied Mosca to a number of meetings at the Bergin with Gotti. Several incriminating conversations by Gotti were sufficient for the Task Force to obtain a court order for a bug its technicians cunningly concealed in the annex of the Bergin club—the perfect spot to record Gotti, who had a habit of conducting sensitive conversations just inside the annex door.

Another low-ranking Bergin crew member had also been recruited via a drug arrest: Salvatore Polisi, known as "Sally Upazz" (Sicilian slang for "crazy") because of his generally loony behavior and his feat of faking his way out of the Marine Corps by a sham psychiatric disorder, and later beating a bank forgery case by faking a psychiatric illness that fooled an entire staff of psychiatrists. Arrested in a 1983 cocaine deal, Polisi spurned an offer to cooperate by the Queens D.A.'s Office—the word on the street among the *Mafiosi* insisted that the office was corrupt—and made a deal with the Eastern District Organized Crime Strike Force. Set up with a wire, Polisi immediately ensnared Queens State Supreme Court Judge William Brennan, who was later convicted of taking bribes from criminal defendants—most of them *Mafiosi*—for fifteen years. Then he was set loose against his old acquaintances in the Bergin crew.

Polisi's contribution was mostly in the form of relatively low-level tidbits about Gotti and the Bergin, but another informant, James Cardinali, was potentially a much more damaging witness. In 1976, in prison on a robbery charge, he met John Gotti and Angelo Ruggiero, and begged them for a job at the Bergin once he was released. In 1979, Cardinali, back on the street, showed up at the Bergin, and was given the most menial jobs, including sweeping out the club. Gotti felt sorry for Cardinali (who had a pronounced limp from a childhood bout with polio), and he would occasionally give him cash. He also began training him to become an apprentice hood.

As he had learned from Fatico, Gotti paid special attention to the training of new recruits. They were first tested by being given an envelope stuffed with large bills, told to go to the bank and cash them in for smaller bills. When the apprentices arrived at the bank, they discovered that the envelope, which they had been told contained five thousand dollars, in fact contained seventy-five hundred dollars. What they brought back from the bank constituted an important test of loyalty.

If they brought back five thousand dollars, they were immediately banished; if they returned with the full amount and announced that whoever gave them the envelope made a mistake, they were marked as capable of further training.

But Cardinali, without bothering to inform Gotti, began killing drug dealers. Arrested in 1983, he agreed to provide information on what he had heard and seen around the Bergin, including much about John Gotti.

Another informant extended far back into Gotti's past. He was Matthew Traynor, the former street gang member in Ozone Park who had become friends with the Gotti brothers Richard and Gene when the Gottis drifted into Ozone Park. Since then, Traynor had gone on to bigger and better things, mainly bank robbery. He had also drifted into drug dealing, and would occasionally serve as courier for narcotics being sold by Gene Gotti.

Traynor had a string of successful bank robberies, but the expensive lifestyle they bought soon began adding a considerable number of pounds to his body, all of it flab. In 1984, while trying to repeat his favorite bank robbery tactic of vaulting the bank counter at a Long Island bank, his bulk got stuck on the counter's glass partition. A gun he was carrying went off, a bullet struck a young woman teller, and Traynor was in deep legal trouble. He immediately offered a deal to the FBI and police, agreeing to provide information against John Gotti and his brother Gene, and citing as motivation a seven-year-old grudge. In Traynor's account, he had made twenty-four thousand dollars in a 1977 bank robbery, and when he went to Ozone Park to celebrate at a local bar with a predominantly Mafia clientele, Gene Gotti approached him. "Gimme ten thousand dollars," Gotti ordered. "We're a little short of money to put on the street right now." Traynor, noting the four grim hoods behind Gotti, complied, but never forgot the gross insult.

This motley collection of lowlifes represented the central human thrust of the developing case against John Gotti. He was unaware that such witnesses even existed, nor did he know, as yet, of Willie Boy Johnson's betrayal. He was certain that the developing federal case would also use some wiretap evidence, but he could not conceive of any bug that could have picked up his most revealing conversations. He remained confident; there was no way they could get him.

But, as things turned out, when the boom was finally lowered, the case that emerged did not emanate from the Bergin, but from an ordinary middle-class Brooklyn house. There, a heroin junkie one day reached into a footlocker and took out twelve thousand dollars in cash. That would come to ignite one of the strangest criminal cases ever seen, *United States v. Aniello Dellacroce, et al.*

8

Our Lady of Wisdom

When the lions fight, the Christians cheer.
—OLD SICILIAN PROVERB

EVEN IN THAT SEMIDARKNESS, with the overhead mirrored light flashing blue and green, and the bodies writhing on the floor, she spotted them somewhere in the middle of that mass. April Ernst did not like what she saw: there he was, dancing with that long-legged blonde whose body seemed ready to pop out of her little white dress. When the throbbing disco music paused momentarily, she saw him grab the blonde and run his hands over her body.

That's it, April Ernst decided. She made a beeline for them across the floor and planted herself in front of her boyfriend, Andrew Curro. "You cocksucker!" she screamed at him. "I'll fix you!" Curro, dressed in standard disco uniform of black shirt open to the navel, gold chain, and white pants, regarded his live-in girlfriend with disinterest.

"Hey, cunt, you don't own me!" he growled at her, and put his arm around the blonde. With that, April Ernst stalked off, calling back over her shoulder, "I told you, I'll fix you!"

Curro shrugged, but during the next few hours, even the presence of the blonde could not prevent his mind from beginning to concentrate on the implications of April Ernst's furious confrontation with him. Given Curro's circumstances, the old saying about scorned women—hell hath no fury, and so forth—now assumed large dimensions. Depending on the extent of her fury, April Ernst was in a position to wreak terrible vengeance on Andrew Curro.

Among other things that New Year's Eve of 1980, April could call the police. She could tell them that her boyfriend, Andrew Curro, worked in a chop shop run by a notorious Queens *Mafioso* named John Carneglia and his brother, Charley. She could tell the police how her boyfriend helped the Carneglias steal cars, then cut them apart to sell the parts. Or, if she were really angry, she could tell police that Andrew Curro and two other men had robbed two armored cars that year and gotten over a million dollars. Or, she might reveal how some of that money was paid to certain people in the Mafia "out of respect."

April Ernst, in her raging fury over catching her boyfriend with another woman, might do any of those things. Any one would cause Andrew Curro a very big legal problem, and he decided to forestall that possibility. April Ernst knew too much.

Later that night, Curro, accompanied by a friend, presented himself with something of a hangdog look at the apartment he shared with April Ernst. Assuming Curro had come to make amends, she let him inside. It was the last mistake of her life, for Curro strangled her. He and his friend then dragged the body to the bathtub, and hacked it into pieces with machetes. When they were finished, Curro scooped up a cup of April Ernst's still-warm blood and offered his fellow murderer a drink.

With pieces of her body placed in plastic bags and disposed of all over New York City, April Ernst disappeared forever from the fast lane. But she was not forgotten: Detective Robert Kohler, one of the police department's most noted homicide investigators, began working from virtually microscopic clues. Within a year, he solved the case, in the process uncovering the link between April Ernst's murder and the armored car robberies. But that was just the beginning of what would prove to be something much more than a homicide case.

Among other things, Kohler discovered that in July 1980, Andrew Curro, Peter Zuccaro, and Joseph Calvacante, local Queens lowlifes, held up an IBI Securities armored car and got away with three hundred ten thousand dollars. Several months later, they grabbed another IBI armored car, escaping with seven hundred fifty thousand dollars. This vast pile of cash, more money than any of them dreamed they would ever see in their entire lives, ignited a mad spending spree, including jaunts to Las Vegas and Atlantic City to gamble away some of the money. The three girlfriends of the robbers, including April Ernst, were perfectly aware of the source of all the sudden wealth; they had watched while the three robbers occupied most of a day just counting it. Bored with the task, and unwilling to bother counting a huge pile of small-denomination bills, the robbers simply gathered up the pile and threw it at the girlfriends, telling them to go shopping. The three women were delighted, since they discovered there was forty-seven thousand dollars in the pile.

A year after the armored car robberies, Kohler's investigation of April Ernst's murder led to its connection with the IBI thefts. The theft case wound up in federal jurisdiction—some of the money was from interstate shipments—assigned to a young Assistant U.S. Attorney named Diane Giacalone. In a deductive process that was to have an important impact on the life of John Gotti, Giacalone very quickly concluded that she was not prosecuting an ordinary robbery case.

Giacalone's background made her almost the perfect prosecutor to understand certain aspects of the IBI case. Born in Ozone Park, she was a product of that second-generation Italian neighborhood and its two-story row houses with small yards and aluminum awnings over the windows, small mom-and-pop stores, and the Italian butcher shops with long links of sausages hanging in the windows.

As a young girl walking to school at Our Lady of Wisdom Academy, a Catholic parochial school for girls, she wondered about some other buildings in her neighborhood: those social clubs where men always seemed to be hanging around, not really doing anything. The daughter of a hardworking civil engineer, she was puzzled: why didn't these men have jobs? Her parents—and other adults in the close-knit neighborhood—did not seem to have an answer, and it was a subject they clearly did not want to discuss at any length.

Although she was considered an oddity in her family because of her desire to go to college, Diane Giacalone had a rock-hard stubborn streak, and not only went off to college, but to law school as well. She joined the Justice Department's Tax Division, and in 1979 returned to her roots by securing an appointment as an Assistant U.S. Attorney in the Eastern District, the federal court jurisdiction that includes Brooklyn, Queens, and Long Island (whose collective population of five million people is larger than most U.S. cities).

Assigned the IBI robberies prosecution in 1981, Giacalone, who bore a striking resemblance to the comedienne Lily Tomlin, was presented with the kind of fairly routine case on which new prosecutors cut their teeth. At first glance, it seemed quite simple: Andrew Curro and his two confederates were facing a mountain of evidence, chief among it the testimony of Gerald Curro, Andrew's brother. Gerald, a heroin addict, resisted his brother's suggestion to join the robbery gang, but witnessed their triumphant return, when they walked into the Curro home with a large mail sack stuffed with cash. Gerald found out that his brother kept some of the robbery proceeds in a footlocker in his bedroom. Short of cash to score some dope, Gerald one day reached into that footlocker and pulled out twelve thousand dollars. Furious at the theft, Andrew suspected that his brother and a friend, Peter Sacco, had stolen the money, whereupon he shot Sacco and planned to do the same to his brother Gerald. Terrified at this prospect, Gerald ran to the authorities and told them the whole story.

And yet, as Giacalone discovered, there were some oddities in the case. For one thing, after Andrew Curro was arrested, a bail bondsman received a phone call from Angelo Ruggiero assuring him that the bail would be guaranteed by "some people" he did not identify further. Why, Giacalone wondered, would an infamous *Mafioso* like Ruggiero become involved in a case with defendants having no known connection to the Mafia?

Then there was the incident involving Joseph Calvacante, one of the robbers. Following his arrest, he was being taken past a holding pen that at the moment contained John Carneglia, another Bergin *Mafioso*. "Keep your fucking mouth shut!" Carneglia yelled as he saw Calvacante, who visibly paled at the sight of Carneglia. Why would a man like Carneglia be concerned what Calvacante might say about the robbery?

From various informants, the answer to both those questions began to emerge. Andrew Curro, it developed, was a car thief, his primary vocation. Recruited by Carneglia in his teens, Curro (who ironically had never learned to drive) demonstrated aptitude in the business of chopping up stolen cars for their parts, and selling them to crooked auto parts dealers at immense profit. Although he did not tell Carneglia about his successful IBI robberies, the wild spending of the three robbers soon made it clear to everyone in the neighborhood that they had carried them out. Charles Carneglia, business partner and occasional spokesman for his brother John, called Andrew Curro with the pointed advice to "drop by" the Bergin and "pay respects" to *capo* John Gotti.

Curro, not especially agile mentally, did not get the message, and told Carneglia he saw no reason to go to Bergin and talk with John Gotti, a man he didn't know. Carneglia was displeased by this reaction; Calvacante and Zuccaro, the other two robbers, had caught on fast and made the proper obeisance: each gave a pile of cash to the Carneglias for eventual transfer to John Gotti as "symbols of our respect." Now it was Curro's turn, but even repeated mentions by the Carneglias of his obligation to "do the right thing" failed to move him. "I ain't givin' no money to John Gotti," he told his brother Gerald.

Charley Carneglia was growing steadily angrier at Curro's obstinacy, and sought to use an extended metaphor to convey his (and presumably Gotti's) displeasure. "Look," he told Curro, "you may be writing a book, but you won't finish it; this isn't the end of the chapter." Curro ignored the warning, but any possible further consequences were rendered academic by his arrest on murder and robbery charges.

All of this was technically hearsay evidence against John Gotti, but there was something that Giacalone, the trained tax attorney, found very intriguing: the numbers didn't add up. Although all defendants claimed that they had not paid a cent in tribute to John Gotti or the Carneglias or anybody else, Giacalone realized they could not account for how all the robbery proceeds disappeared. Even after subtracting the money spent for cocaine, parties, travel, clothes, cars, and other doodads in an orgy of conspicuous consumption, that still left several hundred thousand dollars unaccounted for. Giacalone also consulted a calendar, and realized that the robbers had less than eight months to spend all that money; even the most profligate spending by unimaginative crooks during that period would not account for all of it. (Andrew Curro sought to explain away at least part of the missing money by claiming to have lost one hundred twenty thousand dollars at craps one night in Atlantic City—but FBI agents discovered that a loss of that size, which casino employees tend to remember, was a fiction.)

However convinced Giacalone was that tributes of some size had been paid to Gotti, there was not enough to merit prosecution—for the moment, at least. The three robbers were convicted; Curro snickered when Federal District Court Judge Eugene H. Nickerson sentenced him to twenty-four years in prison. But as far as Giacalone was concerned, that was not the end of the case. For months on end, including weekends, she pored over old files, FBI reports, and every scrap of paper she could get her hands on. Slowly, as she absorbed the details of Aniello Dellacroce's career and that of his favorite *capo*, John Gotti, there dawned in her mind an ambitious plan: the tributes exacted by Gotti from at least two of the robbers were only the tip of a large iceberg. That sort of thing had been going on a long time—in other words, a "pattern of racketeering," enough for a RICO case against Dellacroce and the man who ran the Bergin.

Giacalone did not know it, but a group of federal prosecutors in the same building where she worked were already hard at work on a vaguely similar case, one aimed at the entire Gambino Family structure, including Dellacroce and Gotti. Despite their proximity, however, these prosecutors might just as well have been on the moon, for they worked for an entirely separate organization, the Eastern District Organized Crime Strike Force. And that fact illustrated a persistent problem.

The problem was that the federal government's prosecutorial army arrayed against the Mafia in New York was divided into three sometimes-competing forces. There was

the Southern District in Manhattan, whose territory included
Manhattan, the Bronx, and Westchester County. That district,
particularly when Rudolph Giuliani became the U.S. Attorney
for the jurisdiction, had a reputation for aggressiveness,
spurred in part by the fact that it operated in the world's
greatest concentration of media. The Eastern District operated
in Brooklyn, just across the East River on the other side of
the Brooklyn Bridge. The U.S. Attorney for that jurisdiction,
which functioned in a media backwater, tended to regard
himself as a rival to his Southern District counterpart.

Further complicating things was the existence of the Organized Crime Strike Force in Brooklyn. One of fourteen such
groups spread throughout the country, the Strike Force had
a mandate to put together major white-collar and organized-
crime cases, using the pooled resources of federal and local
agencies. But the Strike Forces worked directly for the Justice
Department; in Brooklyn, as in other areas, the U.S. Attorney
often found himself competing with the head of the local
Strike Force for high-profile cases.

As Diane Giacalone began to formulate her RICO case, the
delicate tendrils of the federal prosecutorial structure began to
vibrate. At first, Edward A. McDonald, head of the Strike
Force, saw no difficulty: his own, much broader, RICO case
was strengthening by the day, as the FBI began bringing him
the treasures from their bugs inside the homes of Ruggiero,
Castellano, and Dellacroce. Further, the state's Organized
Crime Task Force was bringing him their own treasures,
including two cooperating witnesses willing to testify about
John Gotti. Giacalone did not have those precious tapes; as
for her intent to prove that Gotti received cash tributes from
the IBI robbery, McDonald regarded that task as "virtually
impossible."

McDonald's criticism of Giacalone set off a deep personal
animosity on her part for the tall, former college basketball
player who became head of the Strike Force in early 1982.
Noted for his store of Irish charm that he could ladle out in
heaping amounts as the mood struck him, McDonald was a
highly regarded prosecutor who had won fame for his prosecution in the ABSCAM case, notably Senator Harrison Wil-
liams of New Jersey. Extremely fast on his feet, McDonald

and his dozen handpicked prosecutors were cutting a wide swath through the Mafia. Now armed with the RICO statute—"the prosecutor's Louisville Slugger," as it was sometimes known—McDonald intended to take down the entire middle and lower echelons of the Gambino Family.

This idea did not sit well with Raymond Dearie, then the U.S. Attorney for the Eastern District. A cautious man, Dearie thought the idea of charging an entire Mafia family with a crime an "FBI fantasy," and was convinced that "FBI con men" had sold this fantasy to their favorite prosecutors, men like Giuliani and McDonald, who would indict a tuna fish sandwich if the FBI told them it was a criminal. (For his part, McDonald privately referred to Dearie as a "wimp.")

With tensions already building in this tangle of jurisdictions, Giacalone's stubborn insistence on bringing her own case against the Gotti crew began to create serious problems. In a memo to Dearie, McDonald insisted that such a case had "very little likelihood of success," and the FBI began to exert pressure to get her to drop the case. All to no avail, for Giacalone was determined to move forward.

No agency was more uncomfortable with this development than the FBI, which normally brings cases to prosecutors, not the other way around. What was happening represented the FBI's greatest fear in New York: getting caught in a whipsaw between competing jurisdictions and egos. In the FBI's perception, it was often in a no-win situation: bringing a big case to one U.S. Attorney was almost certain to antagonize the other; often, the cases involved crimes that did not fit neatly into geographic categories (citywide Mafia conspiracies represented a classic example of that problem).

To make matters worse, the FBI suffered a deepening estrangement from Giacalone. Two agents working with her reported that she was impossible to deal with; this was followed by an even more disturbing piece of news from James Abbott, Willie Boy Johnson's control agent. Abbott reported that in one meeting with Johnson, the informant began to ask him about a developing racketeering case against John Gotti in the Eastern District. Abbott asked how Willie Boy came upon this confidential information; Johnson wordlessly threw a document in his lap. It was a copy of Giacalone's memorandum to the Justice Department on how she proposed to present her prosecution case. Johnson would not say how he obtained this highly confidential document, and the FBI began a massive in-house investigation to trace the source of the leak. The leak was traced to Giacalone's office, and although the FBI was never able to pinpoint the exact source, it was decided to sever all further connections with Giacalone.

Giacalone decided to press ahead without the FBI, despite advice from one of the Eastern District's most noted prosecutors, Charles Rose, who handled narcotics cases. Rose liked Giacalone, and he sought to deflect her away from her single-minded course: "You *cannot* win a RICO case without the FBI." But Giacalone had a powerful ally: Susan Shepard, a close friend and head of the Eastern District's Criminal Division. Coincidentally Dearie's fiancée and an important influence on him, Shepard became Giacalone's advocate, arguing to FBI officials that she deserved to put her own case forward because of the "sweat equity" she already had invested.

Much of this had to do with Giacalone's stubbornness, and perhaps also something more subtle. Giacalone tended to regard the male prosecutors and FBI agents as some sort of private men's club; they had forged close working bonds, and often socialized together. It annoyed her to see McDonald's back-slapping camaraderie with FBI agents who openly admired his abilities; similarly, she could not understand why DEA and FBI agents practically kissed the ground that Charley Rose walked on, or spoke of Guiliani in terms of "a pair of steel balls."

Sensing emerging disaster, the FBI, especially its resident guru on organized crime, James Kossler, tried to work out a compromise: Giacalone and McDonald would work together on a single RICO case against the Gambino Family. Giacalone would have none of it; she refused to go to McDonald's office (an elevator ride away) to hear his tapes, and demanded that if anybody was going to take an elevator ride, it was McDonald. Privately, she began to talk of McDonald as some kind of monster intent on destroying her. "That goddamn Irish charm doesn't fool me for one minute," she said, and claimed that all the Strike Force's lavish press publicity was solely the result of McDonald's seduction of reporters dazzled by his ability to talk the birds out of trees.

The bitterness was touched off by McDonald's complaint to the Justice Department about the Giacalone situation. To McDonald's fury, however, the department said it agreed with his position, but that Dearie himself would be permitted to make the final decision. Dearie decided to fold McDonald's case into Giacalone's, and now there was real trouble brewing.

It began in Queens. Giacalone, insisting she could make a RICO case stick without any help from the FBI, had asked the Queens District Attorney's Office what it could provide in the way of information about the Bergin crew. To her amazement, she learned that Willie Boy Johnson, among John Gotti's closest *goombata*, had been an informant for them—and, simultaneously, the FBI. (A fact the FBI had concealed from her.) That astonishing piece of information led Giacalone to a critical strategic decision: she would indict Willie Boy Johnson on several RICO counts, and tell him that such an action would reveal his informant status. And that, Giacalone was convinced, would push Willie Boy to become a witness against Gotti—a witness so compelling that the conviction of Gotti (and others) would be assured.

The FBI, informed of this strategem, was enraged, but every effort to block what the Bureau regarded as an appalling maneuver failed. Martin Boland, Willie Boy's original FBI control agent, was flown up from Tampa for an interview with Giacalone on the subject of Johnson as informant. He discovered that she was supremely confident Willie Boy would become a witness; besides, she told Boland, the FBI had allowed him to get away with murder: "Look, the FBI has been letting Johnson do whatever he wants to do, and that crap has to stop!"

Boland bristled. "In the first place, that isn't so. Second, you're a dreamer if you think by doing this, you'll get Willie Boy to testify. Willie will *never* testify."

"Just you wait," Giacalone insisted.

A session with James Abbott, Willie Boy's controller, was even uglier. A man with a short fuse, Abbott quietly listened as Giacalone yelled at him about how the FBI was a virtual partner-in-crime with Johnson, then snapped at her, "You know, if you were a man, I'd knock you on your ass."

To Abbott's astonishment, Giacalone immediately jumped up from behind her desk, assumed a boxer's stance, and with her fists cocked, said, "Okay, let's go at it right now! C'mon!" In spite of everything, Abbott had to laugh.

An uncomfortable observer to all this was John Gleeson, a young prosecutor only three weeks on the job. Considered a brilliant legal mind by his contemporaries, Gleeson had turned down a job at the prestigious Manhattan law firm of Cravath, Swaine and Moore to become a federal prosecutor. His assignment as coprosecutor with Giacalone was an attempt by Dearie to introduce a calming influence beside Giacalone, known for her abrasiveness. Additionally, Gleeson's legal abilities would be needed to work through the intricacies of the RICO law. At the same time, it would not hurt for a jury to see Gleeson—a slender, scholarly looking man with an earnest expression—seated at the prosecution table beside Giacalone, who fairly radiated rampant aggressiveness.

Told only that he was to participate "in an interesting criminal case," Gleeson discovered he had been thrust into a war zone, with "scorched earth," as he put it, everywhere. While McDonald was sulking like an angry bear, his equally angry minions were carrying over to Giacalone the essence of the case they had worked so hard to put together. The FBI agents were all in a rage; from the glares they directed at Giacalone, Gleeson began to imagine the possibility of some of the more angry ones picking her up bodily and throwing her off the Brooklyn Bridge (precisely that possibility, in fact, had occurred to several agents).

Despite Giacalone's belief that Willie Boy Johnson could be persuaded to become a witness, there appeared no prospect of it in the preliminary phases of her case as she began to move toward indictment and trial. Called into a session with Giacalone and two FBI agents, Johnson was informed that Giacalone planned to indict him, during which process it was "likely" his informant status would be revealed.

"I'll be slaughtered!" an anguished Johnson replied. "My family will be slaughtered! Why are you doing this to me?"

Willie Boy knew the answer, but, as he repeatedly insisted to Abbott, his control agent, "There is no way I'll ever testify, no matter what she does." Later that day, Johnson encountered Gotti, and told him, "Johnny, they're accusing me of being an informant." Gotti hardly appeared to be paying attention. "Well, I don't believe it," he said.

But Gotti would learn soon enough that Willie Boy was an informant. In March 1985, he, Dellacroce, and eight members of the Bergin crew, including Johnson, were indicted for violation of the RICO statute. Gotti was arrested at four o'clock one morning in the Bergin while playing cards (with Willie Boy Johnson, ironically enough). Simultaneously, Gene Gotti was arrested at his home; the ever-dimwitted brother, informed he was being arrested for violation of the RICO statute, asked, "Say, who is this Mr. Rico, anyway?"

The first order of business was a bail hearing, presided over by Eugene Nickerson, the judge assigned the trial. He approved a million-dollar bail for Gotti, but then was confronted by a puzzling move by Giacalone: she wanted Willie Boy Johnson remanded to jail. Why, Nickerson asked, would Giacalone allow bail for such dangerous characters as John Gotti, yet oppose bail to a man so low ranking—and presumably less dangerous—as Johnson?

"The reason," Giacalone said, "is that Mr. Johnson has been an informant for the Federal Bureau of Investigation for a period of over fifteen years, including a period up through the present time."

In the stunned silence that followed, it seemed as though everything had suddenly stopped. "Not true, your honor!" Willie Boy blurted, his large hands gripping his chair so tightly that the tattoos on his fingers stood out in a field of white. Slowly, Gotti turned his head to stare at him for a full moment. "So youse the reason we're here, huh?" he said, quietly. Willie Boy just shrugged, his characteristic response to any question he did not want to answer.

Nickerson immediately convened a closed hearing in his chambers to get to the bottom of whatever was happening. During the hearing, he appeared to be puzzled when Johnson admitted, "I spoke to the FBI many times," but then added, "I never gave them any information" about Gotti, Dellacroce, or anyone in the Bergin crew. Johnson also insisted, "My life is not in danger."

Giacalone argued that Willie Boy indeed was an FBI informant, a fact sufficient to cause him to be remanded in "administrative segregation" in prison so as to protect him from other inmates in the general population who might try to kill him. Actually, Giacalone was being disingenuous: as she well knew, putting a man in that prison status, commonly used for criminals who have turned witnesses, was an open advertisement that he was a snitch. Locked up twenty-three and a half hours each day, with no family visits permitted, a man in administrative segregation tended to look toward prosecutors for salvation.

Out on bail, Gotti was back at the Bergin, and clearly in a foul mood. He said nothing about Willie Boy, but that development, combined with his own indictment and other dark clouds on the horizon, caused crew members to tread softly around him. The clouds were many: his brother Gene, Angelo Ruggiero, and six others had been indicted for heroin-trafficking; Willie Batista, a veteran Bergin crew member, had suddenly dropped out of sight amid reports he was an FBI informant; Gotti's conversations in Dellacroce's home had been recorded by an FBI bug; and there were rumors that Paul Castellano was so furious at the turn of events that he was planning to kill Gotti. Worse, from Gotti's standpoint, was the sudden halt to his vaulting ambitions. With Dellacroce dying of cancer in his Staten Island home, it was rumored that Castellano planned to name his chauffeur, Thomas Bilotti, as the new underboss, and Thomas Gambino (son of the late Carlo Gambino) as designated successor to himself as boss of the entire family. Obviously, Castellano's succession plan had no place for Gotti, who apparently was presumed to be eliminated by the time these changes took place.

In that atmosphere, Gotti's volcano seemed to erupt almost hourly. Informed that a loan shark debtor had missed a payment despite rumored wealth, Gotti screamed, "I'll kick his fucking brains in!" And another faulty debtor incurred a similar outburst: "I told him, you better come and check in every week. You miss one week, and I'll kill you, you cocksucker, fucking creep!"

Gotti's mood did not improve until some of the pretrial hearings on his case revealed a number of curious aspects to the government case. Most significant, there was no sign of the FBI; as Gotti noted, he had been arrested by Edward Magnuson, a DEA agent who had been investigating him for some years as a suspected narcotics trafficker. Since then, as the case developed, it was clear that the FBI had nothing to do with it, an unusual situation in a RICO matter. Additionally, although Giacalone had moved to place Willie Boy Johnson in prison segregation—the normally certain sign that he would become a government witness—there was as yet no indication that he planned on doing any such thing. Likewise, Willie Batista had been revealed as an FBI informant, but there was no sign he was about to testify, either—and no sign of Batista himself, for that matter.

Actually, Batista at the moment was at an FBI safe house in Pennsylvania, where Patrick Colgan of the FBI was telling him that Giacalone wanted him to testify. At sixty-one years old, Batista was an old hood who knew the score, and he was well aware of what had happened to Willie Boy Johnson. "Don't try to shit me, Pat," he told Colgan. "As far as I'm concerned, Giacalone is something laying in the grass, just waiting to get me. I'm not testifying against John Gotti. You know it and I know it. If she pushes, I'm into the wind." Sure enough, a few days later, Batista slipped out of his safe house and has not been seen since.

As Gotti deduced, the odds were getting progressively better that the only two possible witnesses who could really hurt him—Johnson and Batista—would never testify. Still better, pretrial hearings on the question of the informants featured the extraordinary sight of Giacalone directing hostile questions at FBI agents who testified; obviously, there had been a bad falling-out between her and the FBI. At one point, Colgan, testifying about Batista, was asked his opinion about the decision to disclose Batista as an informant. As the defense lawyers beamed in satisfaction, Colgan replied, "I am both personally and professionally devastated by the actions of the government in this matter." (Out in the hallway during a recess, Gotti sidled up to agents James Abbott and Bernard Welsh, nodded toward the courtroom, and said, "Some cunt, huh?")

Although there was cause for optimism on the defense side, Giacalone could point to some positive developments for the prosecution as the assorted pretrial maneuverings droned on throughout 1985. Dellacroce, the chief defendant, had been adjudged guilty in a higher court; wasting away with cancer, he would be dead by the end of the year. His son, Armond, known as "Buddy," had been among the ten persons indicted; he pled guilty, but then fled. (Three years later, he would be found dead in Pennsylvania of a cocaine overdose and acute alcoholism.) Charles Carneglia, another of those indicted, similarly fled after indictment.

Giacalone also scored some preliminary victories for the prosecution, including an order by Nickerson that the names of government witnesses be kept secret until they were about to testify, and an anonymous jury. This latter move really exercised defense lawyers, for an anonymous jury—known only by numbers—tends to impress on jurors' minds that the defendants are very bad people in some way; otherwise, why would the judge go through such efforts to protect the identities of jurors?

The jury selection process itself revealed that the defense might have problems: despite an unusually large jury pool, it was difficult to find any potential juror who did not admit "bias" against John Gotti because of all they had read and heard about him as a Mafia *capo*. One prospective juror, asked if he had read anything about murders, car-bombings, and other violence in Brooklyn and what impression he gained as a result, replied dryly, "I got the impression that there was some sort of crime problem in Brooklyn."

Actually, as the trial finally was scheduled to open some-time early in 1986, both sides were fairly well balanced, with a roughly equal number of assets and debits. Given the death, in December 1985, of Dellacroce, the lead defendant, the remaining roster of defendants did not constitute the stuff of intense media interest—certainly not to the extent of the highly publicized "Commission Trial" against the top eche-

lon of the New York Mafia due to get under way across the
river in the Southern District of Manhattan, with real godfathers on trial. But that was about to change, for John Gotti
would dramatically alter the tenor—and the stakes—of the
trial in Brooklyn.

"Everybody's running scared, John," said Gene Gotti
worriedly to his brother.

"Well, fuck 'em, we ain't," John replied, with characteristic bravado.

The strategy session at the Bergin in early December of
1985 was a gloomy one, for there was no question that the
Gottis were in trouble. Dellacroce, their long-time protector,
was dead, and there were whispers throughout the Gambino
Family that Castellano had decided to solve the Gotti problem
once and for all by killing him. The most immediately obvious solution—kill Castellano before he could kill John
Gotti—was not as simple as it appeared. Murdering the boss
of a family required careful attention to politics, for the other
capi in the family would not support such a move unless
there was sufficient economic or other reasons for it. Moreover, tacit approval was needed from the other bosses of the
Commission that such a drastic measure was justified in some
way.

For more than a year, Gotti had been working hard to
establish those essential political conditions, in the process
discovering that Castellano often played into his hands. For
example, the family boss, worried about adverse publicity as
his trial in the auto theft ring case was about to begin, decided
not to attend Dellacroce's funeral. It was a colossal political
blunder, for many of the long list of *Mafiosi* who attended
were offended at this gross violation of Mafia protocol. Gotti
poured as much kerosene as he could on the fire, telling
mourners, "I told you, the fuckin' guy's a bum; he don't
even come to his own underboss's funeral."

Castellano committed another error, this one fatal. Preoccupied with his legal troubles, he delayed action on the danger represented by John Gotti's ambitions, which allowed
Gotti breathing space to undercut the family boss throughout
the rest of the Mafia. By mid-December of 1985, Gotti, hav-

ing achieved the necessary political foundation, now moved to the next phase, which was to penetrate Castellano's inner circle.

The key was to turn Frank DeCicco, Castellano's protégé, and James (Jimmy Brown) Failla, a Gambino *capo* and former chauffeur for Carlo Gambino who later became close to Castellano. Both men were completely trusted by Castellano, but seduced by Gotti's arguments that Castellano's days were finished and that new leadership was necessary to reinvigorate family business, they came to see the necessity of betraying the man they usually called "Big Paulie."

On December 14, Failla and DeCicco had a lengthy meeting with Castellano to discuss the "Gotti problem." Both men counseled a diplomatic solution, arguing that the entire problem could be solved by a major sitdown between Gotti and Big Paulie. Castellano agreed, and told them to make contact with Gotti to set it up. A dinner meeting was arranged between the two men for two days hence, at Sparks Restaurant in midtown Manhattan.

Castellano's willingness to seek a diplomatic solution was a reflection of the state of his mind at that point. Simply, Castellano knew he was through. There was no question he would beat the charges against him in the car theft ring case. That trial, with its distinctly bizarre overtones—including the chief government witness, a hideous man and admitted homosexual who testified about trying to get "the fat sucked out of my face" to make himself more attractive to his jailhouse lover—presented thin evidence of Castellano's direct involvement in the ring. But the so-called Commission Trial was a more formidable barrier. As Castellano was aware, there was no way he could beat that case: the FBI tapes of conversations in his home, during which he was heard clearly discussing Mafia business, were irrefutable. He would be convicted, at which point the seventy-four-year-old godfather, plagued with illnesses and besieged by ambitious hoods from below, would face forty years in prison—a death sentence.

The growing sense of fatalism seemed to hang on him like a funeral shroud when Kenneth McCabe, a former police detective and later federal investigator for Giuliani's office, led him to his arraignment on the Commission case. McCabe, who spent virtually his entire police career fighting organized crime in Brooklyn, had known Castellano for years, from the time when Big Paulie was just another waterfront hood. Now, he heard the godfather pant with effort as he slowly climbed the courthouse stairs; he had aged badly, and sagged beneath some invisible great weight. He looked like a man giving up on life.

Castellano chatted with his old enemy, then said, "Well, at least I was always a gentleman, Kenny."

McCabe smirked. "You're no gentleman, Paulie. I know what you are."

Castellano stopped dead in his tracks. He looked pained, as though his last shred of dignity had been stripped away. "My God, Kenny, how can you say that? I *was* a gentleman, no doubt about it." McCabe did not reply, but noted Castellano's use of the past tense.

It is entirely possible that the fatalistic Castellano knew that he was to be killed the early evening of December 16, 1985, as he headed for his rendezvous with Gotti, for he had been around long enough to realize that a man like Gotti was only rarely predisposed toward diplomatic solutions. Possibly, that is why the godfather pulled up before Sparks Restaurant in his black Cadillac accompanied only by his chauffeur, Thomas Bilotti.

What was going through Castellano's mind as he left his car and encountered several familiar faces standing there on the sidewalk? Seeing Gene Gotti, Anthony Roach Rampino, and Bartholomew (Bobby) Boriello, John Gotti's chauffeur, all dressed in identical overcoats and fur hats, he probably realized what would happen next. Boriello and Gotti fired six shots into Castellano's body. He died instantly. Rampino ran to the driver's side of the car and shot Bilotti to death. The three killers walked quickly away from the murder scene and, a block away, were picked up by Salvatore (Sammy the Bull) Gravano in a Lincoln and disappeared into the rush-hour traffic.

Police detectives knew exactly where to look first in investigating the murder. At John Gotti's home in Howard Beach, Queens, they found him casually attired and relaxed, absorbed in watching one of the nearly forty channels his rooftop satellite dish provided. "Paul got hit?" he asked, repeating the news detectives had broken to him. "Gee, that's too bad." He said it with the tone of a man expressing regrets about the death of a neighbor's cat.

Whatever his public regrets, Gotti pointedly was not at Castellano's funeral. The affair was marked by relative simplicity, as befitted Castellano's low-key style: twenty cars in the funeral procession, a modest amount of flowers, and several hundred attendees, all described as "mourners." For those with long memories, it certainly paled beside the standard set for such occasions, the 1928 funeral of Brooklyn mobster Frank (Yale) Uale after he was shot to death, which featured two hundred cars in the procession (thirty-eight of which were used just to carry all the flowers), thousands of mourners, and burial in a fifteen-thousand-dollar silver and nickel casket, part of an overall two-hundred-thousand-dollar cost.

Instead of attending the funeral, Gotti was busy politicking. In lengthy rounds of meetings with the other twenty-two *capos* of the Gambino Family, he carefully explained the reasons why Castellano had to be killed, adding how that change in leadership would benefit the street crews. From now on, Gotti vowed, there would be greater sharing of family wealth with the front-line troops and, unlike Castellano, the new godfather would be much more accessible. For good measure, Gotti vowed that he would cease his compulsive gambling. To his wife, Victoria, who nagged him incessantly about all the hours he devoted to these meetings and never being home, Gotti snapped, "If I don't do this, I won't be around to come home at all."

But Gotti had done his politicking well, for on Christmas Eve, he hosted a reception at the Ravenite. As he waited for the other family *capi* on the invitation list to arrive, Gotti and DeCicco strolled down Mulberry Street. "They've got to come to me," Gotti said.

And they did. As in a royal coronation, the Cadillacs, Lincolns, and Mercedeses pulled up to the Ravenite and disgorged the powers of the Gambino family, all dressed in their Sunday best. They practically fell over each other in the rush to go to Gotti and kiss him, the traditional sign of respect.

And in that symbolic rite, John Gotti became boss of the most powerful group of organized criminals in the United States.

The entire ritual was filmed surreptitiously by the ubiquitous John Gurnee and a surveillance team lurking nearby. When the kissing and fawning signs of respect finally ended, Gurnee announced, "It makes you want to vomit."

Two weeks later, Gotti showed up in Brooklyn for the reconvening of the preliminary phases of his trial. He was surprised to see a vast, sprawling media circus waiting to record his arrival; he did not realize that in the city of the Power Lunch, the Power Tie, and the Power Haircut, he was now very big news indeed. No longer was he a middle-level *capo* on trial for being a mobster; now he was The Godfather fighting for his legal life.

To a media bored with the gray personalities of godfathers like Castellano and Anthony (Fat Tony) Salerno, who dressed conservatively and looked for all the world like the owners of Italian delicatessens, Gotti became hot copy. He dressed in flashy suits (he was immediately dubbed "the dapper don" by the tabloids as a result), and instead of the time-honored Mafia media relations technique of holding hats or newspapers over faces to foil photographers, Gotti strolled jauntily across a small park on his way to court, allowing the television cameramen and photographers plenty of time to get pictures. He was always good for a one-liner or quip on his way inside, sufficient to lead the local news shows that night.

"Yeah, I'm a boss—the boss of my own family," he said to a forest of microphones that first day of his trial following his elevation to boss. There was a responding chorus of "Thank you, Mr. Gotti," as though the president of the United States had just announced some major initiative.

Inside the courtroom, even one as cavernous as the place where what had become known as "the Gotti trial" was held, things seemed a little crowded. There were seven defendants and their lawyers, the prosecution team of Giacalone and Gleeson, the jury, and a packed audience—many of the latter large men with no necks in leather jackets, who tended to mutter ominously every time Giacalone got up to say something.

Giacalone, attired the first day of the reconvened trial in what the local media approvingly noted as "a power red dress," was one of the main focuses of attention, along with Gotti. But as things developed, four other personalities in that courtroom eventually came to dominate the trial—and its outcome.

One was the most famous lawyer among the defense team, the original defense attorney for Dellacroce, now representing John Gotti: Barry Slotnick. Bearded and slightly stoop-shouldered, Slotnick often had a hangdog look that conveyed the impression of a scholarly rabbi crushed by the burden of considering Talmudic matters of life and death. A media superstar because of his highprofile defenses of leading politicians, *Mafiosi*, and the "subway gunman" Bernhard Goetz, Slotnick was razor-sharp, known for his meticulous cross-examinations that reduced prosecution cases to ribbons. His partner, Bruce Cutler, was a very different kind of lawyer. A former college football player and wrestler, Cutler was loud and flamboyant, with a reputation for hitting below the belt in a courtroom. He had replaced Bergin crew lawyer Michael Coiro on the defense team after Coiro was indicted on obstruction of justice charges in connection with Gene Gotti's drug case. Cutler's courtroom style could be divined from his opening statement, when he slammed chairs, pounded the podium, pronounced the indictment as "something to make anyone retch and vomit," tore it up, and threw the shreds into a wastepaper basket. Then, as jurors stared, open-mouthed, he fondled the microphone and grabbed his backside.

Another striking character was Richard Rehbock, Willie Boy Johnson's lawyer. A Vietnam combat veteran, Rehbock had a certain nihilism instantly recognizable to all other Vietnam veterans; he was proud to say that, unlike most defense lawyers, he had never served as a prosecutor. He was a perfect example of a type of defense lawyer known as "gunslinger," an aggressive, restless man who seemed to enjoy criminal cases mostly for the pure blood sport they offered. With his rimless glasses, Rehbock conveyed the impression of college professor; he liked to further lull opponents by referring to himself as "just a Jewish kid from Great Neck." But he was a savage infighter and a real terror to prosecutors.

Gene Gotti's lawyer, Jeffrey Hoffman, was another of the Manhattan defense attorney superstars. Although not as well known as Slotnick, he had a nearly equal reputation for courtroom brilliance. Smooth and always on top of his case, Hoffman, a former prosecutor in the Manhattan District Attorney's Office, was regarded as a skilled surgeon. Hoffman was sensitive about being called a "mob lawyer," a pejorative term meaning a lawyer whose business is exclusively Mafia clients, with the further implication that such lawyers often move beyond advocacy to something approaching complicity. Hoffman was not a mob lawyer, but his growing reputation had brought Mafia defendants to his law-office door, where they confronted a lawyer with a pronounced streak of independence. He had told one prominent mobster-defendant, "Go fuck yourself," and in some circles of the Mafia, Hoffman was known as a lawyer who "shows no respect."

Presiding over all this was Federal District Court Judge Eugene H. Nickerson, a millionaire former county executive of Nassau County on Long Island, where he still lived on a walled mini-estate. A patrician of the WASP establishment, Nickerson spoke in an upper-class accent known in New York as "Locust Valley lockjaw," but he was known as a talented, scrupulously fair judge who seemed partial to young prosecutors and lawyers just beginning their legal careers.

Like all federal judges, Nickerson would have preferred not to have drawn the assignment of a RICO case. Such cases, known among judges and lawyers as "Godzillas," had all the elements of trouble: multiple defendants, a whole squad of aggressive defense lawyers, and a legal thicket that had yet to be fully explored. Not to mention length: RICO trials tended to be measured in terms of months or years instead of the usual weeks for most trials.

In the case of the Gotti trial, there was an additional complication: a strong personal animosity between Giacalone and the defense. Hoffman, whose smoothness and negotiating skills made him a natural choice to serve as the defense team's liaison with the prosecution, discovered that Giacalone treated him contemptuously, believing that anyone affiliated with defendants she clearly hated was also a criminal. In response, defense lawyers began to refer to Giacalone openly as "the lady in red" or "the dragon lady." Very early on, there were nasty confrontations, and Cutler at one point said, in a voice loud enough to be heard at the prosecution table, "See if the tramp will give us an offer of proof." On another occasion, Giacalone waved her finger in the face of George Santangelo, one of the defense attorneys, and yelled at him, "You're lying!" Santangelo stared at her, then said, "Take your finger out of my face and stick it up your ass."

Even in the most hotly contested trials, this sort of open, personal animosity between prosecution and defense was extremely rare. Nickerson struggled to maintain the peace amidst constant squabbling, which worsened when Giacalone moved to revoke John Gotti's bail. Nickerson was not very impressed with her arguments about Gotti as Public Enemy, but was persuaded of the necessity of putting him in jail on the basis of one very stupid mistake Gotti had committed.

The mistake had been made in 1984, when a Queens refrigerator mechanic, blocked by a double-parked car, impatiently pressed the horn of his truck. A man came out of a nearby bar, smacked him in the face, then reached into his shirt pocket and took $325, representing his just-cashed paycheck. The mechanic leaped from his truck and began fighting his assailant, only to be smacked by a second man who came out of the bar. "You better get the fuck out of here," the second man said.

Police arrested both assailants, and the mechanic found himself before a grand jury, told by the Queens D.A.'s office only that he was to testify "against some punks." But the mechanic had read in that morning's paper that one of his assailants was John Gotti. Understandably, he immediately suffered a memory lapse, and claimed he could not recall the men who assaulted him, a testimony summarized in the immortal *New York Post* banner headline, I FORGOTTI!

The incident was sufficient for Nickerson to order Gotti to jail as a menace to the public order, but while Gotti was free pending an appeal of that order, a much more disturbing incident took place, this one severely rattling Gotti's customary bravado.

One morning in April 1986, Frank DeCicco opened the glove compartment of his car. At that moment, a remote-control bomb exploded, blowing DeCicco and the car to pieces. Several hours later, a visibly shaken Gotti arrived at the Bergin to find an equally rattled crew. Was this the beginning of the long-feared war against the new godfather by Castellano's diehard supporters?

Gotti demanded that the crew find the murderers of DeCicco as soon as possible. He might just as well have asked them to master the theory of relativity, for their blank looks suggested they didn't have the slightest idea. "We don't know," Angelo Ruggiero said, adding they didn't have the first clue of where to begin looking.

"I was doin' good until a coupla hours ago," Gotti said, morosely. He surrounded himself with a phalanx of bodyguards and waited for what he assumed would be an all-out mob war. But it never came; apparently, the remote-control bomb, never before seen in Mafia hits, was the work of expert assassins hired by relatives of the slain Bilotti. Their anger was directed against DeCicco, the Judas who had betrayed Castellano and Bilotti; once their notion of revenge was satisfied, that was the end of it.

A relieved Gotti, his appeals exhausted, went off to the Metropolitan Correctional Center in Manhattan in May, there to join Willie Boy Johnson while the trial was in progress. Each day of trial, Johnson and Gotti rode together in a prison van to court (where they sat near each other), a circumstance that was downright bizarre, since each man acted as though absolutely nothing had happened. Judging by appearances, with both men talking and joking like old *goombata*, it could not be guessed that John Gotti knew his *goombah* had betrayed him for almost sixteen years.

The entire question of Willie Boy as informant hovered over the trial like a wayward balloon. Rehbock, who had become Willie Boy's lawyer after he was remanded to jail, had tried to resolve that issue earlier by asking his client directly about being an informant. "I ain't no informant," Willie Boy said flatly, a position he maintained in the face of a stack of FBI reports Rehbock had subpoenaed, which indicated he had been precisely that. More to the point, he made it clear to Rehbock that he would not testify under any circumstances, period.

"All right, that's it, then," Rehbock said. "You say you weren't an informant, then you weren't. You refuse to testify, and so you will not; you cannot be forced to."

That left the problem of the charges against Johnson. Like his codefendants, he was accused of committing crimes as an "enterprise" through a "pattern" of racketeering. There were two types of evidence: tapes of FBI bugs, and direct testimony of crooks turned into prosecution witnesses. The defense lawyers were most concerned about the tapes, for unless the conversations recorded were ambiguous or virtually inaudible, there wasn't much of a defense against a defendant's own words. But the witnesses were quite something else again, and that is where Giacalone's case began to fall apart.

Her star witness was James Cardinali, the murderer with a limp whom Gotti had given a job at the Bergin. Cardinali, facing a life sentence in Brooklyn during 1983 for murder, turned state's witness, and later was enlisted by Giacalone in her case. Cardinali seemed to be a damaging witness, for he testified that John Gotti got a cut of illegal gambling operations; described a supposed admission by Gotti to him of participating in the murder of McBratney, the kidnapper of Emanuel Gambino; and provided eyewitness accounts of a number of felonies that transpired at the Bergin. For good measure, he claimed to have been taught criminal arts by Gotti personally, and to have been at Gotti's house.

Cardinali as witness most concerned Rehbock, because Cardinali testified that he had direct knowledge of Willie Boy Johnson's crimes, including an incident in which Willie Boy supervised the severe beating by Cardinali and two other hoods of a Staten Island man who infuriated Dellacroce by running a nonsanctioned gambling operation. Indeed, Cardinali really amounted to the entire case against Johnson.

Before cross-examination, Rehbock consulted the woman he sometimes called "my secret weapon," his wife, Sylvia, whom he would occasionally introduce as "the former Miss Sylvia DiPietro"—adding, jokingly, "she's *Sicilian*," as if in warning. Sylvia, whom Rehbock considered the world's leading expert on Italian mores and culture, was consulted on the credibility of Cardinali's claim to have been inside John Gotti's house. No way, she replied; John Gotti would never let a man like Cardinali inside his house.

At the same time, Rehbock was bothered by Cardinali's claim to have known Willie Boy intimately, including the distinctive finger tattoos, which Cardinali identified as "love" and "hate." There is an old lawyer's saying, *Falsis inumum omnibus* (roughly, "If you lie about one thing, you lie about everything"). On that theory, Rehbock began to demolish Cardinali's credibility, climaxing a merciless grilling with a demonstration that most impressed the jury: Willie Boy was asked to show his large hands to the jurors, who had no trouble making out the tattoos "true" and "love." A small point, but like all good lawyer tricks, an extremely impressive one; the jury would not forget that a witness who claimed intimate acquaintance with a defendant could not even get the man's distinctive tattoos straight. And as for Cardinali's claims of a close relationship with Gotti, Rehbock got him to admit that he had never appeared in the many police and FBI surveillance photographs taken of Gotti over the years.

Cardinali's ordeal at the hands of defense lawyers lasted two weeks and, to the distress of Giacalone and Gleeson, he had the bad habit of shooting himself in the foot. To persistent questions from Slotnick about his credibility, Cardinali blurted out, "Mr. Slotnick, I lie a lot." During a wild, high-decibel cross-examination by Bruce Cutler, Cardinali conceded that his criminal record included the savage pistol-whipping of a priest, a point Cutler emphasized for several Catholics on the jury. Cutler also brought out that Cardinali had a stormy relationship with Giacalone, revealing only after getting his deal that he had killed several drug dealers in Florida. (No wonder: Florida has a death penalty for murder.)

Of the half-dozen former criminals who testified against him, Gotti was clearly most exercised about Cardinali. "He was the fucking sweeper!" he hissed to the lawyers as Cardinali began testifying, and immediately scribbled a note to be handed around: "I WANT THIS GUY *MOTHER-FUCKED!!*" Like most *Mafiosi*, Gotti was much taken with flamboyance in lawyers, and much preferred the Cutler style of savage attack, leading questions, and grand gestures. (The jury did not: at one point, the jurors sent a note to Nickerson asking him to turn down Cutler's volume.)

Gotti disliked the more subtle (and quieter) methods of attack by Slotnick and the other lawyers, and when Hoffman began a low-key, surgical dismemberment of Cardinali, Gotti handed him a note, which read, "SIT DOWN OR YOU'RE DEAD." Characteristically, Hoffman rolled the note up into a small ball, and swallowed it. He then continued his attack on Cardinali, which amounted to a series of cuts with a scalpel; he did not confront Cardinali, but quietly worked him into conceding a long list of damaging admissions, including his plan to write a book whose success, obviously, would be predicated on Gotti's conviction. As Hoffman understood, although Gotti did not, the drum roll of admissions from Cardinali's own mouth shattered him as a witness in the jury's eyes.

"Hey, John, how come you guys use a piece of shit like Cardinali?" Gotti asked Gleeson during a recess in Cardinali's demolition.

"Well, John," Gleeson replied, stiffly, "as you are no doubt aware, we have to use the witnesses we can get, whatever their criminal past."

Gotti grunted. "Well, I don't want you to get the idea that all of us are like Cardinali."

Gleeson, who regarded the conversation as extraordinary—criminal defendants normally do not talk to prosecutors during trial—considered a moment before answering. "Here's what I think, John. One thing I don't want to happen is that no one doubts the main point of this indictment, which is how you are described."

Gotti just smiled and shrugged, but he was determined to make his point. He approached the press row. "Mendacity," he said to the startled reporters. "The word for today is mendacity. It's the art of being mendacious."

The lesser criminals-turned-witnesses, like Cardinali, demonstrated a tendency toward self-destruction. One of them, a punk named James Sanetore, during a cross-examination on the details of his criminal career, was asked, "Mr. Sanetore, didn't you burn a woman's breasts with cigarettes?'' Sanetore replied indignantly, ''Absolutely no. All we did was tie her on the bed and throw burning matches on her breast. That's all we did.''

Then there was the untalented hijacker-turned-dope-dealer, Salvatore Polisi, who had bargained away a stiff prison sentence for his testimony about the Bergin crew. Noticing John Gotti making the sign of a pistol with his forefinger and thumb under the defense table as he took the stand, Polisi nonetheless did his best, although he really didn't know much. He was unprepared for an attack by Slotnick from an unexpected direction: his hatred of blacks. ''I believe,'' Slotnick said in his quiet way, ''I asked you whether you had expressed some opinions about the fact that you believed that black people were the lowest form of humanity?''

''That is correct,'' Polisi replied, as Slotnick noted the look of repulsion that crossed the face of one black juror, the real focus of the question. Giacalone tried to salvage what was left of Polisi on recross-examination, but she only made things worse.

''Mr. Polisi,'' she asked, ''are you proud of the way you played your life in the past twenty years?''

''No,'' he answered to an obviously rehearsed question. ''I think it's completely un-American, and I'm ashamed of the way I've lived my life.'' Gotti and the other defendants groaned loudly.

Cutler went into one of his performances, shouting at Polisi, ''Tell us how you acquired this new religion! Tell us so we can free the jails of people like you!''

''Attaway, Brucie, *Brucify* him!'' the defendants would congratulate Cutler after such routines, but Nickerson was less pleased. He and Cutler found themselves in a running battle over Cutler's habit of hitting below the belt or asking improper questions, then hastily apologizing when Nickerson admonished him. ''I am astonished,'' the gentlemanly Nickerson said at one point, ''with my moderation in dealing with you in this case, sir.''

But Cutler was a hero to the one man whose vote counted most on the defense side, John Gotti. They drew closer during the trial, and a gradual, but astonishing transformation came over Bruce Cutler: he began to imitate John Gotti. The evolution amused some of the defense attorneys who knew Cutler well, including Jeffrey Hoffman, who took one look at what he called a "*capo* outfit" Cutler wore one morning—blue suit, blue socks, blue shirt—and asked, "What is this, are we having a sitdown at the Ravenite this morning?"

Cutler's worst tormentor was his friend, the irrepressible Richard Rehbock, who occasionally would rush toward him, drop to one knee, and elaborately kiss his hand, murmuring, "Ah, *Don* Brucino." On other occasions, when he thought Cutler was too wrapped up in his own oratory, he would interrupt to hand him a note. Assuming it was some important legal point, Cutler would stop, open the note and find that it contained only two words: FUCK YOU.

As Cutler and Gotti became close friends—the lawyer later described him as "my role model"—other lawyers were annoyed to discover that Gotti had become chief counsel of the defense team, and Cutler would make no move without Gotti's direct approval. During one defense strategy session, Hoffman realized nothing was happening because Gotti was missing. Hoffman sought to proceed, but Cutler said, "No, let's wait for Johnny Boy."

"*Johnny Boy?*" Hoffman asked, incredulous that Cutler was now using Gotti's Mafia nickname. "Fuck this crap." He decided to have some fun at Cutler's expense.

Spotting Gotti holding court with some cronies and reporters in the rear of the courtroom, Hoffman strode up to him and said loudly, "Listen, John, I told you to get your ass over there. And when I tell you to move, you better move!"

The color drained from Cutler's face, but Gotti, instantly getting the joke, adopted a sheepish look. "Okay, Jeffie boy. I'll do whatever you say. Sorry."

Cutler looked stricken. "Jesus Christ, Jeff," he begged, "please don't ever do that again."

Such antics helped relieve the tension at the defendants' table as the case dragged on for weeks, then months. Although the defense was confident they had irretrievably damaged the prosecution witnesses, there was still deep concern over the impact of the tapes on the jury. The only real optimist was Rehbock, whose client, Willie Boy Johnson, was worried sick over the prospect of a lengthy prison sentence. "I can't do no heavy time," Johnson fretted, but Rehbock told him, "You are not going to do *any* time, Willie, because there is no case here. I'm telling you straight out: there is no case here."

Willie Boy did not seem entirely convinced, and he settled into an even deeper gloom when in January 1987, with the case seemingly winding down, Hoffman brought disturbing news. He had called his Manhattan office during a recess and was told that the judge in the Commission case in the Southern District had just sentenced each of the godfathers convicted in the case to one hundred years in prison. "A century!" Hoffman exclaimed.

The news put the entire defense team into a state approaching depression. But Gotti remained supremely confident. He walked over to the court railing, and addressing the entire press corps, announced, "We're walkin' *out* of here!" He returned to the defense table to nibble on the vast stores of white chocolate kept in the drawers to slake the defendants' apparently unlimited appetites. (Lawyers were astonished at how those same appetites were capable of also devouring gargantuan Italian lunches; these men seemed never to stop eating.)

There were two last acts in the drama as it headed toward final curtain. One was a series of police witnesses, among them Detective Michael (The Falcon) Falciano, whose appearance was eagerly anticipated by Gotti and the other defendants. In a mood of predominant pessimism at the defense table, a witness with Falciano's noted ability as a standup comic was to be welcomed, no matter what he said.

Falciano did not disappoint. As part of his testimony about the abortive Operation Wedge in Queens seven years earlier, The Falcon was asked to describe Angelo Ruggiero. "Oh, heavy," he said. "Bullface. You know, he wasn't a handsome guy. How would I describe him? Animal or human? He looked like a fire pump." Gotti and the other defendants rocked with laughter. Rehbock, cross-examining Falciano about his testimony concerning notes he occasionally scribbled on the backs of his hands during surveillances, could not resist the question, "And do you still have those notes, Detective Falciano?"

"No," Falciano replied in perfect deadpan. "I bathe a lot; I have an Irish wife."

The defendants, especially John Gotti, were less amused by the appearance of another police witness, Detective John Gurnee. "Uh-oh," Rehbock murmured as Gurnee stalked into the courtroom. "Dick Tracy." The name of the comic-strip character signified a defense lawyer's term for that most dreaded of all witnesses, an impressive-looking police or FBI witness whose cool appearance and crisp testimony tend to impress juries.

Gurnee came with his videotapes from the 1979 surveillance operation at the Ravenite Social Club. As he played them for the jury, identifying the various mobsters as they moved across the large television screen ("That's Frank LoCasio, picking his nose"), Gurnee became aware of John Gotti staring fixedly at him. Gurnee stared right back, and in that exchange of glares was signified a curious mutual respect. Part of it stemmed from an incident two years before, when Gurnee, strolling on the street near the Ravenite, just barely managed to evade an attempt to injure him seriously: a local punk ran a car in high-speed reverse at him. The punk roared off in a squeal of tires, but Gurnee was determined that this sort of attempt to intimidate police would have to be nipped in the bud. He stormed into the Ravenite, where he encountered John Gotti sitting at a table.

"I want the name of that punk!" Gurnee yelled, as, with one swift movement, he grabbed Gotti by the throat and lifted him out of his chair. There was a hushed silence inside the club as a half-dozen men simply stood quietly, waiting for Gotti to tell them what to do (possibly, it suddenly occurred to Gurnee, an order to kill the detective on the spot).

But Gotti was eager to defuse the situation. He smiled, and as Gurnee's grip relaxed, sought to soothe the infuriated detective. "Hey, no problem, John," Gotti said, adding that the offending driver would be "taken care of." Later, Gotti passed the word that although Gurnee was a pain in the ass intent on putting the *goombata* in jail, he was an honest cop

who played the game straight, and therefore was always to
be treated "with respect."

Bruce Cutler did not share Gotti's respect for Gurnee. Cutler loathed Gurnee—the feeling was mutual—for a number
of reasons, chiefly the discovery that among the records subpoenaed by defense were surveillance reports by Gurnee.
Several pointedly mentioned Cutler's regular visits to the
club, and Cutler was most exercised about Gurnee reporting
that he had "huddled" at the Ravenite with known mobsters,
and "sped off" in a chauffeur-driven car with some of them.

Intent on berating Gurnee for reports he believed to be
deliberately provocative, Cutler committed a grave tactical
error. The general defense strategy in such situations would
be to leave a witness like Gurnee largely unexamined; his
testimony was not especially damaging to the defendants, and
continued explorations of what had been going on at the
Ravenite would only further arouse jurors' curiosity about
why John Gotti would spend time at a social club far from
his own home. But Cutler plowed ahead, laughably claiming
that the Ravenite was nothing more than a club for innocent,
old Italian men to gather and socialize. Gotti went there only
to socialize, he claimed.

Gleeson spotted the mistake immediately, and with Cutler
having opened the door, he was then able to introduce several
interesting facts, especially the information that virtually all
of the club's official "members" had lengthy criminal
records. In other words, clearly the Ravenite wasn't a social
club at all, it was a clubhouse for gangsters—and John Gotti
and his *goombata* didn't go there merely to socialize.

What impact all this had on the jury is impossible to say,
but the jurors' attention certainly was fixated during the next
and last act in this legal drama, one that had taken nearly
two years, from indictment to final trial. And this last act
was a truly bizarre one: the appearance of defense witness
Matthew Traynor.

The former Ozone Park teenage gang member and later
bank robber originally was to be a prosecution witness, but
later balked after a series of confrontations with Giacalone.
Accurately described by Giacalone as "some strange uncle

you can't keep in the closet,'' Traynor demonstrated a criminal mind of odd proportions.

Seeking to demonstrate that Giacalone's overzealousness was in fact the real impetus for the case, the defense presented Traynor as a typical example of the lengths to which she was willing to go to get John Gotti.

In testimony that was patently perjurious from the first sentence, Traynor claimed that he had been given narcotics, promised virtual forgiveness of all his crimes, and offered sexual release if he agreed to testify falsely about John Gotti. As a final, and repulsive, flourish, Traynor claimed that Giacalone had given him a pair of her panties and told him that would be his sole sexual release until he testified falsely.

Gleeson was on him like an enraged wildcat, and to everyone's surprise, he appeared to have lost control of himself. Actually yelling, the normally cool Gleeson dragged Traynor sentence by sentence through FBI reports of his conversations with the Bureau, all of which flatly contradicted his present testimony. Traynor explained it all away by saying he either (1) was on drugs, or (2) was lying to reduce his sentence on bank robbery charges.

Barely able to control her anger, Giacalone asked that Nickerson strike Traynor's entire testimony. When he refused, Giacalone announced a rebuttal case—of seventeen witnesses.

"Seventeen?" a distressed Nickerson asked.

The resulting testimony was a bad tactical mistake by Giacalone, for it simply raised a natural question in the jurors' minds: if Traynor was such a dirtbag, why had Giacalone considered using him as a witness in the first place?

And, at last, it was finally over. On March 6, 1987, the case went to the jury. While the lawyers fretted and endlessly debated and redebated the wisdom of various moves, Gotti sat unconcernedly in a small conference room set aside for the defense, watching soap operas on television. To skeptical Bergin crew members and the men in leather jackets who showed up at trial every day to line up and kiss Gotti as he entered and exited the courtroom, he insisted that all defendants would be acquitted on all counts.

After a week of deliberations, the jury returned with a

verdict. To the astonishment of the defense lawyers, Gotti turned out to be absolutely right: the jury acquitted all defendants on all counts. It was Friday the thirteenth.

Laura Brevetti, one of Edward McDonald's Strike Force prosecutors, had been observing the trial. As the verdict was read, she went to a phone and called him. "They beat the whole case," she said, simply.

"Okay, thanks," McDonald said. From his office window, he could see Gotti and his crew, surrounded by television cameras and reporters, whooping it up as they walked across the park as free men. He watched for a while, then retrieved a copy of his 1981 memorandum warning that the likelihood of success in Giacalone's case was minimal. He read it again, and threw it on the floor.

Outside, a jubilant Gotti told his crew, "I told you guys, we're the toughest fucking crew in the whole fucking world. Nobody can touch us now!"

9

The Godfather

I try to do the right thing with everybody. I wind up with nothing. Everyone else winds up with the buttercup.

—JOHN GOTTI

JUST BEFORE NIGHTFALL, it began. Like the sound of approaching battle, there were the first sounds of isolated explosions, then, as darkness arrived, it had grown to a din.

Not a bad time for shooting somebody, given all that noise, and the thought seemed to have occurred to John Gotti. A few minutes before midnight, when he emerged from the front door of the Bergin Hunt and Fish Club like some Florentine prince to wave majestically to the crowd, there were eight bodyguards around him. That praetorian guard was somewhat unusual, for in a criminal career of thirty years, Gotti seldom felt the need for such staples of movie melodrama (and what some Mafia bosses regarded as an important status symbol), the collection of grim, silent hoods who oversaw the safety of the boss.

But things were different now. John Gotti was a godfather, a man of status, power, importance, and respect. In Gotti's view, a godfather required certain symbols of authority to let everyone know that he was a godfather: having a group of bodyguards was one sign, and the new three-thousand-dollar diamond pinky ring he now wore was another.

The ring glinted in the light as he waved to the crowd of more than two thousand people gathered along a six-block stretch of 101st Avenue to celebrate the two hundred eleventh birthday of the United States of America on the hot night of July 4, 1987. They cheered, as though Gotti was some kind of hometown hero, newly returned from a mission into space, or fresh from hitting that ninth-inning home run to win the World Series for the Mets. If the people of Ozone Park were cheering his accession to power in the Mafia and his victory in a federal racketeering case a few months before, then there was cause to wonder about the civic education of citizens who thought it worthwhile to cheer a murderer, heroin trafficker, and extortionist.

More charitable minds, however, might conclude that the cheering was not for who John Gotti was, but his generosity. After all, for more than ten years, in what had become a local tradition, he had underwritten the cost of Ozone Park's annual celebration of the nation's birthday. No one knew how much "Johnny Boy"—as he was almost invariably called in the community cowering in the main flight paths of Kennedy Airport—shelled out for the bash, but there were whispers around the neighborhood that it amounted to quite a bundle. Obviously, there were heavy expenses, including the crews of muscular men who wrestled big garbage dumpsters into the middle of the street to block it off to traffic, the carnival operators who set up rides and games, and the platoons of young boys who, for ten-dollar bills pressed into their hands, cleaned up the area afterwards, so thoroughly that not even a cigarette butt marred a spotless urban vista. And, of course, there were the fireworks that Gotti somehow had obtained, the finest pyrotechnics available: splitting comets, exploding torpedos, twinkling stars, Roman candles, weeping willows, and supersize cherry bombs. It required hours for this spectacular collection to be shot off or exploded.

As every attendee of this annual celebration knew, it was all quite illegal. No permit had been obtained to block off the main thoroughfare of 101st Avenue, there was no license to shoot off those fireworks, and the fire department had no official notice that, contrary to city and state law, somebody would be shooting off rockets and bombs to fall among one of the most crowded concentrations of wood-frame homes in the country. Local police seemed to hold an amazingly benign attitude toward such disregard for the law; they demonstrated

equal disinterest in the practice of the Bergin crew to se
aside personal parking spaces along 101st Avenue, where
parking space for other citizens was at a premium. (Shamed
by public disclosures of their tolerance, the police the previous year tried to close down Gotti's fireworks—only to
encounter a virtual urban riot, when residents of Ozone Park
seized the fireworks and threw them into a fire built in the
middle of the street. However, the police did manage to prevent Peter Gotti from enlivening things by seizing from him
two sticks of dynamite he sought to throw into the exploding
conflagration.)

Gotti's regal deportment at such occasions was very much
a reflection of his general behavior as Mafia boss. In fact,
his approach represented a very sharp break with tradition.
Gotti was a public figure, a man who disdained the prevailing
Mafia wisdom about the necessity of godfathers' maintaining
virtually invisible profiles. He was as publicly visible as a
movie star; whether strolling into the city's finest restaurants
(with what headwaiters carefully described as a "party of
six," all of whom demanded to be seated with their backs
to a wall), occasionally accompanying his elder son, John
Jr., to the trendiest nightclubs, or generally just being *seen,*
Gotti seemed to revel in his status as *Pontifex Maximus.* In
the city that worships power, the New York City tabloids
chronicled every move and public utterance of the man they
called "the Dapper Don." He was the subject of cover stories
in *Time, People,* and the *New York Times Magazine,* a tribute
to the phenomenon of national media, whose nerve centers
are in Manhattan, transforming New York infamies into matters of national consequence. Gotti was also chronicled in
that ultimate tribute to fame in America, the "Doonesbury"
comic strip.

Not everyone was impressed with this perverse American
success story, however. The waiters at Gotti's favorite restaurant, a generic Neapolitan dump in Queens, still greeted him
and other patrons at the door with the challenging question.
"Hey, you hungry, or what?" Old-time *goombata* of Gotti'.
from the Bergin crew and elsewhere chuckled at the newspaper stories about the man they still called "nigger" behind
his back, including the one noting that Gotti berated a

reporter for writing that one of the godfather's suits cost a thousand dollars: "That suit cost eighteen hundred dollars! Get it straight!" (The joke, of course, was that no one in the Bergin could recall the last time that Gotti actually *bought* a suit: he was still building a wardrobe by the expedient of selecting the finer items from hijacked shipments.)

One class of people, particularly, did not find this flashiness so amusing. The old-line godfathers and the more senior members of the Mafia establishment regarded Gotti as a loose cannon. Anthony (Tony Ducks) Corallo, boss of the Lucchese Family, considered Gotti's high visibility a guarantee of unwanted attention on the Mafia. In addition, he continually criticized Gotti as "too young" for such lofty rank, and further derided him as a "punk." Corallo was not alone in that opinion: Anthony (Fat Tony) Salerno, boss of the Genovese Family—the second most powerful Mafia organization after the Gambino Family—also thought Gotti was a punk, and senior *dons* around the country, such as Nicodemo Scarfo of Philadelphia and Raymond Patriarca of New England, worried that Gotti's flashiness would ignite some kind of official crackdown.

But what the old godfathers did not understand was that Gotti was a hero of the new generation of *Mafiosi* just then beginning to move into middle-management positions. For the most part, they represented something that the Mafia had never seen before, mob yuppies unhappy with the old ways.

'We're in the fucking wagon-wheel business," many of them would complain about an organization that had one foot in the modern corporate world, and another in the time long since past. They were tired of the elaborate hypocrisy the elders of that world represented: family men who claimed to despise anything having to do with narcotics, yet maintained elaborate facades behind which to sell tons of heroin; men of the old school of gentlemanly behavior who strictly prohibited off-color language around women, yet who in their private conversations managed to use "fuck" as every fourth word of a sentence; Runyonesque characters who loved to sit around by the hour and tell funny stories about life in the Mafia, and at the same time were capable of inhuman savagery, beating people they hardly knew to death with hammers and baseball bats, or cutting them into pieces, or torturing them brutally for hours on end.

The new generation of *Mafiosi* were scornful of what they most often called "all this stupid *Cosa Nostra* crap," the elaborate rituals of friendship and respect the older generation demanded, including the Old World habit of kissing each other. The new generation was devoted exclusively to materialism. They could be seen outside the social clubs, toothpicks in their mouths, hands in the pockets of their hand-tailored suits, occasionally touching up their hundred-dollar Power Haircuts. While the older generation worried about whether their demonstration of respect to a fellow godfather at that wedding or funeral had just the right touch so as not to offend delicate sensibilities, the new generation was devouring the financial pages, and discussing the merits of offshore bank accounts and Caribbean tax havens.

The yuppie generation snickered at some of the obsessions with elaborate respect and noblesse oblige among the older generation: godfather Tony Corallo, walking into a restaurant with a camel's-hair coat draped over his shoulders, casually throwing the coat away, confident that one of his minions was guaranteed to catch the coat before it hit the floor; or Aniello Migliore, a multimillionaire *capo* of Corallo's with a lucrative loan shark racket, who bought a huge, two-million-dollar mansion on Long Island—on whose roof he built a complex of coops for the pigeons he brought from his old Queens neighborhood.

The new generation paid careful attention to the latest fashion trends explained each month in *Gentleman's Quarterly,* and saw no point in the low-key lifestyle of their elders, some of whom persisted in wearing what in Italian neighborhoods were known as "Don Cheech clothes": baggy pants belted somewhere around the chest, baggy off-the-rack jacket, shirt of ancient vintage, and a tie of uncertain ancestry—the full effect topped by an old fedora which appeared to have been broken in first by a cement mixer. And the new generation saw no sense in the elaborate efforts to hide money and adopt a low profile: money was to be spent as conspicuously as possible, on clothes and the flashiest cars. (A fair number of the new generation liked to drive that ultimate yuppie-mobile, the BMW.)

Just prior to his elevation as head of the Gambino Family, Gotti occasionally remarked that he was "their last hope," referring to the new generation of yuppie mobsters. He was quite right, for John Gotti was a man who best demonstrated their wish for a Mafia devoted exclusively to the business of organized crime. While the older *dons* clucked about Gotti's glittering public persona, the new generation approved of a man who seemed to have little interest in the obsession over old feuds and rituals, who seemed to have no qualms about being known as a mobster chieftain, who seemed to have no intention of adopting a low profile, and who seemed concerned exclusively with business.

Among other things, Gotti's age—forty-six years old when he became family boss—promised a change in the way that the Gambino Family, at least, would be doing business. And that is exactly what happened: within three weeks of Castellano's murder, Gotti took on the family's old guard.

His first, and most prominent, enemy was the family's longtime *consigliere,* Joe N. Gallo, at age seventy-seven considered among the Mafia's senior statesmen. Gallo disliked Gotti intensely, a man he regarded as a street hood who had advanced too fast, and had committed the cardinal sin of "raising his hands" to a boss. For his part, Gotti called Gallo an "asshole weak cocksucker," and was determined to remove this symbol of the old ways.

The climactic confrontation came during a meeting of Gambino *capi* in early January of 1986, when Gallo hoped to rally them behind him in an attempt to brake the rapid ascent of the ambitious Gotti. Gallo's strategy, like a new president coming into the White House, was to ask all the *capi* to resign: those meeting with his favor would be reappointed. The move was designed to create an element of uncertainty: if Gallo had that sort of power, would it be wise to anger him by indicating any support for Gotti?

"I'm right," Gallo said in a short speech to the assembled *Mafiosi*. "I can break [demote] the captains, I can break the underboss anytime I want."

But Gotti was ready for that move. "Joe, don't flatter

yourself," he said, aiming directly for Gallo's weakest point, his reputation as a weak-willed accommodator. "You ain't no Paulie [Castellano]."

"What are you talking about?" Gallo asked.

"I'll getcha voted in or voted out," Gotti said. "Joe, you think you're dealing with a fool. I break them twenty-three captains. I put in ten captains that I promote tomorrow . . . they vote you down. I break them, put my original captains back and you ain't no *consigliere*."

There were knowing smiles all over the room as Gallo was reduced to speechlessness; he had been neatly outmaneuvered by a man he made the mistake of underestimating. Gallo paid the penalty for his political error: in short order, he was removed from his prestigious post and replaced by Salvatore (Sammy the Bull) Gravano, a young (forty-one) Staten Island hood very much in Gotti's own image. This was a politically shrewd choice, for it achieved two political objectives at once. Gravano, one of the hit team that assassinated Castellano, was being rewarded for his role in the murder, and at the same time, it was a signal to the younger generation that men of Gravano's age would be moved into powerful family positions. (Normally, the *consigliere* post is given to a senior member of the family, but younger family members often complained they could not communicate with a man often old enough to be their grandfather, a prisoner of the old ways who did not understand the problems of younger mobsters.)

Gotti also demonstrated a sure political touch in deciding who would be the new underboss of the family to replace Dellacroce. Originally, Gotti named Frank DeCicco to the post. After DeCicco himself was murdered, Gotti then named a veteran Gambino *capo*, Joseph (Joe Piney) Armone. Another shrewd choice, for Armone, sixty-six years old, was regarded as solid throughout the Gambino organization, and had a strong reputation as an earner.

But there was a more subtle political signal Gotti was sending. Armone had been among those convicted in the famous "French Connection" case fifteen years before, and was widely suspected of continuing heroin deals. Clearly, a family boss who appointed a notorious heroin trafficker had no compunction about his crews' becoming directly involved in narcotics. If anyone failed to get the point, Gotti made it even clearer when he decided to bestow formal "made" status on two Gambino Family associates: Eddie Lino and Peter (Little Pete) Tambone, whose involvement in narcotics had touched off Gotti's serious political crisis with Castellano.

These moves were part of a general political realignment of the family, and when it was finished, Gotti created a small palace guard: Gravano as *consigliere*, Armone as underboss, and four key, more-equal-than-other *capi:* Gene Gotti; Angelo Ruggiero, among his closest *goombata;* Joseph (Joe Butch) Corrao, a Little Italy *Mafioso* who would keep the loyalty of the Ravenite crowd for Gotti; and James (Jimmy Brown) Failla, the betrayer of Castellano, who was expected to keep Castellano's old supporters in line.

Gotti's biggest problem for the moment was training Angelo Ruggiero in the arts of becoming a *capo*. This was no easy task, for in addition to an inability to keep quiet for any portion of his waking hours, Ruggiero was especially thickheaded; trying to teach him something was akin to training an especially dimwitted animal not to urinate on the rug. "You got to learn to keep your motherfuckin' mouth shut!" Gotti shouted at him on several occasions, hoping it would stick. "You was a soldier three days ago; you're a captain now. Keep quiet; they know you there . . . you gotta forget them liberties you take. Take 'em when we're alone."

Gotti was especially angered when, shortly after his appointment, Ruggiero brought him some minor problem involving a family loan shark. "I don't deal with this anymore," Gotti snapped, trying to teach Ruggiero that a family boss was not to become so directly involved in minor administrative matters: that's what a boss had *capi* for. And as far as that was concerned, Gotti made it clear that Ruggiero himself had a lot to learn about how to conduct himself as a *capo:* "You got to make your men know their fuckin' place, How many times I gotta tell you that, Angelo?"

Given the requirements of plausible deniability for Mafia bosses, Gotti had to impose some distance between himself and the lower ranks, including some of his *goombata*. "I can't socialize with these guys," he said regretfully to a friend. "I'm a boss, you know what I mean? I gotta isolate myself a little bit."

His isolation was not of a type that made Paul Castellano such a remote figure, for Gotti continued to appear almost every day at the Bergin, and, more infrequently, at the Ravenite. His presence now tended to be somewhat more regal than in the past. He traded in the Lincoln given to him by Castellano and Dellacroce, and began moving about in a black Mercedes sedan with every possible option, including tiny wipers for the headlights. The sixty-thousand-dollar car was provided, officially, by Gotti's employer, the Arc Plumbing and Heating Corp., which apparently wished to reward its star salesman. (And no wonder: for reasons which later intrigued investigators, Arc managed to win over twenty million dollars in city contracts coincidental with Gotti's service as salesman. Those contracts included, to the mortification of the New York City Police Department, work on several police precincts. Arc also won the contract for the toilets at Shea Stadium in Queens, the revelation of which led an anonymous sports fan to erect the following sign in some of the men's toilets at the stadium: REMEMBER: THIS PISS COMES TO YOU COURTESY OF JOHN GOTTI.)

Gotti never drove the Mercedes himself—he had three different chauffeurs for that task—because he had learned the hard way he should not be behind the wheel of any vehicle. A maniacal driver, he had been stopped four times in two years, from 1984 to 1986, on speeding and drunken driving charges, and finally took some sage advice from fellow *capi:* given the fact that police were now lying in wait for him, and would happily write a ticket for even the tiniest violation, it would be smart to leave the driving to somebody else. But he still liked to get behind the wheel of the Cigarette speedboat he kept berthed in Sheepshead Bay. Other boaters learned to be someplace else when Gotti wanted to indulge in water sports, for he drove the boat like a crazy man, with a penchant for attempting to drive through anybody in his way.

The modest home in Howard Beach and the speedboat did not bespeak the lifestyle of a Mafia boss, but Gotti began to accumulate a few other, less visible, signs of upward mobility. One was a four-hundred-thousand-dollar vacation home in the Pennsylvania Poconos; another was a condominium in Montauk, on the far tip of Long Island's southern fork. (None of these, for obvious reasons, was in Gotti's own name: his home was officially owned by his wife, the Pennsylvania house belonged to his son, and the Montauk condominium belonged to other family members.)

Gotti spent very little time at either of his vacation retreats, for above all else, he was a workaholic. Police and FBI surveillance teams for years marveled at his work schedule, often running to fourteen hours a day and more; after he became family boss, he seemed to work even longer hours. Most of that time was spent in the sometimes-intricate political maneuvers that accompanied his consolidation of power.

One important such maneuver centered on the ambiguous figure of Thomas Gambino, eldest son of the late Carlo Gambino. Although Gambino was listed in the FBI files as a *capo* in the family that bore his father's name, he had no arrest record. Officially, Gambino was a Garment Center businessman, operating a trucking firm, and serving as an officer of the Greater Blouse and Undergarment Association, which represented five hundred manufacturers that employed over twenty thousand people. The association, which negotiated industrywide collective bargaining agreements with the International Ladies Garment Workers Union, was considered by both the FBI and the New York City Police Department's organized crime experts as mob-dominated. Gambino had always denied having any connection to organized crime, but John Gotti, in a conversation with one of his mob friends, operated on the assumption that Carlo Gambino's son was in fact a fellow mobster.

"I'm gonna suggest to Tommy [Gambino]," Gotti said, "we're gonna beef up his *regime* [crew] . . . but we're not giving him no fuckin' hotheads or any of those scumbags; we can't fuck up his mind with these bullshit street sitdowns . . . he's gonna give us 100 percent, you know what I'm saying."

Gotti's concern for Gambino was related to the political maneuvering aimed at Gotti that took place shortly before Castellano's death. Gotti had heard reports that Castellano intended to name Gambino as his chosen successor, and fretted even after Castellano's death that Gambino would attempt to make some kind of move. But Gambino told Gotti he had no such ambition, and when he appeared with Gotti at the funeral of Frank DeCicco, the political signal was very clear: Gotti and Gambino had made some kind of arrangement. At the same time, Gotti determined that Carlo Gambino's three other sons would not place any obstacles in his way. Two of them were businessmen, one running a poultry-distribution firm, the other a Staten Island cement-mix outfit. As for the third Gambino son, Joseph, he was a subject of much talk in the Mafia, which was everlastingly bemused by the fact that his life centered on one passion: pastry cooking. A man who had devoted his adult life to mastering this difficult art, Joseph Gambino worked as a pastry chef and taught classes in his particular specialty—rugelach—at a fancy cooking school.

Once Gotti had set his political foundations firmly in place, he moved aggressively to expand and reorganize family operations, which had begun to atrophy in the last year of Castellano's reign, when the then-godfather was preoccupied by his legal troubles. Gotti's attention was focused southward, toward New Jersey, a traditionally racketeer-ridden state where there were lucrative Mafia operations in the waterfront, transportation, and garbage disposal industries. However lucrative, those operations were loaded with delicate political considerations, since not only were two other families of the New York Mafia—Lucchese and Genovese—involved, but also the Philadelphia Mafia organization.

Even more delicate political problems were connected with the Mafia's greatest prize in New Jersey, Atlantic City. The gambling mecca had been the focus of intense Mafia interest from the first moment of its creation in 1977. But unlike Las Vegas, where the Mafia had concentrated on gaining footholds in the gambling casinos and skimming the profits, in Atlantic City the mobsters faced elaborate machinery designed to thwart any mob influence in the casino's management. The Mafia then switched direction, gaining control over corrupt unions involved in the casino industry, and organizing large loansharking, narcotics, and prostitution rings that amounted to a multimillion-dollar money machine.

The Philadelphia Mafia had overall control of these rackets, but worked out elaborate share agreements with the New York Mafia, chiefly the Gambino Family. The Philadelphia organization's interests were overseen by its leader, Nicodemo (Little Nicky) Scarfo, who established a close working partnership with Paul Castellano. However, the murder of Castellano and the turmoil within the Philadelphia organization—a dozen murders marked an ongoing war over division of spoils from narcotics and Atlantic City rackets—presented Gotti with a major diplomatic problem. He would have to renegotiate the Gambino Family's arrangement in Atlantic City.

The negotiation promised to be difficult, for not only had Gotti contrived to murder his own boss—a move usually regarded with uneasiness by other Mafia leaders—he was generally considered throughout the rest of the Mafia's upper establishment as too young and too flashy for such high rank as family boss. And among the Mafia senior leaders who shared that uneasiness was Nicodemo Scarfo.

In January 1986, a month after Castellano's murder, Gotti convened a secret summit meeting in New York. With elaborate efforts to evade the presumed police and FBI surveillance teams, Scarfo slipped out of Philadelphia and made his way to a nondescript house on a dead-end street in Staten Island. Accompanied by his underboss, Philip Leonetti, Scarfo met Gotti—who was flanked by Frank DeCicco and Angelo Ruggiero—in the home's dining room. Scarfo had come prepared to be unimpressed by Gotti, but after thirty minutes of conversation, concluded that he might have underestimated the Gambino Family's new boss. Gotti was sharp, very quick-minded, and appeared to have solid command of various items on the summit's agenda—notably among them, how both sides would carve up Atlantic City into respective spheres of influence.

Apparently aware that the question of Castellano's murder was on Scarfo's mind, Gotti launched into a lengthy analysis of that event. He took full credit for arranging the murder, then startled Scarfo by claiming, "I got full Commission approval.'' (A slight untruth, for in fact other Commission members had never given formal approval, but a form of tacit consent.) Gotti went on to explain the economic and political reasons for his decision to get rid of Castellano, and announced, ''I'm fully in charge.'' That out of the way, Gotti and Scarfo settled down to a discussion of Atlantic City and related matters.

Scarfo came away from the meeting deeply impressed, although Leonetti confessed some nervousness about Gotti's naked ambitions. It was a feeling heightened during three subsequent summit meetings in New York during the next six months between the Scarfo and Gambino organizations to hammer out the final details of their cooperative arrangements in Atlantic City. But neither Scarfo nor Leonetti was able to profit from the new arrangement: a year after the summit meetings, both men were swept up in a furious FBI offensive against the Philadelphia organization. Scarfo was hit with a fifty-five-year prison sentence for racketeering (plus a life sentence in state court for murder), and Leonetti was sentenced to forty-five years in prison for racketeering and narcotics dealing. Gotti immediately moved to take control of the entire Atlantic City rackets.

Meanwhile, Gotti was busy further south, in Florida, site of the Gambinos' Fort Lauderdale subsidiary, established years before by Carlo Gambino and later given to Aniello Dellacroce. Gotti determined that the subsidiary was not earning sufficiently high profits from its specialties, loansharking and illegal gambling. Part of the reason for the operation's relatively low performance stemmed from the low energy level of the man in charge, a seventy-year-old *capo* named David (Fat Dave) Iacovetti, who was replaced by one of the younger mobsters Gotti was advancing to *capo* positions, Natale (Chris) Richichi. In turn, Richichi was to be overseen by Joe Armone, Gotti's new underboss (and reputed within the Gambino Family to be a man who knew how to make operations earn). Iacovetti was kept on as subordinate to Richichi.

The Florida matter was solved easily enough, but Gotti faced a number of difficult problems closer to home in New

York, ones that required more drastic solutions. One of them went under the name of Robert DiBernardo.

Known as "Dee-Bee" in the Gambino Family, DiBernardo was its presiding genius over the pornography racket. He had made the family millions in the trade and, at one point, controlled a network of Times Square bookstores that sold pornographic material at immense markup. That part of his life was a deep secret hidden from his suburban neighbors on Long Island: they knew only that this "real estate investor" who worked in Manhattan could afford a sprawling ranch home and a white Mercedes, seemed devoted to his family, and was a friendly man who spent some of his spare hours serving as a Little League coach.

The irony of this typical suburban father serving in any capacity whatsoever with anything connected to children was perverse, for DiBernardo was the biggest child pornographer in the entire United States. He had sought to control that immensely lucrative trade for the Gambino Family.

But DiBernardo was also to play an unwitting role in the course of American history. In 1984, when Geraldine Ferraro was the vice presidential candidate on the Democratic ticket, news reports revealed that Congresswoman Ferraro's husband, businessman John Zaccaro, was manager of a Manhattan building in which a DiBernardo company leased space for pornography operations. Zaccaro denied knowing DiBernardo, and said he had attempted to terminate the lease. The media furor damaged Ferraro's campaign.

A year later, DiBernardo was in deep trouble: an FBI sting operation directed against the pornography trade, code-named MIPORN, ensnared him. Convicted, he stayed out of jail pending a long series of appeals, but when those finally ran out, he faced a five-year prison sentence. Moreover, still another federal investigation began to focus on his role in the child pornography racket.

Despite his troubles, DiBernardo was known within the Gambino organization as a ferocious money-earner, and he was entrusted with investing the organization's rich cut from the concrete industry bid-rigging scheme. That reputation for making money grow on trees led Gotti to promote him to *capo* shortly after taking over the family, but almost at once, he realized his mistake. The problem was that DiBernardo actually led a triple life, the third as a secret real estate magnate: he was skimming a good portion of the payoff money entrusted to his care, and building his own personal real estate portfolio, which by 1986 amounted to over four million dollars. Much worse, there were rumbles that DiBernardo had tried to deal his way out of his imminent prison sentence by attempting to become an FBI informant. And to top it all off, he was also reputed to be attempting to forge some kind of secret partnership with the Genovese Family's New Jersey division.

In sum, enough malfeasances for a death sentence. In June 1986, DiBernardo and his white Mercedes disappeared. Men of the Westies, the eager gang of killers from Manhattan's West Side, carried out the murder after their leader, James Coonan, huddled with Gotti and told him the Westies could use all the murder contracts they could get. Given his new position, Gotti no longer handled the actual specifics of the contract killings, a job now assigned to Angelo Ruggiero. But Ruggiero, who often let his emotions (and his mouth) run away with him, occasionally would demonstrate a less than firm grasp of the arcane art of contract murder. He successfully arranged for the disappearance of DiBernardo, but his next contract was a mess.

The intended victim in that case was Anthony (Gas Pipe) Casso, a Lucchese Family soldier and heroin trafficker, who openly called Ruggiero an "idiot." Insulted, Ruggiero decided to have him killed, a task entrusted to Michael (Mickey Boy) Paradiso, one of John Gotti's oldest *goombata*, who had drifted from gambling to narcotics trafficking. Paradiso, in turn, assigned the actual task of killing to three hoods, including a Staten Island thug named James Hydell, a Neanderthal. Hydell shot Casso five times, but failed to kill him, a mistake that proved costly: kidnapped by Lucchese hoods, Hydell was hideously tortured for twelve hours, then killed, all as a warning to Ruggiero.

The incident further rattled Gotti's faith in Ruggiero's abilities as a *capo*, and created a major managerial problem: as family boss, Gotti was being ushered into the great riches of the upper-level rackets, ones that required *capi* with some intelligence and business sense who could help him run the organization.

When he was a *capo,* Gotti was given modest pieces of family business operations, including a New Jersey ice-cream company obtained from a businessman drowning in loan shark payments. The company proved unprofitable, and as Gotti complained, "This is pathetic. I don't even get any ice cream out of it." But when he became boss, Gotti was introduced to a world where the *real* profits of organized crime existed, sometimes in mind-boggling amounts.

The most prominent example was the concrete industry racket, which was so vast that it was shared equally by all the Commission hierarchy. Beginning in 1981, at the same time as a huge building boom in New York City, the Mafia took control of the Concrete Workers Union. With that wedge, it then created a "club" of six major concrete contracting firms who were the only ones allowed to bid on major projects (two million dollars or more). With the bids rigged, the Mafia imposed a "tax" of one percent of the total contract, plus two dollars for every cubic yard of concrete poured. For such huge projects as the Javits Convention Center and Trump Tower, the "tax" meant immense profits for the mob. Before the scheme was finally ended by a combined attack of the FBI, the State Organized Crime Task Force, and the New York City Police Department, the hierarchy of four Mafia families split profits of at least eight million dollars. (The fifth Mafia family, the Bonanno organization, was temporarily banished from the Commission and did not share in the spoils.)

Surprisingly little mob muscle was required to make this scheme work, and even less was needed for another scheme, this one producing an ocean of money. Its founding genius was an émigré Israeli electrical engineer named Michael Markowitz, who discovered that wholesale gasoline dealers were supposed to collect federal and state taxes on each gallon they sold, which was to be turned over to tax authorities. Markowitz then devised a complicated scheme under which the gasoline would pass through a daisy chain of dummy companies; in the process, some of the money collected for taxes never found its way to the federal and state treasuries.

It was not necessary to steal all the tax money; even a penny a gallon was sufficient to generate a flood of cash, for passing through the Port of New York every year are hundreds of millions of gallons of oil. In fact, Markowitz and a small group of like-minded Israeli émigrés were making so much money that they had no objection when the Colombo Family discovered the scheme and sought to take a slice. Markowitz happily worked out a turf arrangement, ceding Long Island to the Colombo Family, represented by a prototypical yuppie mobster of the new generation named Michael Franzese. Within two years, the Colombo-Markowitz combine split somewhere around three hundred million dollars.

Gotti was astounded when he learned of the vast profits even a few cents a gallon could generate. He was further astounded when he learned that Michael Franzese was the Colombo Family's representative for its interest in the scheme; he and Gotti had had a contretemps a few years before, during which Gotti concluded that Franzese was a punk with no future. Gotti now realized he had badly underestimated the yuppie mobster, son of Colombo *capo* John (Sonny) Franzese.

The Gotti-Franzese confrontation was sparked by a flea-market operator who counted Gotti among his friends. He had sought to open a flea-market operation on Long Island, and was informed that the territory had been promised to someone allied with Michael Franzese. The flea-market operator warned Franzese that he was a friend of John Gotti, the Gambino *capo,* who would not tolerate having his friends pushed around. Franzese was unimpressed: "Fuck John Gotti."

That statement, conveyed to Gotti, caused him to have Franzese summoned to a meeting at the Bergin, during which an infuriated Gotti threatened him: unless the flea-market operator was allowed to set up shop on Long Island, Franzese was in trouble. Franzese, realizing he was in far over his head, apologized abjectly, but Gotti wasn't through yet.

"You know, Michael," Gotti said, with that baleful stare, "I hear there's somebody goin' around New York sayin' 'Fuck John Gotti.' I think a guy like that ought to be shot down like some fuckin' dog, what do you think?"

Not surprisingly, Franzese agreed wholeheartedly with this proposal, and left the Bergin on shaky legs. Later, he assiduously avoided Gotti, but while the Gambino *capo* was sweating every dollar he could earn from the hard work of loansharking, gambling, and narcotics, the college-educated yuppie *Mafioso* hardly lifted a finger and was earning millions. To be sure, Franzese was not destined, finally, to enjoy the fruits of the gasoline scheme. The Organized Crime Strike Force in Brooklyn found out about it, and by the time they were finished, one of the Markowitz's business partners was found strangled to death after the revelation in court that he was an informant, and Franzese pleaded guilty to an airtight case and received ten years in prison (plus a five-million-dollar fine). And some time later, Michael Markowitz, having confessed all to authorities, was found shot to death inside the one single symbol of his success in the New World that most pleased him: his hundred-thousand-dollar Rolls-Royce.

Still, Gotti found the entire episode instructive. One of the great perks of being a godfather was an end to the necessity of serving in the Mafia frontline trenches amid the petty squabbles, trouble from law enforcement, hustling after every dollar, and sheer grind of it all. Godfathers could sit back and preside, with the money brought to them. Godfathers didn't have to bother with such mundane duties as smashing a recalcitrant debtor in the face until he came up with the money; above all, a godfather collected.

The Gambino Family was considered within the Mafia as the most adept at making a lot of money, and just about everybody in the family had heard of such classic operations as the famed Westchester Premier Theater caper in the 1970s. Arranged by Carlo Gambino and Paul Castellano, the operation consisted of obtaining control of a large dinner-theater in Westchester County, just north of New York City, which featured top-name entertainment, including Frank Sinatra. At root, it was a simple "bust-out" operation: Gambino and Castellano paid no bills while skimming the receipts, in the process collecting nine million dollars before the place collapsed into bankruptcy. Meanwhile, patrons could have no doubt about the change in managerial atmosphere: there were mobsters in eight-hundred-dollar silk suits selling popcorn, men with distinctly apelike appearance working as "security guards," and parking lot "attendants" who would shout at the drivers of arriving cars, "Get the fuck out, and I'll park this fucking piece of shit!" (One mobster, watching a performance of *The Nutcracker*, asked, "Hey, how come there's no talkin' in this thing?")

As Gotti further discovered, a godfather did not have to worry about storing all the money he was earning; each family had a "money-mover," an expert at hiding and reinvesting profits. When Gotti took over the Gambino organization, the family's chief money man was Seymour Rand, who managed a dizzying array of sixty-five separate bank and financial accounts, along with a dozen large safe deposit boxes. Rand was responsible for "moving" at least ten million dollars a year in family proceeds; some of the money was returned to the family boss in the form of return from legitimate investments, or alleged business profits.

Gotti was much attracted to this lifestyle, for he no longer had much desire to spend so much time in the streets (nor, significantly, did Victoria Gotti want him to spend so many hours away from home). Gotti was never what might be called a homebody, but his family was now beginning to drift away. By 1984, both his daughters were married, one of them to a Queens junkyard dealer named Carmine Agnello. Their courtship was not without irony, for some years before, two local hoods had approached Gotti with complaints that Agnello was guilty of a long list of transgressions worthy of capital punishment; they asked Gotti's approval of their plan to murder him. Gotti heard out the details, then ruled Agnello had not sinned to the extent of deserving death, but could be beaten to within inches of his life. Subsequently, Agnello was seen around Queens looking like one of the wrecked and dented cars brought into his junkyard.

Politely, Gotti did not mention his role in this event when his daughter introduced Agnello as her fiancé, and her father underwrote an elaborate wedding and reception for eleven hundred guests. The manager of the vast catering hall where the reception took place was able to handle a number of curious aspects of the affair, including a sensitivity about photography among the guests, and the hovering presence of police detectives and FBI agents who seemed to have a consuming curiosity about the guests' identities and the license numbers of their cars.

In 1984, at the age of forty-four, Gotti became a grandfather, when his eldest daughter Angela gave birth to a baby boy. Gotti was deeply touched when she named the baby Frank, for if there was one memory that haunted him, it was the loss of the boy in whom he had reposed so much hope. The Gotti home still contained a shrine to the boy, complete with black velvet curtains and votive candles; every Christmas, his parents wrote out an elaborately affectionate greeting card and put it away in a drawer, among the others of previous Christmases Frank Gotti would never receive. At home, Gotti was never far away from the memory of his lost son, and seemed unable to relax completely, even when absorbed in his favorite reading matter, books of Roman history, works that apparently provided him inspiration through the blood-curdling tales of Caligula and Nero. A man who rarely vacationed, he had no hobbies or other interests, and puttering around in the garden outside his home held no appeal. (For security reasons, the cutting of his lawn was entrusted to several hoods from the Bergin, who seemed to spend most of their time during this task arguing about the proper procedure for trimming ''Johnny Boy's grass,'' lest he be offended in some way and they wind up underneath it.)

Gotti's older son, John Jr., had followed the path trod by the sons of other *Mafiosi* to military school, but never demonstrated even a glint of interest in anything academic. According to whispers around the Bergin, John Gotti, Jr.'s chief claim to fame was genetic: he had inherited his father's violent temper, liable to erupt at even the slightest provocation, and he had been arrested for his role in two brawls. (To her husband's dismay, Victoria Gotti fired off a letter of complaint to the *New York Daily News*, furiously protesting that newspaper's characterization of her son as ''baby mobster'' following one of those brawls.) By 1984, at the age of twenty-two, he was the president of a Brooklyn trucking company that capitalized on certain convenient connections with a number of Teamsters Union locals. Business conversations with his father revealed a pronounced similarity of

approach to problems. For example, there was the day when
Gotti Sr. was enraged because a Bergin hood, who had been
given a job at Gotti Jr.'s firm, incautiously used the father's
name on the telephone.

"I'm gonna give him a kick in the fuckin' ass!" Gotti
screamed at his son. "The fuckin' guy uses my name on the
fuckin' phone!"

"You serious?" Gotti Jr. replied. "This guy's so full of
shit, it ain't funny."

"You tell him," his father ordered, "next time, don't be
mentionin' no fuckin' names on the phone or I'll put him in
the fuckin' hospital!"

Gotti's connections with the rest of his family were
marked, above all, by his continuing strained relationship
with his brother Gene. During Gotti's racketeering trial,
defense lawyers were amused to see Gene sink lower and
lower in his seat as wiretap tapes were played, during which
an angry Gene Gotti was overheard referring to his brother
as a "fuckin' shithead" and "asshole." As John Gotti fixed
a withering stare on him, Gene continued to sink lower in
his seat. "Is he lookin' at me?" he whispered as the tapes
repeated what he assumed were private conversations with
Angelo Ruggiero and others about assorted grievances concerning John Gotti.

Hearing some of the bitter comments directed at him by
his brother did not help John Gotti's already rocky relationship with Gene, who in turn seemed to resent the meteoric
ascent of "Johnny Boy." To members of the Bergin crew,
Gene Gotti often would sardonically refer to his brother during the *capo* days as "powerhouse fucking captain John
Gotti," and himself as "in the doghouse Gene Gotti."

Still, Gene Gotti was blood, no small matter among Italians. And no one, aside from Gene Gotti himself, was more
concerned than John Gotti about the heroin trafficking case
that confronted his brother, Angelo Ruggiero, John Carneglia, and several other defendants. The case opened in 1983,
and months dragged by as the pretrial maneuvering droned
on in Brooklyn federal court. The chief problem for the
defendants was contained in a large box carried by FBI agent
William Noon every day into court: cassette copies of tapes

recorded by the FBI from its bugs inside the loquacious Angelo Ruggiero's house.

When the trial finally began, there was trouble right from the outset, for presiding was Judge Mark A. Costantino, known to lawyers as a terror. "Sit down and shut up!" Costantino was apt to shout at a lawyer whose objections he found unpersuasive. A product of city asphalt who still retained a rich city accent, the sixty-seven-year-old Costantino was a grandfatherly type who maintained a dictatorial rule over every minute of a trial and demonstrated low tolerance for anything he felt was dilatory. Noted for his off-the-cuff speeches from the bench that occasionally bordered on the bizarre ("I am not in Central Park, I am in Brooklyn federal court. I know what is happening"), Costantino was presiding over a case that, despite the multiple defendants, was at root fairly simple.

The core of the case was the Ruggiero bug: either the conversations reflected extensive conspiracies to distribute heroin, or they did not. Defense lawyers concentrated their energies on the tapes, working to get as many of them excluded as possible, and dropping occasional hints that the FBI might have faked them (an allegation the FBI found vastly amusing, since to fake the stream of consciousness that was Angelo Ruggiero's daily conversation would have been the greatest forgery in history). All the while, the lawyers engaged in a running war with Costantino. "Respectfully . . . ," one lawyer began, and was immediately squashed by Constantino, who snapped, "Sit down respectfully."

In the end, despite what was clearly an irrefutable case, one juror refused to believe a single word on the tapes and the testimony of several coconspirators. He held out against all attempts at persuasion by his fellow jurors, and finally a mistrial was declared. A second trial, several months later, raised serious questions about the jury-selection process in the Eastern District of New York: one juror in this trial of alleged narcotics conspiracies was caught attempting to have cocaine smuggled to him by a girlfriend. A second mistrial occurred, and now Gotti and his codefendants faced the ordeal of a third trial, for the U.S. Attorney's Office for that district was determined to hold as many trials as necessary to achieve a resolution.

For the moment, John Gotti had no solution for this ongoing problem. Meanwhile, he was confronted with a problem of more immediacy, one that caused him to revert to his roots. Indeed, it was vintage Gotti.

When construction began on the new Bankers and Brokers restaurant in the complex known as Battery Park City on the tip of Manhattan in late 1985, the owners knew they could expect a visit at some point from John O'Connor, vice-president and business manager of the Carpenters Union in New York City. Notoriously corrupt, O'Connor routinely shook down construction projects, threatening to put up picket lines of union carpenters (which unionized workers of all other trades would not cross) unless a bribe of some dimension was paid to him.

O'Connor made his anticipated visit in early 1986, during which he noted that the crews working inside the new restaurant were nonunion, and that there could be a "problem." The restaurant owners immediately got the point, and a payment of five thousand dollars to O'Connor was deemed sufficient to resolve the matter. On reflection, however, O'Connor wanted more, but when he tried to collect it, the owners threw him out. O'Connor then sent a squad of goons to the restaurant to trash the place; in less than an hour, they caused thirty thousand dollars' worth of damage.

This was a fairly typical incident in a city of almost totally corrupt labor practices, but the difference was that the restaurant in question was under the aegis of the Gambino Family. A complaint to the family's new boss set off his short fuse, and in a subsequent meeting with Ruggiero, Gotti ordered that O'Connor be severely disciplined: "Bust him up! Put a rocket in his pocket!" In his fury, Gotti overlooked the fact that he had issued that order in his Bergin office; increasingly security-conscious since his elevation, normally he conducted such sensitive conversations away from the Bergin, most often on the sidewalk or street, presumably safe from police or FBI eavesdropping.

At any rate, Ruggiero approached the Gambino organization's favorite disciplinarians, the Westies, for some original ideas on how properly to discipline O'Connor. The Westies leader, James Coonan, taking his cue from some of the savagery afflicting Northern Ireland, suggested "kneecapping," the practice, pioneered by the IRA, of shooting suspected informants and other people the organization didn't like in the kneecaps to cause permanent, crippling injury.

Four Westies gunmen were subsequently dispatched to carry out the mission, but betrayed a certain confusion about human anatomy: they shot O'Connor in the buttocks and both legs. In the hospital a month recovering, O'Connor no sooner could walk again when he was arrested on labor racketeering charges. He professed innocence of the charges, and continued to insist to skeptical police detectives that he had been shot by a "Puerto Rican" gunman for some unknown reason.

And that, as far as John Gotti was concerned, was the end of the incident. His authority as godfather had been challenged directly by this "fuckin' Irish punk," and John Gotti had showed him he was not a man to be taken lightly.

Gotti thought no more of it as he continued to consolidate his power and lay plans for further expansion of family operations into such lucrative areas as New Jersey. Thus far, all seemed to be going well. His brother and Angelo Ruggiero still faced that heroin case, but there had been two mistrials already; with luck, they might actually beat the case, or the government would finally give up.

"We got a fuckin' good thing goin' here," Gotti remarked one night to his old friend, Joe Massina of the Bonanno Family, as they strolled the sidewalk outside the Bergin. "If we can keep goin' and they leave us alone for five years, we got somethin' that can last a hundred years."

"It's a hell of a legacy to leave," Massina said.

But to achieve that legacy, Gotti needed time—and that was something his law-enforcement adversaries were not about to give him. Gotti had made many enemies in the law-enforcement establishment, and one of the ironies of his success was that the more publicized he became as godfather and reputed "untouchable," the more determined his enemies in the New York City Police Department, the Eastern District

U.S. Attorney's Office, the FBI, and a half-dozen other agencies were to destroy him.

Their strategy was to concentrate on what they perceived as Gotti's chief vulnerability, his *goombata*. Initially, that strategy met with only limited success, for while some of them harbored deep resentment toward Gotti for his imperious treatment of even his closest *goombata*, they also retained a curious loyalty toward the man they continued to call "nigger" behind his back.

An interesting example was one of Gotti's oldest *goombata*, the dimwitted hood Alphonse (Funzi) Tarricone. Sent to jail in 1981 for running a huge loan shark racket using $600,000 of John Gotti's money, Tarricone had been arrested by the FBI after telling one slow-paying victim, "I'll pull your fuckin' eyes out of your fuckin' head!" FBI Special Agent Bernard Welsh, a long-time nemesis of Gotti who had handled the Tarricone case, was aware that in view of Tarricone's limited mental capacity, there was no way he could have accumulated all that capital himself. But Tarricone claimed not to know what Welsh was talking about when the FBI agent raised the subject; he went off to jail insisting that it was all his money, and John Gotti had nothing to do with it.

But three years later, released early on parole, Tarricone was a desperate man. His operating area had been the New York racetracks, where he specialized in providing loans to horseplayers. Now, he wanted to get back in action at the tracks, but state law, which barred convicted felons from entering any racetrack, stood in his way.

"Bernie, listen, you *gotta* get me back in the tracks," Tarricone pleaded to Welsh.

"I could arrange it, Funzi," Welsh replied, carefully baiting the hook. "Of course, I have to get something in return. You follow me, don't you, Funzi?"

"Yeah, sure," Tarricone said, aware that Welsh was making the terms clear: a return to the tracks, in exchange for which he would become an FBI informant. Tarricone seemed to have no qualms on that score, but then Welsh raised the stakes.

"Look, we don't want a lot of little bullshit things. This

is a serious step for the FBI, let me tell you. And for that, we have to receive equal value, Funzi."

"Like what?"

"Like John Gotti," Welsh said.

Tarricone was silent for a full moment. "I gotta think about that, Bernie," he said.

The next day, Tarricone met with Welsh again. "I can't do it," he said, clearly torn. "I can't go against John."

Welsh shrugged. "Okay, that's your choice, Funzi. Now you have to live with the consequences: we catch you loan-sharking, we throw you in jail. Simple."

Similarly, another Gotti *goombah*, Leonard Dimaria, found himself confronted with the same choice. In another of those temper tantrums that seemed to erupt every time he encountered a New York City Police Department detective, the inveterate cop-hater Dimaria one day beat up a detective he felt was giving him a hard time. Dimaria immediately realized his mistake, for even the most dimwitted hoods understand that detective squads (and cops generally) amount to very close fraternities of men who become very angry when one of their own is attacked. Accordingly, an entire squad of Brooklyn organized crime detectives, considered the biggest and toughest in the entire department, went looking for Dimaria, intent, as the quaint police phrase had it, on providing him with an "attitude adjustment" (meaning they would beat him into a pulp).

Dimaria went into hiding, and passed the word that he would emerge to surrender on an assault charge—provided that he be permitted to give up only to Detective John Gurnee, who had a reputation as a by-the-book cop who did not use any rough stuff. Gurnee guaranteed Dimaria's continued good health, and as a result, the grateful *Mafioso* indicated he owed the detective a favor. Gurnee had one in mind.

"I want you to help me, Lenny," Gurnee told him. "You'll work directly for me; nobody else will know about it. You'll never have to testify. You know the people I want to know about."

"I hear you," Dimaria replied, then asked for time to think about it. A few days later, he told Gurnee no; aware that at some point he would be asked to give information

about John Gotti, he announced that he could not bring himself to rat on the man he had known for nearly thirty years.

But the constant pressure at all points of the compass
directed at Gotti's crew and friends began to score some
successes—as James Cardinali learned. Cardinali, the killer
who became a federal witness against John Gotti after being
arrested on a murder charge, at one point was sent to talk
with FBI agents. Cardinali tried to impress them with his
knowledge of what was going on inside the Bergin crew, but
sensed that the agents were not particularly overwhelmed
Indeed, they began correcting him on several minor points,
indicating detailed knowledge of what was going on among
the men of the Bergin. In other words, they had managed to
convert some of the crew members into informants. When
Cardinali revealed a tidbit he thought might be interesting,
the agents hardly blinked an eye. "Look," one of them
snapped, "don't try to impress us. If you knew some of the
people around Gotti who are working for us now, the fucking
hair on the back of your head would stand up."

Perhaps so, for some extraordinary events were about to
take place in the criminal career of John Gotti. In the end,
they would destroy him—ironically enough, just as he
reached the apex of that career.

10

Requiem

We only kill each other.

— BENJAMIN (BUGSY) SIEGEL

WHEN THE TENNESSEE STATE POLICE found Michael McCray early one spring morning in 1988, he was sitting in a parked car in the Cherokee National Forest, reading his Bible. The troopers approached his car cautiously, having been warned by their colleagues in New York City that the man wanted there was not playing with all fifty-two cards in his deck at any given time, and further was to be considered armed and dangerous.

That warning seemed to be justified by what the troopers found in McCray's car: one shotgun, one rifle, one crossbow, ten explosive-tipped arrows, five skyrockets, several hundred rounds of ammunition, and a machete. Asked why he felt constrained to carry this impressive arsenal in his car, McCray replied, "I wanted to meet with John Gotti, and you never know the way the wind blows."

The troopers nodded solemnly at this apparently reasonable explanation, for even as far south as Tennessee, everybody seemed to know that this man John Gotti was some kind of big-time Mafia godfather reputed to be a very tough customer indeed. Therefore, McCray could hardly be blamed for wishing to arm himself sufficiently for an encounter with the man called by *Time* magazine the "overlord of crime."

McCray, a thirty-seven-year-old born-again Christian with mental problems, was wanted on a charge of aggravated assault in New York City, where he had created quite a ruckus. First, he sent a letter to John Cardinal O'Connor, head of the Roman Catholic Archdiocese of New York, criticizing Gotti for trafficking in narcotics. Three days later, he quit his job as a photo technician, and planted a package containing what he described as a bomb outside the Ravenite Social Club in lower Manhattan. While a fascinated audience of Mafia hoods looked on, the police bomb squad put to work one of its favorite toys, a robot bomb-retrieval device that picked up the package and carried it away. "I don't see no wires, so how can they make it move around like that?" one hood asked a uniformed cop on duty nearby. "There's a tiny little cop inside," the cop replied, deadpan.

As things turned out, all the bomb squad's elaborate work was hardly necessary; the "bomb" turned out to be mostly salt. John Gotti, waylaid by newspaper reporters outside his home, had a one-liner ready, as usual. "Do I look worried?" he asked, somewhat rhetorically. True, not a line of concern seemed to crease his face, but in fact at that moment, John Gotti was a very worried man. His concern was not because Michael McCray planted a bomb outside the Ravenite, or wanted to hold a discussion about narcotics while brandishing a crossbow armed with explosive arrows, but because Gotti suddenly had come under assault from his presumed friends and his known enemies.

Although Gotti had obtained tacit, if not enthusiastic, approval from the Commission members for his disposal of Paul Castellano, a powerful member of that body began to have second thoughts about the new Gambino boss. Vincent (The Chin) Gigante suddenly recognized that the flame of ambition which had driven Gotti to the momentous step of killing his own boss would not be confined, necessarily, to the question of leadership in the Gambino organization.

"Chin," as he almost always was addressed, was something of an expert on the subject, for he had risen to leadership of the Genovese Family because of the very same burning ambition. A former bodyguard and chauffeur for Vito Genovese, Gigante carefully cultivated a facade of stupidity, which tended to make people underestimate him (for one thing, Gigante, a pug-nosed ex-boxer, *looked* stupid).

Gigante's *naif* act helped him survive the internal upheaval that tore the family apart during power struggles following Genovese's death in 1969. Meanwhile, Gigante proceeded quietly to develop a reputation as an efficient earner, and performed a number of intricate maneuvers that brought him to the top leadership level of the family. When the family boss, Anthony (Fat Tony) Salerno, went to prison for one hundred years after conviction in the Commission case in 1987, Gigante succeeded him.

All the while, Gigante conducted one of the most amazing acts in the history of organized crime: he pretended he was totally insane. Aware of police and FBI surveillance, he strolled around the streets near his home in bathrobe and slippers, talking to himself. When two FBI agents served a subpoena on him, Gigante walked naked into the shower, holding an umbrella. Whenever any form of legal retribution drew near, Gigante's family (not his Mafia one) moved to have him declared mentally incompetent.

Gigante was not incompetent, and as he watched Gotti consolidate his power, he correctly estimated that there would be trouble. Gigante deduced that with the concrete racket ended, the Gambino and Genovese organizations would seek new sources of cash. Given the deep inroads the Mafia had made into the construction unions, construction was the logical next target. But Gigante's organization, traditionally strong in that field, was busily attempting to reestablish its preeminence; it did not welcome competition from the larger Gambino organization. In addition, the Genovese organization had strong roots planted in New Jersey, but Gotti, armed with his alliance with Scarfo of Philadelphia, was already moving to expand significantly Gambino influence in that state. So there was certain to be trouble there, too.

A series of meetings among worried Genovese captains and their boss took place at Gigante's headquarters, a small social club in Greenwich Village. As was his custom, Gigante continued playing what apparently was a nonstop game of gin rummy during the discussions. As was also his custom, Gigante periodically would announce "gin," without showing his cards, at which point the other players immediately would throw in their hands, never bothering to ask Gigante to show his alleged winning hand. (It was considered incautious to do so, or to wonder about Gigante's amazing winning streak, since he once severely beat a hood who dared to demand that Gigante show his cards.)

As he played cards, Gigante listened to the counsel of his most senior *capi*, who advocated the negotiation of some sort of arrangement between the Genovese Family and Gotti. Gigante shook his head no, and noted that he did not trust Gotti: given the Gambino Family leader's reputation for violence—and the murder of his predecessor—what evidence was there that Gotti could be trusted to uphold his end of a bargain? Besides which, Gigante argued, there was no guarantee that Gotti would be around for much longer; he really didn't have the "right stuff" to be a godfather, and lacked sufficient stature to run the Gambino criminal empire. No, there would be no negotiation with a man like John Gotti.

For the moment, there was no final decision on what to do about Gotti, but events soon forced a decision. Within six months of Gotti's accession to power, Genovese operatives in New Jersey began to complain of growing Gambino encroachments in their territory. The loudest complainant was John Riggi, a Genovese *capo* who despised Gotti as a street thug with no class—and an overly ambitious man certain, sooner or later, to take over the entire lucrative Genovese operation in New Jersey. It turned out to be sooner: Riggi began to hear reports that Gene Gotti, his brother's emissary, was making diplomatic overtures in New Jersey, attempting to find allies willing to desert the Genovese organization in favor of Gotti's. A Riggi meeting with Gigante concluded with a decision that the only solution to the problem was to murder both John Gotti and his brother, thereby eliminating a festering sore that threatened eventually to subsume the Genovese organization.

In August 1987, Louis (Bobby) Manna, a Genovese *capo* who was on-site supervisor for the Genovese Family's New Jersey operations, met in Cassella's Restaurant in Hoboken with Martin (Motts) Cassella, owner of the restaurant and a Genovese soldier; Frank Danello, a soldier; and Richard (Bocci) DeSiscio, another soldier and a leading Genovese executioner. As usual, the group met in the restaurant's ladies room, presumed to be safe from any possible FBI bugging. Interrupted occasionally by a female restaurant patron who did not know of the meeting—she would be told, "Go piss in the street, lady, this is a fucking business meeting!"—the three men discussed how the Gottis would be disposed of.

"Wear a disguise," Manna advised DeSiscio, who was to carry out the hit. "It's [101st Avenue in Ozone Park, Queens] an open area." (By which he meant the area was a busy commercial area, with many potential eyewitnesses.)

"Do you know where you're going to do this guy?" Danello asked.

"Yeah, on the corner," Cassella said, apparently referring to a major intersection near the Bergin club. He went on to discuss how John Gotti and his brother Gene would both be shot by DeSiscio on some unspecified morning when they exited the Bergin.

DeSiscio never got a chance to carry out his murder assignment, for although the Genovese men assumed they were safe from prying ears inside the ladies' room of Cassella's Restaurant, in fact the FBI had it bugged. As a result, the Bureau was now presented with a moral dilemma: if Gotti was warned about his upcoming assassination, that would tip off Gigante and Riggi that the FBI had an active bug inside the secret meeting room of the family's New Jersey division. The revelation would preclude any further, incriminating, conversations in the room. But the alternative was to permit the murder of John Gotti.

"We have no moral choice," James Kossler, the Bureau's organized crime guru, announced to his troops. "Even at risk of losing an extremely valuable electronic source, we are compelled to warn Gotti." Accordingly, two agents visited Gotti and told him that he was the subject of a murder plot by the Genovese faction in New Jersey. Not a flicker of emotion crossed his face as the agents told him in specific detail what had been planned—obviously, the result of a bug—and when the agents were finished, Gotti expressed an elaborate thank you.

The agents were no sooner out the door when Gotti, working himself into one of his monumental temper tantrums, ordered a hit on Gigante. But Gigante, anticipating such a move, had beefed up his security, a screen that could not be penetrated. So Gotti settled for a consolation prize: Vincent (Jimmy) Rotondo, Gigante's underboss and a leading waterfront racketeer, who was found shot to death in his car, a bag of fish thrown on his lap—a distinctly Sicilian touch meant as a message to the Genovese organization, whose leadership was dominated by men of Sicilian descent.

Gotti himself did not move anywhere without a phalanx of bodyguards, and there was greatly increased tension at the Bergin, whose habitués knew a mob war was now imminent. Into this tense situation, tragically, wandered William Ciccone, a mildly retarded young man from the Ozone Park neighborhood near the club. What he hoped to achieve by standing on the other side of the street from the Bergin and staring at it for hours on end will never be known. But inside the club, tense men noticed him, and assumed he was probably the vanguard of some massive Genovese assault. A group of them rushed out, beat him unconscious with baseball bats, and threw him into a car. Then they shot Ciccone to death and dumped his body in the basement of a Mafia-owned Staten Island candy store, preparatory to disposing of the body the next day. The broken body of William Ciccone, his life snuffed out because he was in the wrong place at the wrong time, was discovered accidentally a few hours later by a uniformed patrolman checking out a report of a prowler.

Preoccupied with his security in the face of an anticipated all-out war with Gigante, Gotti did not concern himself with the murder by his men of Ciccone, a crime he considered merely as the swatting of a pesky fly. But Gotti's law-enforcement adversaries were infuriated, for the cold-blooded slaughter of Ciccone in broad daylight summarized to them the *real* John Gotti, the thug behind the fancy suits and the tabloid gossip column items about which fancy restaurant he had been seen in. Already intent on putting Gotti in jail, they were now galvanized into action. And just when Gotti assumed the only real threat to his existence came from his enemies in the Genovese organization, both he and his organization were suddenly struck by a series of body blows. The first came from Edward McDonald's Organized Crime Strike Force, which convicted Joe N. Gallo of racketeering. The so-called Mr. Untouchable, who had not seen the inside of a prison for thirty years, was sentenced to ten years in the federal penitentiary; at seventy-six years old, Gallo faced death in prison.

Gotti, who had demoted Gallo, was not especially disturbed about the conviction, but was upset when McDonald then went after Armone; "Joe Piney" was also convicted of racketeering. And to make matters worse, an unrelated, joint FBI-police operation in Florida took down the entire Gambino Family operation in Fort Lauderdale, with nearly every member of the crew arrested, including Armone. In one swoop, Gotti's profitable Florida subsidiary was decapitated—with attendant loss of income.

Next came bad news in an even more lucrative area of Gotti's business, narcotics. Mark Reiter, the operation's link with black dealers, was caught in Manhattan dealing one hundred pounds of high-grade Sicilian heroin; he was accused of selling seventeen million dollars' worth of heroin over a three-year period to a network of black dealers from Harlem to Boston. Reiter was still a defendant in the Gene Gotti–John Carneglia case in Brooklyn; he had a slim chance of beating that case, but any chance of winning in Manhattan disappeared when James Jackson, a black heroin dealer jailed in the same case that involved Reiter, suddenly was removed from the general prison population. Reiter received a phone call from the ever-loquacious Angelo Ruggiero, who told him, "You got a problem. You better get a lawyer and come see me. The guy is no longer there."

Ruggiero apparently had learned nothing from his experience at the hands of FBI techies, for his incautious call was made over an FBI-tapped line. William Noon, the FBI agent who had become a walking data bank on the Ruggiero-Gotti narcotics operation, immediately deduced the meaning of Ruggiero's call: Jackson had turned snitch, and was being transferred to a section of prison set aside for informants. And that meant Jackson would be the chief witness against Reiter. It also meant that Reiter had no hope of beating the case, and faced forty years, or worse, in prison. Out on bail, Reiter made precisely the same deduction, and fled to California. He was arrested there and shortly afterward, the roof fell in on him in New York: with Jackson as star witness, Reiter was convicted, and sentenced to two life terms, plus sixty years, with no parole.

His flight and subsequent conviction in Manhattan created one of those odd little footnotes that occasionally lend Kafka-esque aspects to federal criminal jurisprudence. In fleeing to California, Reiter had evaded trial in the Brooklyn case. Now, the government wanted its pound of flesh, and charged a man already in prison forever with the crime of bail-jumping.

In a hearing before federal judge Joseph McLaughlin, Reiter decided to act as his own lawyer—and proved anew the old legal adage that the man who represents himself has a fool for a client. McLaughlin, noted for his ability to keep an absolutely straight face despite the most outrageous legal gambits directed at him, betrayed a slight flicker of incredu-lity as he listened to Reiter's defense, which consisted, in the main, of a claim that he jumped bail only because he was driven half mad by the pain of "cluster headaches." Reiter went on to claim that these blinding headaches usually occurred every time he drank champagne. It went downhill from there, and McLaughlin wound up sentencing Reiter to a year and a day, consecutive to the infinite sentence he was currently serving.

Noon and Robert LaRusso, the prosecutor in the Gotti-Ruggiero case, could barely keep straight faces during this proceeding. They welcomed such comic relief, for the entire narcotics case was about to drive both of them insane. By 1988, having lasted five years, it was the longest pending criminal matter in the history of the federal judiciary. The case always had some jinx or other afflicting it: a thickheaded juror, another juror who tried to get cocaine into the jury room, and a defendant suffering cluster headaches from drinking champagne. On top of that, there had been at least two attempts to fix the jury. Although the jurors were anony-mous—increasingly standard procedure in Mafia or Mafia-related trials—one juror made any tampering effort that much easier by driving to court every day in his car with vanity license plates spelling out his last name. What next?

The answer came soon enough, as the third trial opened

in early 1989. During LaRusso's opening statement to the jury, the new judge presiding over the trial, ninety-one-year-old John Bartels, fell sound asleep. The judge's nap probably had less to do with the vitality of LaRusso's speech than it did with the fact that this apparently never-to-be-resolved case was now unfolding for a third performance. Like a long-running play seen for the umpteenth time, all the performers involved looked tired in their roles.

To be sure, it was a reduced cast of characters: the original case had been divided into several smaller cases, and the one that LaRusso now was attempting to prosecute featured only John Carneglia and Gene Gotti. Angelo Ruggiero, who was to be the third defendant, was in a Manhattan hospital, being treated for heart problems and spots on his lungs—the latter malady not surprising in view of his habit of smoking four packs of Marlboros a day. His doctors were rendered speechless when Ruggiero announced he was giving up his Marlboros and replacing them with a recessed-filter brand that, Ruggiero insisted, in the face of all medical evidence, would not harm his lungs. (The doctors turned out to be right: Ruggiero died of lung cancer a year later, at the age of forty-eight.)

But the lines were the same in the play, and Noon once again was on the stand for hours at a time to discuss the central issue of the case, recordings of blabbermouth Ruggiero's indiscreet conversations. Ronald Fischetti and Gerald Shargel, two highly regarded gunslingers, had little to work with in the way of a defense, so they attacked the tapes, hoping to create in the jury's mind some doubt as to their veracity. Much was made of various periods of time between the tapings and the hours later when they were sealed, the implication being that the FBI might have altered them. Much was made also of the FBI's Enhancement Center, where technicians attempt to screen out background noise on tapes to bring out voices; again, the implication was that the evil geniuses in the FBI cunningly had managed to fake the crosstalk among three heroin traffickers.

Noon, as the FBI's resident expert on the tapes, tried not to look bored as he was asked, for the hundredth time, about the precise circumstances of every tape. At one point, Shargel asked a tedious series of questions about the color and type of a locked cabinet in the office of Noon's supervisor, Bruce Mouw. When Noon answered he did not know, Shargel thundered, "Well, Agent Noon, aren't you trained as an FBI agent to be observant?" To his cost, Shargel immediately learned that Noon was an effective counterpuncher: "Yes, but not to the extent of my supervisor's office cabinet."

And so the trial droned on for a few more weeks, until the old jinx took hold again. First, one juror was dismissed when it turned out he had forgotten to mention he was the relative of a federal prosecutor in the very same building. Then, apparently convinced he was staring conviction in the face, Gene Gotti attempted to help his own case by tampering with the jury. Private detectives hired by Gotti had discovered the identity of one of the anonymous jurors, and the old heroin trafficker Eddie Lino—now blessed with the honor of made man by John Gotti—was dispatched to handle the matter. Gotti might as well have sent a retarded child, for Lino proceeded to foul up his assignment.

It had been learned that one of the jurors lived in the Long Island suburb of Kings Park, where Noon also lived. Lino was to tack an unsigned letter on the man's door, telling him that as a neighbor of Noon (although Noon in fact didn't know the juror), it was "not proper" to sit on the case, and that he should do "the right thing" and remove himself from that jury. This latter phrase, a common expression in the Mafia world, was a dead giveaway to the letter's genesis. But Lino also erred by tacking the letter on the wrong door; the puzzled man who read the letter immediately called the FBI, and Lino and Gene Gotti were in even more trouble.

It turned out that the real reason why Gotti wished to remove that particular juror was because two of Gotti's scariest-looking hoods had managed to identify one of the alternate jurors. Further, they had terrified him by approaching him at home, announcing that they knew he was a juror in the Gene Gotti trial, then walking away. When deliberations began, the alternate, now a full-scale member of the jury, flatly refused to participate in them. Sobbing in terror, he admitted that he was afraid for his life if he voted his convictions, which were that Gene Gotti and John Carneglia were guilty of trafficking in heroin. He was dismissed, and after only thirty minutes, an eleven-person jury announced it had reached a verdict: guilty on all counts.

As are all criminal defendants, Gene Gotti was given the standard advice by his attorney not to say anything to waiting reporters, and to let the lawyer do the talking. Gotti appeared to agree, but the moment he walked out of the courtroom, he apparently could not resist giving the assembled media his succinct comment on the course of events. Throwing his hands in the air, he shouted, *"What the fuck is this fucking shit?"* The comment did not make the evening TV news shows. Carneglia, noticing two FBI agents who were sniffing around suspiciously, said, "Fucking FBI pain in the ass." He regarded the agents, both of football tight-end size, and said to one of them, "Hey, why don't you get somebody bigger down here?"

"Bigger than me?" the agent asked.

"Yeah," Carneglia, ever the hood, snarled. "Bring all your big guys down here. I'll get my big guys, my biggest guys." The agent smiled at the prospect: a rumble, right in the federal courthouse, between FBI agents and the Bergin crew. Given the size of men the FBI had been recruiting lately, it would have been no contest.

Some weeks later, Gotti and Carneglia were remanded to jail, their bail revoked when Noon testified that in the several years since their indictment in 1983, both Gene Gotti and John Carneglia had continued to traffic in narcotics. Noon stopped just short of stating the obvious: Gene Gotti and Carneglia, extremely close to John Gotti, would not have dared to continue dealing in heroin without the direct approval of the family boss—who, according to the whispers of informants, was getting his cut of the vast profits.

There was no proof of that, of course, and neither Gene Gotti nor Carneglia was about to discuss the delicate question of John Gotti's involvement in narcotics dealing. In the spring of 1989, anticipating the worst from Judge Bartels, notoriously merciless in narcotics cases, both men appeared before him to hear the sentences. They got the book thrown at them: Bartels sentenced them each to fifty years in jail.

Gotti was disturbed by the sentences, for not only was his middle-aged brother Gene going to prison—probably for the rest of his natural life—but close *goombah* Carneglia was also going away. Carneglia, with a reputation as a buffoon, nevertheless was a huge money-earner for the Gambino organization, and demonstrated unexpected talents in the art of laundering money at compound interest.

Coincidentally, Gotti was hit with another blow from the Eastern District's U.S. Attorney's Office. The prosecutors there had been concerned with severing all the tentacles of the Gotti-Ruggiero narcotics operation, among them Arnold (Zeke) Squiteri, the New Jersey *Mafioso* and close friend of John Gotti. There had been brief conversations on the Ruggiero bugs about Squiteri, not quite enough to make a case. But just as the prosecutors despaired of nailing Squiteri, the FBI learned of a curious development in New Jersey: a low-level hood named Richard Pasqua had been arrested by U.S. postal inspectors in a mail fraud case. Facing heavy charges, he agreed to cooperate, and began telling the postal inspectors about John Gotti, Arnold Squiteri, and narcotics. His listeners had no idea of what he was talking about, but a call to the FBI brought Noon on the run.

Noon discovered that Pasqua had served time in prison with a number of Bergin crew members, several of whom bragged to him about how much money the crew was making in narcotics. They also boasted about John Gotti as narcotics kingpin. According to Pasqua's account, when he asked them about the long-standing Gambino Family rule against its individual members dealing in narcotics, they laughed, telling him that John Gotti openly encouraged narcotics sales—provided he always got his cut.

Still not enough to make a solid case against Gotti, but Pasqua, who had dabbled in narcotics himself, had extensive firsthand knowledge about Squiteri's heroin dealings. Converted by Noon into a credible prosecution witness, Pasqua testified against Squiteri and his partner, Alphonse Sisca, who were convicted on all counts and were sentenced to forty years in prison. The case was prosecuted in New Jersey by John Gleeson of New York's Eastern District, who like his fellow prosecutors in that jurisdiction, had an abiding interest in the question of John Gotti as narcotics trafficker. In fact, the Eastern District prosecutors had a strong interest in John Gotti as *any* kind of criminal; still smarting over their defeat in the 1987 racketeering case, they were determined to put the most notorious criminal in their jurisdiction behind bars.

The convictions of Gene Gotti, John Carneglia, and Arnold Squiteri all hurt John Gotti, but they were not fatal blows. Still, Gotti began to find himself besieged on all sides as other of his *goombata* came under assault.

One was a close friend, *Mafioso* Giuseppe (Joe) Gambino, cousin of the late Carlo Gambino, who was a major narcotics trafficker with a strong power base in a notorious Mafia stronghold in the Bensonhurst section of Brooklyn. Gambino ran a nightclub-restaurant there, which also served as headquarters for a large-scale narcotics operation linked directly to the "Sicilian Connection" of the Sicilian Mafia. Beginning in 1987, an FBI operation focused on the Gambino empire, and a year later, the axe fell: the FBI rounded up two hundred traffickers in Sicily and this country, saving the arrest of Gambino and his chief confederates for the moment when agents knew they would be in one place.

That moment came one night in December 1988, when Gambino hosted an elaborate party at the nightclub for his fellow traffickers and their friends. Just as the party was going full blast, teams of FBI agents strolled into the place. One agent walked up to a microphone used by a band providing musical entertainment and announced, "This is the last dance. We're the FBI and you're under arrest."

The announcement was greeted by tumultuous applause and squeals of delight from the audience, which assumed that Gambino, known as a lavish host, had arranged this "raid" by actors playing FBI agents to enliven the proceedings. But Gambino knew better, and he sat in stunned silence as the agents began their roundup. When it was Gambino's turn to be led away, the agents couldn't resist pulling out FBI microphones concealed in the nightclub's walls and waving the devices in front of Gambino's face. Gambino turned pale, for he had spent a small fortune during the past several years for technicians using electronic "sweepers" to detect such devices; they had pronounced the place free of electronic invaders.

"Like we say, Joe," one FBI agent brightly informed Gambino, "when we put in bugs, *nobody* finds them."

Gotti had no sooner absorbed the news of Gambino's arrest when he learned that another of his close Mafia friends, his newly promoted *capo*, Joseph (Joe Butch) Corrao, had come under attack. Corrao, charged with obstruction of justice in a case in Manhattan, underwent the strain of two mistrials, and was finally convicted during a third trial in July 1989. He was sentenced to two years in prison.

Similarly, Carlo Gambino's son, Thomas Gambino, with whom Gotti had reached a special arrangement, found himself before a grand jury in Brooklyn, which was very interested in the conversations that had been recorded between himself and Paul Castellano in Castellano's home. The grand jury was also intrigued by other FBI wiretaps, in which John Gotti referred to Gambino as a mobster. Gambino was not an impressive witness, at one point telling the grand jury he had "no knowledge" of what Gotti did for a living. Consequently, he was indicted for obstruction of justice for what the grand jury claimed were 140 specific instances during his testimony in which he had given "false, evasive and misleading testimony." (He was later acquitted.)

At the same time, Gotti found himself under assault on suburban Long Island, where a massive federal investigation resulted in a civil RICO lawsuit against one hundred defendants in the garbage collection industry, alleging that forty-four of the largest carting companies, virtually the entire industry, were dominated by organized crime—chiefly Gotti's organization.

The real significance of these assaults was that they directly attacked various sources of Gotti's income, and at the same time put out of action some of his closest allies and *goombata*. Feeling increasingly isolated, Gotti derived little comfort from his brothers: Gene Gotti was in prison, and his youngest brother, Vincent, had finally crashed to earth. John Gotti openly spurned Vincent as he slid ever deeper into a morass of alcoholism and drugs. Brother John finally barred him from the Bergin altogether, and stopped mentioning his name following Vincent's indictment for narcotics trafficking. Vincent fled that indictment, was caught, and later convicted and sentenced to six to fourteen years in prison. No one from the Gotti family attended his trial or visited him in prison; at the Bergin, John Gotti acted as though his brother had died. Curiously, while Vincent was on the lam, he used the alias "Frank Gotti," some sort of desperate gesture toward his older brother John on a level he apparently thought guaranteed to get his attention. It did not.

But of all his troubles, the matter of Willie Boy Johnson bothered John Gotti the most. Ever since the not-guilty verdict in his racketeering trial in 1987, Gotti confronted the problem of Johnson, who clearly had committed the gravest of all Mafia sins: informing. The traditional penalty was death, yet Gotti hesitated: Johnson, whatever the extent of his betrayal, was his oldest and closest *goombah*, and the bond that existed between the two men extended to a depth even beyond their shared experiences, including killing.

What precisely that bond was no one save both men could say, but other *goombata* of Gotti became progressively more agitated as Gotti continued to resist the idea of killing Willie Boy Johnson. For his part, Johnson refused to believe that Gotti would ever issue the orders for his execution. He spurned all talk of police protection or entry into the federal Witness Protection Program. He made no attempt to go into hiding, and spent his days precisely as he had always spent them: a no-show job at a Mafia-connected construction union, with the rest of his time hustling various gambling operations. He never bothered to arm himself with a gun, and moved around his old haunts as though he did not have a care in the world.

In fact, he was facing one troublesome charge: while in prison during the Gotti racketeering trial, he had tried to facilitate a heroin deal involving his son. The men setting up the deal in prison were informants, and Johnson and his son subsequently faced a heroin sales conspiracy charge. Johnson's attorney, Richard Rehbock, worked out a deal: in exchange for lenient treatment for his son, Johnson would cop a plea to a reduced narcotics charge. Since Johnson had served nearly two years in jail during the Gotti racketeering trial, it was anticipated he would be sentenced to time already served.

Johnson was scheduled for a sentencing hearing one fall morning in 1988 in Brooklyn federal court. With the air of a man taking a walk to the corner, he casually strolled through the front door of the federal courthouse, and immediately encountered John Gurnee, who happened to be walking by. Gurnee, who had retired from the police department and was now an investigator for the U.S. Attorney's Office, stopped dead in his tracks.

"Willie, why are you walking around like that?" he hissed at Johnson.

"Like what?" a puzzled Johnson replied.

"Don't you know that John Gotti is going to kill you?" Gurnee asked him. "If I were you, I'd do something to protect myself."

"Protect against what, John?" Johnson said, looking even more puzzled. "Listen, I never hurt Johnny, so why would he try to hurt me? I got nothin' to worry about."

Gurnee shook his head. "Willie, you don't get it, you really don't." When he saw that Johnson had absolutely no realization that his life was in any danger, Gurnee gave up any further conversation.

Upstairs, in a third-floor courtroom, Johnson was scheduled to appear before Judge Costantino, the presiding judge in the Ruggiero–Gene Gotti narcotics trial. By coincidence, that trial was in brief recess while Costantino considered the question of Johnson's sentence for his guilty plea.

"Hey, Willie!" Gene Gotti shouted as Johnson entered the courtroom. He rushed forward and planted a kiss on his cheek. Willie Boy stood stock still, uncertain whether the kiss signified that most ominous of all Sicilian Mafia customs, the kiss of death. Gotti hugged him, and Willie Boy stared into his eyes. The eyes were cold and lifeless, and Willie Boy knew: he was no longer one of the *goombata*.

But he was still alive, despite the prediction of John Gurnee and everybody else in the law-enforcement establishment that it was only a matter of time before John Gotti had him slain. The prediction was based on the irrefutable direction of Mafia logic. First and foremost, Willie Boy was a proven informant, and that alone was sufficient to guarantee his execution. However, even more urgent business concerns dictated his death. Chief among them was the question of Mark Reiter: in prison for life, he was the subject of recurring hints by FBI and DEA agents and police detectives that he could relieve the burden of a life behind bars without parole by cogent discussions concerning narcotics dealing by the Gambino Family—notably, John Gotti. Reiter was clearly frightened of Gotti, and had resisted all efforts to make him talk. Nevertheless, the authorities had persisted and, as Gotti was aware, it might be only a matter of time before Reiter—not a made member of the Mafia—would finally accept a deal. Thus, some direct action was required to remind Reiter of the penalty for talking. Willie Boy Johnson's murder would be that perfect example.

Still, Johnson felt no danger. He continued to move around openly, and to the amazement of his lawyer, Richard Rehbock, showed up for legal strategy sessions at the lawyer's office with the relaxed air of someone who did not have a care in the world. Rehbock was struck by this air of unconcern, another aspect of a personality that fascinated him. He had gotten to know Johnson quite well, and discovered that although Willie Boy presented the classic picture of hulking street hood, he was also a man who had a detailed knowledge of current events (he once flabbergasted Rehbock with a detailed exposition on the question of international tariff agreements), a voracious reader who seemed to remember everything he ever read, and an aesthete whose home was decorated with several pieces of expensive artwork.

Nevertheless, Johnson was also a devoted believer in the occult and assorted quasi-scientific pursuits. He was strongly interested in the work of Rehbock's wife, Sylvia, a practicing numerologist who had her own local cable TV show. Asked by Johnson to divine his future, she set up her paraphernalia, and finally arrived at her conclusion. "You face an uncertain

future," she told Johnson carefully, avoiding mention of what
she had really read in her signs: death.

Several weeks later, on the morning of August 29, 1988,
Willie Boy left his home just before 7 A.M. As he was about
to get into his car, four men suddenly surrounded him and
fired nineteen bullets into his body. Later that morning,
reporters waylaid Gotti outside the Bergin. Asked how he
felt about the death of his *goombah*, Gotti replied breezily,
"Well, we all gotta go sometime." As he spoke, police
homicide investigators sifting through the dead man's pockets
found a four-hundred-dollar offtrack betting ticket. It was a
winner.

And then Tony Roach Rampino. Gotti had always trusted
him with any job, including courier for money or drug shipments. Tony Roach could be depended on to return with
every nickel or every last gram, even though he had become
a stone-cold junkie. Gotti felt sorry for his old *goombah;* the
father of a severely retarded child, Rampino often sank into
deep depressions. He took increasing amounts of cocaine and
heroin to snap out of these depressions, and soon was in
such bad shape that, Gotti discovered, he could no longer be
entrusted with sensitive assignments. (Rampino fouled one of
them up so badly that Gotti felt constrained to administer a
disciplinary beating to him personally. While Rampino stood
there, in the back room of the Bergin, Gotti wept as he
smashed his fists into Tony Roach's body.)

The end was inevitable. Desperate for money to support
his habit, Tony Roach in the fall of 1988 was arrested for
selling one-eighth of an ounce of heroin to an undercover
cop for thirty thousand dollars. Shortly after the arrest, FBI
agent George Hanna was in Tony Roach's jail cell,
attempting to discern whether, having hit bottom, he now
was willing to discuss anything of consequence. Having sam-
pled some of his own drugs, Rampino was high as a kite,
and greeted Hanna like an old friend. Hanna was shocked to
hear Rampino suddenly say, "I can give you the whole case.
I can show you where the guns are." He went on to talk
about the murder of Paul Castellano—how John Gotti ordered

it, who was there, how it was done, who fired which shot. Rampino included his own involvement.

Hanna ran to a phone and called prosecutor Charles Rose in the Eastern District in Brooklyn. "Charley, you better come over here and listen to this," Hanna told him. But by the time Rose arrived, Rampino had come down off his dope high, and no longer wanted to discuss any subject in connection with John Gotti—or anything else, for that matter. Convicted of narcotics trafficking, he silently went off to prison to begin serving a forty-year sentence.

Legally, Rampino's admission could not be used, but a frustrated Rose was able to vent his aggravation upon the person whose case had become an extremely personal one to the Eastern District. It was a perjury case against Matthew Traynor, the Ozone Park teenage gang leader (and, later, bank robber) whose brief moment for the defense in the John Gotti racketeering trial had provided that proceeding with a real low point. Rose, a personal friend of fellow prosecutor Diane Giacalone, was angry at Traynor for a number of things, not the least of which his repulsive claim that Giacalone had given him drugs and told him to sniff a pair of her panties for sexual release. Traynor would pay for that outrage, Rose and his fellow prosecutors vowed; as some of them noted, "Maybe Diane is a bitch, but she's *our* bitch." An infuriated Rose went to see Traynor in his prison cell, where he was serving fourteen years for bank robbery.

Perhaps cowed by Rose's angry intensity, and the intimidating presence of an accompanying federal investigator, John Gurnee, Traynor freely admitted that he committed perjury during the Gotti trial, including lies about Giacalone. Rose, intent on restoring Giacalone's honor, worked out a deal: via an affidavit, Traynor would admit the particulars of his perjury, in exchange for a five-year prison sentence tacked onto his fourteen-year sentence for bank robbery.

That minor matter out of the way, the Eastern District prosecutors now turned to some bigger fish. Chief among them was the pending case of one of John Gotti's closest *goombata*, Angelo Ruggiero.

*　　*　　*

The Eastern District had a pending narcotics case against Ruggiero, but they discovered that the voluble *Mafioso* was suffering from even worse troubles. Hospitalized for heart trouble and spots on his lungs (later diagnosed as cancer), Ruggiero discovered that he was a pariah throughout the entire Mafia. No one would speak to him, no one would visit the man whose inability to keep quiet had caused so much trouble. He did receive one visit from John Gotti. Ruggiero's *goombah* stayed only briefly; it was an awkward moment for both men, and Gotti could not conceal the fury he felt against one of his oldest and closest friends for the damage he had caused. "I can't do anything for you now," Gotti said, and left. Alone again, Ruggiero knew precisely what Gotti meant: if he recovered from his illness and went on trial in the pending narcotics case, in the event of his conviction, he would live and go off to jail to serve forty years. But if he were to be acquitted, Angelo Ruggiero would be executed; his lapses demanded death under the code of the organization by whose rules Ruggiero had played all his adult life.

Given his medical condition and the bleak circumstances of his professional life, it was not a comfortable hospital stay for Ruggiero. It became even more uncomfortable the following January, when a delegation of police detectives suddenly appeared outside his room.

"I would ask that you do not unduly disturb Mr. Ruggiero," one of his doctors fretted as he regarded the hulking, grim-faced group of men.

"Oh, of course not," one of the detectives replied. "All we're doing is telling him he's going to jail for twenty-five years."

The delegation found Ruggiero in bed, hooked up to various monitors. "What the fuck do *you* want?" he said to one of the men he immediately recognized, his old nemesis, John Gurnee.

Gurnee unfolded a piece of paper. "We have a warrant for your arrest," he said formally, then proceeded to read off the particulars of the charge. Ruggiero, Gurnee announced, was being arrested for his involvement, along with John Gotti, in the assault against John O'Connor, the corrupt union official who had the effrontery to shake down the Bankers and Brokers Restaurant. "You," Gurnee concluded, "are in a world of trouble, Angelo."

Ruggiero seemed to have no visible reaction to this news, but Gurnee noticed that the heart monitor connected to Ruggiero registered a distinct coronary disturbance. The monitor's squiggly lines oscillated even more wildly when one of the delegation in the room said, "Yeah, that's right, Angelo, and this time we got you on tape, you cocksucker!"

Of course, this was a strong hint that the case was built around wiretaps. Ruggiero faced the considerable task of convincing a jury that recorded conversations between himself and John Gotti about putting "a rocket in his pocket" had no connection with O'Connor's subsequent wounds. But Ruggiero never did hear those tapes in open court (nor, for that matter, did he ever hear a jury verdict in his heroin case). By the end of 1989, his body lost the fight to cancer, and he died that December, still a pariah in the Mafia, and still technically a man innocent of the charge that he had conspired to commit deadly assault on one John O'Connor.

That left John Gotti, along with Anthony (Tony Lee) Guerrieri, as the remaining defendants. There was a great deal at stake for Gotti: it was a state charge, and under terms of New York State's "predicate felon" law, a twice-convicted felon (such as Gotti) convicted of a third felony faced a minimum of twenty-five years in prison.

"Three-to-one odds I beat this case," Gotti told detectives who arrested him one frigid evening in January, 1989. Given Gotti's poor reputation as a gambler, his adversaries could be forgiven for laughing outright, but Gotti turned out to be right. Throughout the month-long trial, Gotti appeared totally unconcerned, and to the astonishment of his lawyers, devoted lulls to reading Nietzsche.

As Gotti seemed to have anticipated, the prosecution case foundered over the tapes in which prosecutors reposed so much hope. The agency that had installed them, the state's Organized Crime Task Force, was, like every other official entity in the fiscally troubled state, plagued by budgetary cutbacks. It lacked the money to buy the latest bugging technology, and used old, barely functioning equipment to bug Gotti. The result was several hours of poor-quality tapes that the jury ultimately found not very credible. Gotti walked out of court a free man, and on the night of his acquittal appeared at the Ravenite to wave grandly to a celebratory crowd that cheered him as a fireworks display erupted over Mulberry Street.

Gotti did not know it at the time, but his acquittal amounted to only a brief respite from the forces now gathering to bring about his final fall. He was unaware of the main threads of that destruction beginning to take shape in several disparate locations. In no particular order, they included a lonely highway near the Texas-Mexican border, a sparsely furnished room in Philadelphia, and a nondescript van near the tip of Manhattan.

Afterword

"I'm so much better lookin' than him, it ain't even fucking funny," Salvatore Reale said as his Lincoln hummed along the virtually deserted Highway I-10 in Texas. On that stretch of road near El Paso (and just a few miles from the Mexican border), there was not much scenery to be seen that night, so his passenger—who had heard all this many times before—tried to feign some interest in Reale's monologue.

As usual, to pass the time during long drives, Reale was expounding on his grievances. These centered on John Gotti, for Reale, a Gambino Family soldier who once handled the family's operations at Kennedy Airport, was firmly convinced that only bad luck had prevented his own rise to power. An insufferably vain man, Reale remained positive that as a *Mafioso* smarter and more handsome than Gotti, he deserved to be godfather.

Of course, there had been that inconvenient conviction three years before for racketeering at the airport, followed by subsequent banishment on parole to Arizona, but Reale was insistent that not even this obstacle should have prevented his rise to power. He had further complaints: now out of the mainstream, he was a virtual gofer by that spring of 1989, relegated to working as a courier for the family's drug money. (In fact, at that moment, he had four million dollars in narcotics money he was transporting in the trunk of his car to Miami for laundering purposes.)

"Shit," Reale said, bitterly. "If only that airport thing hadn't happened." To reconfirm his image of a man much better-looking than Gotti, he switched on the car's interior light to look at himself in the rearview mirror.

A mistake: just down the road, men working at a U.S.

Border Patrol checkpoint noticed that flash of light. An unusual occurrence that time of night, it was sufficient to convince them the car was worth checking out—especially along I-10, known as "drug highway" for all the drug smugglers who use it to move narcotics in and out of Mexico.

As Reale's car glided to a stop at the checkpoint, Reale committed a second mistake. "Yeah, I'm a citizen," he said when the border patrolman asked him the standard question whether he was an American citizen. "Hey listen, why are you guys stopping me? I ain't got no wetbacks in here."

Unfortunately for Reale, the patrolman was Hispanic. Offended by the ethnic slur, he was determined to dig into that Lincoln more deeply. He brought two drug-sniffing dogs to check out the car, and when they got near the trunk, they began whining. Asked to open his trunk, Reale obligingly complied. The dogs nearly went crazy at the smell of two large suitcases resting there.

With sufficient legal cause to open the suitcases, the patrolman was surprised to find not narcotics, but piles of money— $3,790,200 in U.S. currency and $20,995 in Swiss francs. Reale's explanation—that this cash had been won in Las Vegas gambling and he was merely transporting it to Miami for some unspecified reason—was laughable on its face. For one thing, since when do Las Vegas casinos pay off in Swiss money? For another, tests revealed narcotics residue on the suitcases.

In other words, Reale was in a serious jam. Very quickly, he found himself in jail, and a day later, an angry federal judge revoked his parole and ordered him to prison for ten years. Once there, Reale began talking to federal agents about a number of interesting subjects, including the Gambino Family's narcotics operations, and how the family extorted money out of Kennedy Airport.

At almost the same moment that Reale began to enlighten federal agents about assorted business practices of the Gambino organization, a group of FBI agents and prosecutors were inside a government-issue interview room in Philadelphia, listening intently as a relaxed Philip Leonetti expansively talked about life in the Mafia. As the former underboss of the Philadelphia Mafia organization, Leonetti obviously knew all there was to know about the secrets of that group. Such revelations were of limited interest to some of his listeners—agents and prosecutors from New York—but they came fully alert when Leonetti mentioned several trips he and Scarfo had taken to Staten Island, where they met John Gotti. He went on to recount the deal reached by Gotti and Scarfo to split up Atlantic City, along with an even more startling piece of intelligence, Gotti's defense of the murder of Paul Castellano.

"And you'd be willing to testify?" one prosecutor asked.

"Sure," Leonetti replied. "No problem." The agents looked at one another: Leonetti was prepared to be that most valued of all prosecution witnesses, a man at the top, an insider who could present a priceless portrait of John Gotti the mobster chieftain at work in the higher reaches of organized crime. Or, as listening prosecutors preferred to phrase it, a "pattern of racketeering."

Translated, that meant a RICO case.

The news of Leonetti's conversion to snitch leaked out, and so Gotti became aware that Philip Leonetti, eager to reduce his forty-five-year prison term, would take the extraordinary step for a Mafia senior executive of testifying in open court against a fellow senior *Mafioso*. Similarly, Gotti would read in the newspapers of the arrest of Salvatore Reale, and draw the obvious conclusion, especially since FBI agents had taken the trouble in court to mitigate, as much as possible, the legal punishment against him. Obviously, Reale was helping the FBI.

But Gotti was not aware of a much more dangerous threat that arrived late one summer night in a beat-up van that made its way from lower Manhattan to Mulberry Street. There, it disgorged a team of FBI techies near the Ravenite. In a matter of minutes, they had made their way inside the club and planted a number of sophisticated bugs in the walls of a second-floor apartment where Gotti was known to conduct sensitive business discussions.

The next day, a switch was flipped in a control room over a mile away, and an ocean of conversations began to flow from the bugs. Most of them were from Gotti, who, convinced of the safety of his Ravenite lair—periodically swept for electronic intruders—talked unrestrainedly about family business.

And in that flowing stream of secrets, there was a recurring theme: despite the media portrait of Gotti as the untouchable "Teflon Don," in fact Gotti was at his most vulnerable. Summarily, he had achieved the pinnacle of his ambitions, only to find it turning to ashes. His moods were increasingly somber as he confronted the truth that his way of life—and his organization—was coming apart at the seams. Almost all his old *goombata* were gone now, either dead or in prison, and his brother (and chief partner in crime) was behind bars for the rest of his life. The organization, battered on all sides by a furious assault from the law enforcement establishment, betrayed signs that unlike past crises, it was not reacting well.

The most visible sign of trouble was in the organization's most lucrative enterprise, narcotics. Following the conviction of Gene Gotti, his partner Eddie Lino was annoited by John Gotti with the status of made member and ordered to take control of what was sometimes humorously called the Gambino Family's "Offshore Pharmaceutical Division." But Lino himself faced charges in the same case that ensnared Gene Gotti, and his preoccupation with his legal troubles tended to make executive decision-making very slack. As a result, turmoil broke out, a problem not helped when $4,000,000 in profits fell into the hands of the *federales* after Salvatore Reale so stupidly insulted a border patrolman.

To his surprise, Lino was acquitted of narcotics charges in federal court, a verdict that seemed to unhinge his mind. For months afterward, he appeared unable to function, wrapped in some sort of strange religious mysticism that pronounced his acquittal the result of direct divine intervention. (Actually, it had more to do with the courtroom brilliance of his defense lawyer, Jeffrey Hoffman, who somehow convinced a jury that all those incriminating tapes from the bug inside Angelo Ruggiero's house were total fakes prepared by the FBI.)

In any event, Lino may have misinterpreted the intentions of Higher Authority, for one night in 1990 he was shot to death in his black Mercedes.

Although it was commonly assumed that Gotti had arranged for Lino's murder to solve an intractable organizational problem, there was less certainty concerning the death of a man much closer to Gotti: Bartholomew (Bobby) Boriello.

By early 1991, Boriello had followed the career track of many other *Mafiosi* in the past, cashing in on years of faithful service as the boss's chauffeur to win higher rank. In Boriello's case, Gotti committed a grave blunder, appointing him *capo*, with specific instructions to take John Gotti Jr. under his wing for tutelage in the finer points of organized crime. But Boriello not only proved to be stupid, he was arrogantly stupid, as well. There were growing tensions with business partners in the Lucchese organization involving gambling operations, and in a move that infuriated Gotti when he found out about it, Boriello lured John Gotti Jr. into a New Jersey heroin operation. Not too long afterward, in early 1991, Boriello was shot to death in the driveway of his home by killers he appeared to know.

These murders—and a half-dozen others—were symptoms of a criminal organization suffering from disintegration. Worse, given all the turmoil and law enforcement pressure, income was down markedly. Like a soap opera, this roster of troubles unfolded in conversations at the Ravenite, where the bugs transmitted an emerging portrait of a criminal enterprise in acute pain. By the end of 1990, there were recurring whispers from informants that some factions in the Gambino Family had actually begun thinking aloud about the possibility of murdering their high-profile boss, arranging new leadership, and starting all over again from scratch.

From Gotti's standpoint, all this trouble was bad enough, but he also assumed that at some point, his relentless enemies in the federal constabulary would go after him again in a racketeering case. He was not unduly worried about the prospect: he had already beaten one big federal case, and acquittal meant that he was effectively immunized for all federal crimes committed within the range of that indictment. Further, he was quite certain that he had been kept safe from electronic snooping at his Ravenite headquarters, and was very careful never to discuss sensitive matters in his home.

But the long-anticipated federal indictment that finally surfaced in late 1990 contained a number of shocks for Gotti. The chief one, of course, was the existence of the FBI bugs in his inner sanctum, the basis for charges that Gotti had participated in a "pattern of racketeering." Those tapes, the product of state-of-the-art technology lavished by a beneficent Congress on the FBI, were clear and would prove very difficult to refute. Then there was the matter of the Castellano killing: the government now claimed it had solid proof that Gotti had ordered it, and that there were eyewitnesses, to boot.

The greatest shock in the federal indictment, however, was in an area supposedly immune from federal prosecution: income taxes. Ever since the days of Al Capone, when the Prohibition era gangster went off to prison for the crime of failing to pay federal taxes, *Mafiosi* took special pains never to run afoul of the one federal agency they most feared, the Internal Revenue Service. Yet, federal agents investigating Gotti made the astonishing discovery that the Teflon Don hadn't bothered to file income taxes since 1985. An astonishing lapse, for failure to file amounts to a crime blissfully easy for prosecutors to prove: the law permits no excuse, even death, for failing to file an income tax return. And there is not much room for a defense; either a defendant filed his tax returns, or he didn't. The proof—no income tax return received by the IRS—is an immovable object.

To make matters worse, Gotti was remanded to prison pending the start of his trial on the grounds that he had a record as a perverter of juries. The successful argument for Gotti's incarceration was made by an old Gotti antagonist, John Gleeson, who had graduated to chief prosecutor in the new federal assault. Gleeson followed that up by successfully arguing that Gotti's flamboyant lawyer, Bruce Cutler, should be barred from representing him on the grounds that the FBI bugs in the Ravenite had recorded Cutler so deeply involved in Gotti's business, it made him a potential witness.

While Gotti searched for a new lawyer, he spent almost the entire year of 1991 in the drab confines of the Metropolitan Correctional Center in lower Manhattan. As the prison's star inmate, Gotti did not suffer a terrible penal servitude, but fellow inmates noticed that he seemed to be a more somber man lately. He often seemed to be gripped by some ennui, and there were days that in the midst of his darker moods, he was a man to be avoided.

Everyone who knew Gotti was aware that he especially was to be avoided during the middle of March. Sometime during that period, the following notice would appear in the obituary sections of several newspapers:

> Frank: The pain of losing you never
> leaves our heart. Loving you, missing
> you, always and always hurting.

It was signed by members of the Gotti family. On that day, Gotti was truly impossible and men crossed him at their peril. Morose, seemingly lost deep in thought, Gotti did not look like the feared godfather of tabloid journalism or the "dapper don" of American popular culture.

He seemed somehow older that day; this was John Gotti, the inner man who had arrived at this crossroads of his life suddenly aware of how much he had lost, the middle-aged mourner of a dead son.

Dramatis Personae

James Abbott FBI agent, control agent for top-level informant Wilfred (Willie Boy) Johnson.

Joseph (Joe Piney) Armone Heroin trafficker, underboss Gambino Family, currently serving ten years in prison for racketeering.

William Batista Hijacker, Fatico crew, FBI informant. Dropped out of sight, 1985.

Martin Boland FBI agent, recruited Wilfred Johnson as FBI informant.

James Cardinali Murderer, narcotics trafficker, chief prosecution witness against John Gotti. Currently serving ten years in prison for murder.

Charles Carneglia Brother of John Carneglia, auto thief, narcotics trafficker, close friend of John Gotti. Currently federal fugitive.

John Carneglia Auto thief, hijacker, heroin trafficker, close friend of John and Gene Gotti and Angelo Ruggiero. Currently serving fifty years in prison for heroin trafficking.

Frank (Buzzy) Carrone Hijacker, bank robber. Died in prison, 1973.

Paul Castellano Brother-in-law and successor to Carlo Gambino as boss of the Gambino Family, 1976. Murdered, 1985.

Michael Coiro Gotti crew lawyer. Convicted in 1989 of racketeering and obstruction of justice, now serving 15 years in prison.

Patrick Colgan FBI agent investigating Fatico crew, 1972, narrowly escaped death in shootout with Frank Carrone. Currently FBI Supervisor in the Bureau's Special Operations Division; one of the FBI's top surveillance experts.

James Coonan Leader of Westies gang, forged important alliance with Gambino Family. Currently serving life in prison for murder.

Joseph (Joe Butch) Corrao Gambino Family *capo*, friend of John Gotti. Convicted of obstruction of justice 1990, but case later dropped.

Andrew Curro Auto thief, holdup man affiliated with Carneglia brothers. Now serving twenty-four years in prison for murder.

Gerald Curro Heroin addict, brother of Andrew Curro. Chief prosecution witness, armored car robbery case.

Bruce Cutler Attorney and close friend of John Gotti.

Raymond Dearie U.S. Attorney for the Eastern District of New York, 1980. Now a federal judge.

Frank DeCicco Close associate of Paul Castellano, whom he later betrayed to John Gotti. Murdered, 1986.

Aniello Dellacroce Underboss of Gambino Family, important sponsor of John Gotti. Died of cancer, 1985.

Armond (Buddy) Dellacroce Son of Aniello Dellacroce, narcotics trafficker. Found dead of cocaine overdose, 1988.

Salvatore (Sally) DeVita Transvestite hijacker, Bergin crew.

Robert (Dee-Bee) DiBernardo Gambino Family *capo*, overseer of organization's pornography operations. Disappeared and presumed murdered, 1986.

Leonard Dimaria Loan shark, friend of John Gotti.

April Ernst Girlfriend of Andrew Curro. Murdered, 1980.

James (Jimmy Brown) Failla Ex-chauffeur Carlo Gambino, later important Gambino Family *capo*. Betrayed Paul Castellano and forged alliance with John Gotti, 1985.

Michael (The Falcon) Falciano Legendary New York City Police Department detective, now retired.

Carmine (Charley Wagons) Fatico Gambino Family *capo*, instructor and patron of John Gotti in organized crime. Now retired.

Donato (Danny Wags) Fatico Brother and chief assistant of Carmine Fatico.

Remo Franceschini Detective lieutenant, New York City Police Department, controversial commander of Queens District Attorney's Squad. Retired 1991.

Ralph (Ralphie Wigs) Galione Murderer of kidnapper James McBratney. Murdered, 1973.

Joe N. Gallo Gambino Family *consigliere*, deposed by John Gotti, 1986. Currently serving ten-year prison sentence for racketeering.

Carlo Gambino Boss of Gambino Family beginning in 1957, most powerful organized crime chief in the United States. Died of natural causes, 1976.

Diane Giacalone Assistant U.S. Attorney, Eastern District of New York. Chief prosecutor in racketeering case against John Gotti, 1985. Currently head anti-racketeering section, New York State Metropolitan Transportation Authority.

Vincent (The Chin) Gigante Boss of Genovese Family, bitter enemy of John Gotti.

Rudolph Giuliani U.S. Attorney for Southern District of New York, renowned prosecutor of New York Mafia. Resigned to run as Republican candidate for mayor of New York City, 1989. Defeated by Democrat David Dinkins.

John Gleeson Assistant U.S. Attorney, Eastern District of New York, coprosecutor in Gotti racketeering trial.

John Good FBI Supervisor, directed FBI offensive against Fatico crew, 1972.

Gene Gotti Hijacker, heroin trafficker, brother of John Gotti. Currently serving fifty years in prison for heroin trafficking.

John Gotti Hijacker, heroin trafficker, successor to Paul Castellano as boss of Gambino Family, 1985.

Peter Gotti Hijacker, bookmaker, brother of John Gotti. Manager of Bergin Hunt and Fish Club, Gotti headquarters.

Richard Gotti Hijacker, brother of John Gotti. Minor functionary in Gambino Family organization.

Vincent Gotti Narcotics trafficker and addict, brother of John Gotti. Currently serving twelve years in prison for narcotics.

Salvatore (Sammy the Bull) Gravano Strong-arm artist, stickup man, pretégé of John Gotti. Replaced Joe N. Gallo as Gambino Family *consigliere*, 1986.

John Gurnee New York City Police Department detective, directed extensive surveillance operation against Ravenite Social Club. Retired 1987, later federal investigator with U.S. Attorney's Office, Eastern District of New York. Died of cancer 1990.

Robert Hernandez New York City Police Department detective, played key role in police assault on John Gotti crew, 1980. Retired 1982, currently insurance company investigator.

Jeffrey Hoffman Manhattan criminal defense attorney, played significant role in destruction of government's case against John Gotti, 1986–1987.

Wilfred (Willie Boy) Johnson Hijacker, stickup man, gambler, top-level FBI informant, close personal friend John Gotti. Murdered, 1988.

Robert Kohler Noted New York City Police Department homicide detective, broke armored-car robbery case 1980 that eventually led to racketeering indictment against John Gotti and others.

James Kossler FBI Supervisor, originator of plan for massive federal assault against New York Mafia.

Dominick Lofaro Narcotics trafficker, New York State Police informant, later prosecution witness against John Gotti.

Joseph Massina Leading Bonanno Family *capo*, heroin trafficker, close friend of John Gotti.

James McBratney Gangster, murderer, kidnapper of son of Carlo Gambino. Shot to death, 1973.

Kenneth McCabe New York City Police Department detective, noted organized crime investigator. Retired 1986, later federal investigator, U.S. Attorney's Office, Southern District of New York.

Edward A. McDonald Chief, Organized Crime Strike Force, Eastern District of New York, 1982. Resigned 1988, now in private practice.

Bruce Mouw FBI Supervisor, head of Gambino squad.

Eugene H. Nickerson Federal judge, presiding judge at Gotti racketeering trial, 1985–1987.

William Noon FBI agent, key figure in destruction of Gene Gotti–Angelo Ruggiero narcotics organization.

Michael (Mickey Boy) Paradiso Heroin trafficker, friend of John Gotti.

Salvatore (Sally Upazz) Polisi Hijacker, narcotics trafficker, later prosecution witness against John Gotti.

Anthony (Tony Roach) Rampino Murderer, narcotics trafficker, close friend of John Gotti. Currently serving thirty years in prison for narcotics.

Seymour Rand "Money-mover" for Gambino Family.

Richard Rehbock Manhattan criminal defense attorney, defeated government racketeering case against Wilfred Johnson.

Mark Reiter Heroin trafficker, important link with black heroin dealers for Gotti-Ruggiero narcotics operation. Currently serving a life sentence in prison for heroin trafficking.

Charles Rose Assistant U.S. Attorney, Eastern District of New York, chief narcotics prosecutor.

Angelo Ruggiero Heroin trafficker, hijacker, murderer, close friend of John Gotti. Died of cancer, 1989.

Salvatore Ruggiero Heroin trafficker, brother of Angelo Ruggiero. Killed in airplane crash, 1982, while federal fugitive.

Thomas Sheer Assistant FBI director, chief of FBI's New York field office. Retired 1988, currently in private security work.

Barry Slotnick Chief defense attorney, Gotti racketeering trial, 1985–1987.

Arnold (Zeke) Squiteri Narcotics trafficker, close friend of John Gotti. Currently serving forty-year prison sentence for heroin trafficking.

Peter (Little Pete) Tambone Narcotics trafficker, involvement in Gotti-Ruggiero heroin operation led to banishment from Mafia by Paul Castellano. Reinstated by John Gotti, 1986.

Alphonse (Funzi) Tarricone Loan shark, strong-arm enforcer, close friend of John Gotti.

Matthew Traynor Narcotics dealer, bank robber, FBI and police informant, later defense witness for John Gotti. Currently serving fourteen-year prison sentence for bank robbery and perjury.

Bernard Welsh FBI agent, nemesis of John Gotti and Fatico crew, 1970s.

Index

Compelling True Crime Thrillers
From Avon Books

DEATH BENEFIT
by David Heilbroner
72262-3/ $5.50 US/ $6.50 Can

FREED TO KILL
by Gera-Lind Kolarik with Wayne Klatt
71546-5/ $5.50 US/ $6.50 Can

TIN FOR SALE
by John Manca and Vincent Cosgrove
71034-X/ $4.99 US/ $5.99 Can

"I AM CAIN"
by Gera-Lind Kolarik and Wayne Klatt
76624-8/ $4.99 US/ $5.99 Can

GOOMBATA:
THE IMPROBABLE RISE AND FALL OF
JOHN GOTTI AND HIS GANG
by John Cummings and Ernest Volkman
71487-6/ $6.99 US/ $8.99 Can

The Best in Biographies from Avon Books

IT'S ALWAYS SOMETHING
by Gilda Radner   71072-2/ $6.50 US/ $8.50 Can

RUSH!
by Michael Arkush   77539-5/ $4.99 US/ $5.99 Can

STILL TALKING
by Joan Rivers   71992-4/ $5.99 US/ $6.99 Can

I, TINA *by Tina Turner and Kurt Loder*
71992-2/ $5.99 US/ $7.99 Can

PATTY HEARST: HER OWN STORY
by Patricia Campbell Hearst with Alvin Moscow
70651-2/ $6.99 US/ $8.99 Can

SPIKE LEE
by Alex Patterson   76994-8/ $4.99 US/ $5.99 Can

OBSESSION: THE LIVES AND TIMES OF CALVIN KLEIN
by Steven Gaines and Sharon Churcher
72500-2/$5.99 US/$7.99 Can